Edinburgh
CityGuide

The first edition of *The List*'s annual *Edinburgh City Guide* contains information and comment on over 600 venues and locations.

- Independently selected and researched
- Covers all aspects of Edinburgh life
- Easy to use listings format
- Entries organised by theme and include all essential information
- Photographs, favourite places, index, maps and city calendar
- Produced and compiled by *The List*, Scotland's leading arts and entertainment magazine

Edinburgh City Guide Editor
Alice Bain
Contributors
Accommodation Rebecca Ford and Rachael Street **Architecture and Areas** Tim Abrahams
Attractions Anna Miller **Bars and Pubs** James Smart and the Bar Guide team **Castles and Historic
Houses** Kaye McAlpine **Clubs** Henry Northmore **Day Trips** Kaye McAlpine **Festivals** Mark Fisher **Film**
Miles Fielder **Gay Life** Gareth Davies **Kids** Ruth Hedges **Music** Mark Robertson and Doug Johnstone
Museums Anne Marie Gibson **Places of Worship** Kaye McAlpine **Restaurants** Donald Reid and the
Eating and Drinking Guide team **Shopping** Maureen Ellis **Sports and Activities** James Smart and the
Adventure Sports Guide team **Theatre, Comedy, Dance** Mark Fisher **Travel** Kaye McAlpine
Editorial Assistant Emily Jones **Additional Research** Emily Jones, Carolyn Rae and Jay Richardson
Photography
Michael Wolchover unless otherwise credited

Publisher
Robin Hodge
New Projects Director
Mhairi MacKenzie-Robinson
Production Manager
Simon Armin
Design and Art Direction
Krista Kegel-Dixon
Production Assistant
Lucy Reeves
Subeditor
Ashley Davies
Sales and Sponsorship
Amanda Mungall (Sales & Sponsorship
Director), Carol Ferguson, Rachel Shields,
Barbara Crichton, Brigid Kennedy
Circulation
Sheri Friers
IT Systems
Andy Bowles
Maps
Digital Data for the street maps supplied by
Netmaps via. J.S. Graphics
john@jsgraphics.co.uk

Cover photograph: Windows on the Scottish Parliament (page 18) by Michael Wolchover
Back cover photograph: Royal High School (page 16) by Michael Wolchover

**Published by The List Ltd
HEAD OFFICE:**
14 High Street
Edinburgh EH1 1TE
Tel: 0131 550 3050
Fax: 0131 557 8500
www.list.co.uk
edinburghcityguide@list.co.uk

GLASGOW OFFICE:
at the CCA
350 Sauchiehall Street
Glasgow G2 3JD
Tel: 0141 332 9929
Fax: 0141 353 2803

contents

introduction

Welcome to *The List's* brand new guide to Edinburgh. This neat package is crammed with all the combinations you need to crack open the capital. We've included over 600 entries, giving you the low down on architecture, galleries, theatres, shops, hotels, restaurants, bars, places to stay and places to go for the day and more, all in *The List's* easy to use listings format.

We're talking about a superlative city. One of Europe's most beautiful, it has earned UNESCO World Heritage status for both its Old and New Towns. It has more hills than most and an eye-watering view round every street corner. And it has the biggest concentration of arts festivals playing at one time, on the planet. With a ground-breaking new Scottish Parliament building opening in October 2004, Edinburgh is booming.

And why? Surely not because of the weather, although it is astonishing just how many days the Royal Mile is awash with pavement café action. It's the residents who have made this northern city the vibrant capital it is today. Since its heyday as epicentre of the Scottish Enlightenment (1775 until around 1850), Edinburgh has been the birthplace – and place of learning – of many remarkable talents. A book like this might not even exist were it not for the locals who published encyclopedias, invented the colour photograph or wrote their way into the history books. So what better way to introduce this guide than to credit a few of the characters, old and new, who appear in our entries as creators of the things we list.

Actors Alistair Sim (1900—76) St Trinians' star; Sean Connery (1930—) who went from milkman to 007; Ian Charleson (1949—90) *Chariots of Fire*
Architects Robert Adam (1728—92) for Charlotte Square; William Playfair (1790—1857) for National Gallery and Royal Scottish Academy Building; Sir Basil Spence (1907—1976) who built the University Library and a garage in Causewayside (now a wine shop); Malcolm Fraser (1959), Scottish architect of the year 2002
Artists portrait painter Sir Henry Raeburn (1684—1758); Scottish colourists FCB Cadell (1883—1937) and SJ Peploe (1871—1935); artist and arts impressario Richard Demarco (1930—); sculptor Eduardo Paolozzi (1924—); painter John Bellany (1942—); painter Callum Innes (1962—)
Comedians Impressionist Rory Bremner (1961—)

Economist Adam Smith (1723—90)

Encyclopedia publishers William Chambers (1800—83) and Archibald Constable (1774—1874)

Literary giants Sir Walter Scott (1771—1832); Robert Louis Stevenson (1850—94); Sir Arthur Conan Doyle (1859—1930); Muriel Spark (1918—); Norman MacCaig (1910—96); Ian Rankin (1960—); Irvine Welsh (1961—); Alexander McCall Smith (1949—)

Musicians The Proclaimers (1962) honorary sons of Edinburgh for Sunshine on Leith

Philosopher David Hume (1711—76)

Photographers pioneers Hill and Adamson (19th century)

Politicians Robin Cook (1946—) Channel 4 politician of the year, former cabinet minister and student of the Royal High; student rector of Edinburgh University and present chancellor Gordon Brown (1951—); prime minister Tony Blair (1953—) former Fettes College pupil

Scientists Edinburgh student Charles Darwin (1809—82) theorised on evolution; Joseph Black (1728—99) discovered carbon dioxide; Sir James Simpson (1811—70) invented anaesthetics; inventor of the colour photograph James Clerk Maxwell (1831—1879); Alexander Graham Bell (1847—1922), invented the telephone; The Roslin Institute, Edinburgh created 'dolly the sheep' (1996—2002) the first mammal to be cloned

Olympic sportsman Alan Wells (1952—) gold medal, 100 metres, 1980 Olympics

Alice Bain, Editor

The List magazine is published every fortnight and gives comprehensive arts and entertainment listings and reviews for Edinburgh and Glasgow.

Other publications include:

Bar Guide to Edinburgh & Glasgow, latest edition October 2003
The Guide to Scotland's Cities, first edition February 2004
Adventure Sports Guide, *Scotland*, first edition May 2004
Deli & Good Food Directory to Scotland, new edition May 2004
Eating & Drinking Guide, Edinburgh & Glasgow, new edition April 2004

city calendar
of events in Edinburgh 2004/2005

Listed here are just some of the many special events happening in Scotland's capital this coming year.

■ 1st & 3rd Sat every month
Farmer's Market
Fine produce from over 40 specialist producers on Castle Terrace. *See Food and Drink in Shopping*.

■ 6 Mar–9 May
First Scottish show for sculptor **Louise Bourgeois** at the Fruitmarket Gallery. *See Art Galleries*

■ 2 Apr–20 May
178th Royal Scottish Academy Annual Exhibition 2004 at the Royal Scottish Academy Building. *See Art Galleries*

■ 3 Apr–13 Jun
Lucian Freud: The Complete Graphics, Ben Nicholson and the St Ives School at the Scottish National Gallery of Modern Art. *See Art Galleries*

■ 3–14 Apr
Edinburgh International Science Festival
Workshops and events. *See Festivals*

■ 3–17 Apr
The Edinburgh Easter Festival
Performance event. *See Festivals*

■ 10 Apr
David Byrne, Usher Hall
Former Talking Head turned world music guru does his thing. *See Music*

■ 23 Apr
Royal Scottish National Orchestra, Usher Hall
Climax of the RSNO season. *See Music*

■ 25 Apr
Marie McLaughlin, Usher Hall
Scots born international opera star performs. *See Music*

■ 30 Apr
Beltane Fire Festival
Revival of this exciting pagan event on Calton Hill. *See Festivals*

■ 22 May–18 Jul
Artist **Nathan Coley** at the Fruitmarket Gallery. *See Art Galleries*

■ 25 May–2 Jun
Children's International Theatre Festival
Events and performance for young people. *See Festivals*

■ 29 May–31 Oct
Paolozzi At 80
Leith-born artist at the Dean Gallery. *See Art Galleries*

■ 4–6 Jun
Gardening Scotland
Over 400 exhibitors at Ingliston Royal Highland Centre.

■ 5–6 Jun
Caledonian Brewery Beer Festival
Beer sampling, food and live music at Caledonian Brewery. *See Attractions*

■ 6–13 Jun
Leith Festival
A week of community events. *See Festivals*

■ 7–8 Jun
Meadows Festival
Outdoor community event. *See Festivals*

■ 12–13 Jun
Edinburgh Treefest
Outdoor community event celebrating trees and forests. *See Festivals*

■ 13 Jun
Edinburgh Marathon
See Sports and Activities

■ 13 Jun
Red Hot Chili Peppers, Murrayfield
California's most celebrated veteran funk rockers return.

■ 15–26 Jun
Scottish Opera presents La Boheme
Pucini's classic tale by the company lauded for last year's *Ring Cycle*. *See Theatre, Comedy, Dance*

■ 24–27 Jun
Royal Highland Show
Large-scale livestock and agricultural show at Ingliston Royal Highland Centre. *See Festivals*

■ 10–11 Jul
T in the Park, Balado
David Bowie and the Darkness top the bill at Scotland's biggest rock and pop festival just over the Forth bridge from Edinburgh, near Kinross. *See Music*

■ **10 Jul–19 Sep**
Past Things and Present: Jasper Johns Since 1983
at Scottish National Gallery of Modern Art
See Art Galleries

■ **24–25 Jul**
Musum of Flight Air Show
East Fortune hosts Scotland's biggest civil air show. *See Museums*

■ **30 Jul–8 Aug**
Edinburgh Jazz and Blues Festival
International music festival. *See Music and Festivals*

■ **4 Aug–11 Sep**
Painter **Alison Watt**
at the Ingleby Gallery. *See Art Galleries*

■ **4 Aug–5 Dec**
The Age of Titian
Underground link between the Royal Scottish Academy and the National Gallery of Scotland opens with the Titian exhibition. *See Architecture and Art Galleries*

■ **6–28 Aug**
The Edinburgh Military Tattoo
The famous event on the castle esplanade. *See Festivals*

■ **8–30 Aug**
Edinburgh Festival Fringe
The largest cultural festival in the world. *See Festivals*

■ **14–30 Aug**
Edinburgh International Book Festival
International author/book event in the city centre. *See Festivals*

■ **15 Aug–4 Sep**
Edinburgh International Festival
The world renowned performance arts festival. *See Festivals*

■ **18–29 Aug**
Edinburgh International Film Festival
Longest continually running film festival in the world. *See Festivals*

■ **27–28 Aug**
FEDAGA Flower Show
Edinburgh allotment-holders' flower and produce exhibition at the Southside Community Centre.

■ **3–5 Sep**
Mela
Multicultural community event in Pilrig Park, Leith. *See Festivals*

■ **25 Sep**
Doors Open Day
For just one day some of the city's finest buildings open their doors to the public. *See Architecture.*

■ **2 Oct–4 Dec**
New Work Scotland Programme
at the Collective Gallery. *See Art Galleries*

■ **8 Oct**
This is the big one: the opening of the Scottish Parliament. *See Architecture*

■ **17 Nov–3 Dec**
Abstract painter **Callum Innes**
at the Ingleby Gallery. *See Art Galleries*

■ **25 Nov–9 Jan**
Capital Christmas and Hogmanay
One of the world's biggest winter festivals. *See Festivals*

■ **12 Feb–2 May 2005**
Andy Warhol: Self Portraits
at Scottish National Gallery of Modern Art
See Art Galleries

For up-to-the-minute arts and entertainment listings, get The List magazine, published every fortnight.

A Capital Christmas 25 Nov–9 Jan

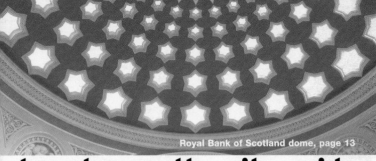

how to use the city guide

Entries are listed first by theme, then by sub-section, then alphabetically. For example:

Theme • **Art Galleries**
Sub-section • **Artist-run**
Name • **Total Kunst**

Each entry contains the following information:

Location
A quick location guide. Note – the areas given corrrespond with general city areas rather than specific neighbouroods.
City Centre
New Town
Old Town
West End
Southside
Leith
Outskirts
Out of town
Citywide

Address and phone number
Multiple branches are listed within one entry. Out of town entries include miles from Edinburgh and the nearest main road.

Opening hours
Hours, days and months where appropriate.

Description
Extra information, and in the case of restaurants and bars a review, completes each entry.

Website
Websites have been included where they exist.

Name
Of venue, event, shop etc.

The Real Mary King's Close
Old Town, Map 2 G6
2 Warriston's Close, Writers' Court, Royal Mile, 08702 430 160
May–Oct Mon–Sun 10am–9pm; Nov–Apr Mon–Sun 10am–4pm
Adult £7, child £5, conc £6
Cunningly hidden under the Royal Mile is an exciting warren of concealed streets where, centuries ago, people lived, worked and died. This tour tells their story from within the dark closes: a grave-digger's family stricken with plague, a grand 16th century townhouse and a small 'laigh' or poor house are all described by characters from the past, including a maidservant, a foulis clenger (cleaner), and the daughter of Mary King herself.
www.realmarykingsclose.com

Map reference
Gives a precise location. Maps are at the back of the guide.

Admission / Room rates / Average meal price
Prices given where available.

North Bridge, Old Town, page 19

the city

the city

architecture

The centre of Edinburgh constitutes a UNESCO world heritage site. This is both confirmation of its worth as a dense historic fabric and a means of conserving that wealth. Consequently, a heritage culture forces contemporary architects into an attitude of modernising by stealth, often with surprising and ingenious results. This selection of Edinburgh buildings offers a dip into capital architecture.

12th Century

St Margaret's Chapel
Old Town, Map 2 E6

Edinburgh Castle, 0131 225 9846
Apr–Oct Mon–Sun 9.30am–6pm; Nov–Mar Mon–Sun 9.30am–5pm
Castle: adult £8.50, child £2, conc £6.25
More myth and sentimental feeling has been generated by this tiny building than any other in Edinburgh. Perhaps it's because of the legendary holiness of the Hungarian-born Queen in whose honour it was first built on Castle Rock some 20 years after her death in 1110. Or maybe it's because St Margaret's is the oldest and smallest building in the city. Only 8.5 metres in length, little of the original chapel remains apart from the chancel arch and three of the outer walls. However, its simple vaulted interior, restored during the 19th century, is a model of medieval Christian modesty.
www.historic-scotland.gov.uk

15th Century

St Giles Cathedral
Old Town, Map 2 G6

High Street, 0131 225 9442
Service times vary. Open Oct–Apr Mon–Sat 9am–5pm, Sun 1pm–5pm; May–Sep Mon–Fri 9am–7pm, Sat 9am–5pm, Sun 1pm–5pm
Free: £1 donation optional
Compared with the great cathedrals of Europe, St Giles is not a classic piece of medieval architecture. This is perhaps because down the years Edinburgh's citizens have either ignored it or fought over it. The 15th century choir is of note but elsewhere only the famous crown of thorns was left unaltered by a huge exterior makeover in

MY FAVOURITE AREA

New Town
'I recommend a walk around the New Town in winter.'
Roddy Woomble, Idlewild

1817. The interior too was drastically renovated in the late 19th century. The Thistle Chapel (1911) is superb, however. More of a Scout hut for the posh than a place of worship, it is packed with the insignia of Scotland's highest chivalric order.
www.stgiles.net

16th Century

John Knox House
Old Town, Map 2 H6

45 High Street, 0131 556 2647
Closed until May 2005
Oddly, no one is quite sure whether Edinburgh's most famous misogynist and Reformation minister lived here or not. What is certain, however, is the fact that even more than nearby Gladstone's Land, this house represents the city as it was over 400 years ago. Although essentially two medieval buildings joined in 1556, it shows how narrow and cramped 16th century Edinburgh was. The wonderfully irrational interior is currently being incorporated into the new Scottish Storytelling Centre (see Theatre, Comedy, Dance) by Edinburgh architect Malcolm Fraser.
www.storytellingcentre.org.uk

city5s

SCOTTISH PARLIAMENT

■ **Site** It is built on the site of an old Scottish and Newcastle brewery.

■ **Model** The main model for the parliament was the federal government of Saxony, situated in Dresden.

■ **Architect** Enric Miralles, the Catalan architect of the Scottish Parliament, completed his doctoral thesis on William Adam, Edinburgh's great 18th century architect, at Columbia University, New York.

■ **Cost** The parliament was originally supposed to cost £40m and be finished in autumn 2001. It will finally open in October 2004 having cost around £500m.

■ **Inquiry** In May 2003 an inquiry was launched into the reasons behind the overspend. It will report after the building is completed.

17th Century

George Heriot's School
Old Town, Map 2 G7
Lauriston Place, 0131 221 6700
Check website for open days and by arrangement

'This statue represents my body, this work my soul.' So reads the inscription, in Latin of course, on the statue of merchant and benefactor George Heriot. Although it has the air of one of the city's Gothic public buildings, Heriot's was begun in the 17th century by William Wallace - no, not that one - funded by a bequest by the eponymous merchant. Although the school is now fee-paying, 'Jinglin' Geordie', as he became known, wanted to create a school for the city's poor. This would have been achieved earlier had not Cromwell used the partially built structure as a military hospital in 1650. Its plan is based on a rational renaissance design for an Italian palace but is decorated in the manner of the Jacobean English country home.
www.george-heriots.com

18th Century

Charlotte Square
New Town, Map 2 D5
It might be hard to believe today, but until 1790 the New Town was not considered a success in terms of design quality. None of the public buildings was celebrated and the private houses were commended for their rationality but condemned for their monotony – a criticism that applied particularly to Princes Street. To address these criticisms the town council invited Robert Adam to create a plan for Charlotte

The Scott Monument frames The Balmoral

Square in 1791 that combined uniformity with finesse. The stunning palace front of the north side, around 100 meters long, is an exact replica of the south.

Old College
Old Town, Map 2 H7
South Bridge, 0131 650 1000
Mon–Fri 9am–5pm
'The buildings in the University of Edinburgh are extremely mean and inconvenient,' ran the opening lines of the subscription in 1789. 'A plan for building a new university has been prepared by Robert Adam which has met with general approbation,' it concluded. The front that runs down South Bridge is the finest work by the great architect of Edinburgh's Georgian revival. Six six-metre columns of buff sandstone from Craigleith Quarry flank three archways, the central one of which gives access to the quad. Over 20 years after Robert Adam died, the internal quadrangle was completed, following a design by William Playfair. Pedestrian access at all times (see Art Galleries for Talbot Rice Gallery opening hours).
www.ed.ac.uk

Royal Bank Of Scotland
City Centre, Map 2 G4
42 St Andrew's Square, 0131 556 8555
Mon–Fri 9.15am–4.45pm
The old guard of the Bank of Scotland are currently battling to maintain their presence at their famous, yet architecturally overrated, head office on the Mound. Meanwhile, the Royal Bank's showcase city centre office continues to be one of the city's undiscovered gems. Incredibly, the spectacular dome in the perfectly square teller's hall was added some 80 years after William Chambers designed the original building as a house for Sir Laurence Dundas. Supported by four wide arches, the dome is a host of star-framed windows that diminish magically to a central point. For sheer drama it just shades the former Royal Bank branch – now the Dome (see Bars and Pubs) – at the east end of George Street.
www.royalbankscot.co.uk

19th Century

The Balmoral
City Centre, Map 2 G5
1 Princes Street, 0131 556 2414
As if apologising for the massive, aggressive bulk of the hotel below, the clock tower of the Balmoral is one of Edinburgh's most famous landmarks. It almost beckons guests of the Caledonian, the Balmoral's rival at the opposite end of Princes Street, to come on over. Formerly the North British, the Balmoral has a far greater amount of surface ornamentation, inspired by French and German

Renaissance architecture. It boasts 168 rooms, 20 of them beautifully refitted by Rocco Forte's sister Olga Polizzi. The Annan Suite, has one of the most amazing views in the world. See Accommodation.
www.thebalmoralhotel.com

The Colonies
New Town, Map 2 D2
Off Glenogle Road, Stockbridge
'If the working people of this country are ever . . . to receive better houses, they must build them themselves.' So said the Reverend James Begg in his history of the Edinburgh Co-operative Building Society entitled *Happy Homes for Working Men*. Taking their cue from a similar project in Birmingham, workers in Edinburgh, under the direction of the good reverend, pooled their savings, bought a narrow strip of land by the Water of Leith and paid for rows of cottages to be built upon it. In 2004 one of these covetable one or two bedroom houses would set you back well over £100,000. Come back Reverend Begg. Your city needs you.

Edinburgh Academy
New Town, Map 2 E2
42 Henderson Row, 0131 556 4603
Check website for open days
This is certainly one of the oddest pieces in Edinburgh's collection of Georgian classicism simply because of its height. William Burn's original two-storey design for the academy was considered to be too expensive, so he converted it to one. Essentially, the building is T-shaped in plan, with the long Doric columned frontage reaching out over the wide assembly area with opened, beckoning arms. The Assembly Hall is the cockpit of the building. An intimate, yet highly formal theatre, it is lit by high levelled strip windows recessed into an oval cupola.
www.edinburghacademy.org.uk

Fettes College
New Town, Map 2 A2
Carrington Road, 0131 332 2281
Check website for opening days
The current prime minister famously despised his time at Fettes College and one can't help but experience a sympathetic shudder of dread passing the imposing Gothic masterpiece which rises imperiously above Inverleith. Designed by David Bryce it is littered with the best work of the sculptor John Rhind who has work in every major Edinburgh building that the Victorians got their hands on. So imposing is Fettes that it is hard to believe that this chateau was not a conversion from a stately home but purpose built for educational purposes. Inside, the detail is considerably sparer but no less dominating in terms of scale.
www.fettes.com

Forth Bridges
Out of town, Map 1
South Queensferry. 9 miles north west of
Edinburgh off A90, 0131 319 1699
It is an important stage in every young
Edinburgher's life: the day he/she realises
that the trains don't actually go over the
arches of the Forth Rail Bridge but
through them. 'The supremest specimen
of ugliness' was the pronouncement of
designer-philosopher William Morris
when he first saw this steel cantilevered
bridge rising from three piers sunk in the
Forth. Built in 1889 with 60,000 tonnes of
steel and the horror of the Tay disaster
fresh in the memory, it is a mighty piece
of Victorian structural engineering. The
Road Bridge is its elegant counterpoint: at
the time of building in 1964, it was the
longest suspension bridge in the world
outside the US.
www.feta.gov.uk

National Gallery of Scotland
City Centre, Map 2 F6
The Mound, 0131 624 6200
Mon–Wed/Fri–Sun 10am–5pm, Thu
10am–7pm
Free (charge for special exhibitions)
One can only guess what William Playfair
would make of it. He began two projects
in 1822 in an atmosphere of civic
enthusiasm for architecture. The first, the
National Monument on Calton Hill that he
designed with Charles Cockerell, has
never been completed. The second, the
Royal Scottish Academy, is now being
linked in an adventurous subterranean
engineering project of no small cost and
no small ingenuity to one of his later
buildings, the National Gallery. The
extension will provide greater revenue
potential for the gallery as well as the
ability to host massive exhibitions, such as
the Titian, opening 4 August. At the same
time, the sanctity of Playfair's Doric
temples will be preserved. See Art
Galleries.

Royal High School
City Centre, Map 2 I5
5–7 Regent Road, 0131 556 1665
Open by arrangement
Alex Salmond, former leader of the SNP,
will tell you that before 1997, Scotland's
senior figures had decided that the RHS
was to be the core of the new parliament
building until Donald Dewar decided it
was associated too strongly with
nationalism. The massively literal Greek
revivalist high school was converted into a
parliament building in 1977 when a pro-
devolution vote looked a cert in the
referendum of 1978. There are plans to
have it converted again into the Scottish
National Photography Centre. Hopefully
these stand a better chance of being
realised.
www.snpc.org.uk

Royal Museum of Scotland
Old Town, Map 2 G7
Chambers Street, 0131 225 7534
Mon–Sat 10am–5pm, Tue 10am–8pm, Sun
noon–5pm
Free
Its exterior may be the least interesting
facade on the south side of Chambers
Street but the Royal Museum's central
hall is arguably Edinburgh's most
dramatic public space. Although now
cluttered with a café and resurfaced with
some oh-so-70s travertine, this stunning
cage of iron and glass, built in 1883, is
still impressive. Once a resolutely hushed
space, enlivened only by the distant
murmur of instruction emanating from the
exhibition spaces mingled with the ripple
of the fountain, the hall is now subject to
five daily interruptions by the incongruous
but stunning Millenium Clock. See
Museums.
www.nms.ac.uk

Scott Monument
City Centre, Map 2 G5
East Princes Street Gardens, 0131 529 4068
Apr–Sept Mon–Sat 9am–6pm, Sun
10am–6pm; Oct–Mar Mon–Sat 9am–3pm,
Sun 10am–3pm
Adult £2.50
The competition organisers for this
memorial to Sir Walter Scott said they
wanted a Gothic monument – and a
Gothic monument they got. The
fantastical spire and buttresses were
designed by George Kemp, an architect
with no formal training but a huge
enthusiasm for the cathedrals of northern
Europe, upon which he modelled the
upper stages of the monument. He used
Scott's beloved Melrose Abbey as a model
for the graceful lower arches. The
monument has 287 steps at the top of
which is a fantastic view of Princes Street
Gardens. Kemp drowned in the Union
Canal before it was completed.
www.cac.org.uk

St Stephen's Church
New Town, Map 2 E3
St Vincent Street, 0131 556 2661
Open by arrangement and during the Fringe
Location, location, location. Although St
Stephen's is not one of WH Playfair's
most famous buildings – the National
Gallery and the Royal Scottish Academy
are better known – it is certainly his most
striking. The tower is a moment of drama
in the uniform New Town and is even
more spectacular when lit up during the
Festival. When first built the octagonal
interior was vast. But the existing main
hall, with its superb Willis organ
dominating, is merely the original gallery
area. A concrete floor was added in the
1950s when the church became too big for
its dwindling congregation. It is now a
major Fringe venue during August.

20th Century

17 Royal Mews
City Centre, Map 2 J4
17 Royal Terrace Mews
Richard Murphy is known for designing arts venues; from the early design of the Fruitmarket and on to the finecikity intelligence of the Tolbooth. He has, however, some equally superb houses in his portfolio. Built in 1993, 17 Royal Mews may not be on the largest scale but when it comes to sheer ingenuity it is his cleverest. With a car port dominating the first floor area, and space in the former stable block at a premium, Murphy pulls out all the stops to create a dynamic, spacious apartment. Cutaways, sliding panels and mirrors, together with a tightly engineered floor plan, make this one of the most desirable properties in central Edinburgh.
www.richardmurphyarchitects.com

Dick Place
Southside, Map 2 off G10
off Kilgraston Road
This is where Edinburgh's architects built for themselves at the turn of the 20th century. Hidden within the plush groves of the Grange, Dick Place is a treasure trove of innovative buildings. Sir William Kininmonth introduced modernism to Edinburgh with the design for his own house at 46a (Kininmonth worked, for a time, in the same practice as Sir Basil Spence, designer of Coventry Cathedral and the Gorbals' highrises). Frederick Pilkington took a rather fanciful shot at art nouveau for his own place at 38 as well as a milder version at 48–50. Nearby on 25 Findhorn Place is a more modest house built for Robert Middlemass, who is credited with inventing the digestive biscuit.

Edinburgh International Conference Centre
West End, Map 2 D7
The Exchange, 0131 300 3000
Open by arrangement
How do you design modern, large-scale buildings in a city dominated by the tenement, a very precise vertical unit? Terry Farrell may have been responsible for the master plan of the Exchange business development of which the EICC is a part, but this was his only building within it. Like the circular corner tower of the Museum of Scotland, Farrell's EICC, completed in 1995, shows how conveniently the cylinder sits alongside Edinburgh's urban cityscape. With some fascinating organisation of space internally, the centre is a valuable addition to the capital's bid to be a world player in terms of business facilities.
www.eicc.co.uk

Maybury Casino
Outskirts, Map 1
5 South Maybury, 0131 338 4444
Mon–Fri/Sun 6pm–6am, Sat 6pm–4am
Membership: free but must be taken 24 hours before visiting
'A distinctly modern note is added to the surroundings at the Corstorphine tramway terminus by the new Maybury Roadhouse,' declared *The Scotsman* in 1936. Although style bars and not roadhouses are all the rage these days, the Maybury is still a superb building, blessed with a miniature Busby Berkeley staircase and a large galleried room designed originally for concerts but now used as a gaming hall. The casino refit is gloriously tacky but there is still enough of the original grandeur to remind you of what was once the place to drink in Edinburgh.
www.galacasino.co.uk

city5s
SCHOOL'S OUT

■ **Fettes** During his time as a milkman, Sean Connery delivered to this exclusive educational establishment. James Bond attended it in Ian Fleming's novels and Tony Blair launched his musical career here.

■ **George Watson's College** Rugby stars Gavin and Scott Hastings both attended.

■ **St Trinnean's** Now part of Edinburgh University's Pollock Halls, this school (1922—1946) was the inspiration behind the famous fictional one headmistressed in film by Edinburgh actor Alastair Sim.

■ **Royal High School** An illustrious role call including novelist Sir Walter Scott, inventor Alexander Graham Bell, poet Norman MacCaig, writer of Taggart Glen Chandler and actor Ian Charleson.

■ **Broughton High** Former pupil Shirley Manson began her singing career in Goodbye Mr Mackenzie which broke up in 1992. Since 1994 she has been a leading light in the band Garbage.

Museum of Scotland
Old Town, Map 2 G7
Chambers Street, 0131 247 4422
Mon/Wed–Sat 10am–5pm, Tue 10am–8pm,
Sun noon–5pm
Free
Remember when Prince Charles spent his
time laying the boot into innovative
architecture rather than fire-fighting
damaging news stories? Then you'll
remember him being sniffy about this new
museum. Since then other critics have
accused it of having a layout as
labyrinthine as the history it depicts, while
others have suggested it draws attention to
itself rather than its collection. Unlike
Charlie boy, they have a point, although
they fail to do justice to a truly superb
modernist building that credits the public
with intelligence while playfully
connecting the original Royal Museum's
Victorian take on the Renaissance with the
Old Town tenements.
www.nms.ac.uk

Royal Commonwealth Pool
Southside, Map 2 J10
Dalkeith Road, 0131 667 7211
Mon–Fri 6am–9.30pm (closed Wed
9am–10am), Sat 6am–8am/10am–4.30pm,
Sun 10am–4.30pm
Swim: from £3.50
Just after the Second World War Professor
Abercrombie published his Civic Survey
in which he recommended that crowded
tenements all over the city be knocked
down. By 1967, a public enquiry had
rejected this plan but not before the
Pleasance had been demolished to make
way for a ring road. The nearby
Commonwealth Pool, completed the same
year, is the upside of this faith in grand
scale urban planning; beautiful volumes of
interconnecting spaces and starkly
simplistic diving boards in which the
masses could spend their leisure time. The
noise generated by hundreds of kids at
busy times is also impressive. See Sport.
www.edinburghleisure.co.uk

Scottish Poetry Library
Old Town, Map 2 I6
5 Crichton's Close, Canongate, 0131 557
2876
Mon–Fri 11am–6pm, Sat 11am–4pm
Browsing and borrowing: free
This unfussy steel framed building,
another designed by Malcolm Fraser (see
Dance Base), is affirmatively modern, but
the oak panelled exterior and Caithness

> ### MY FAVOURITE ROOF GARDEN
> **Museum of Scotland**
> 'This roof garden is a brilliant
> place to just go and see the city
> from a different angle.'
> *Gordon McIntyre, Ballboy*

stone courtyard acknowledge the past.
Opened in 1999, the building's practical
uses are modest. It houses a small but
accessible poetry collection downstairs as
well as discussion and reading areas
upstairs. Its charms lie in the detail: from
the oak leaves carved into the stone in the
courtyard to the further use of wood
within the building, it is a wee poem in
itself.
www.spl.org.uk

21st Century

Dance Base
Old Town, Map 2 F7
14–16 Grassmarket, 0131 225 5525
Mon–Fri 8am–9.30pm, Sat 10am–5.30pm
Don't let the unassuming entrance fool
you. Designed by Malcolm Fraser
Architects, Dancebase is an astonishingly
sensitive piece of architecture, both to the
immediate environs it inhabits and to the
purpose of the building. Sandwiched
between two tenements, the entrance
space unfolds out into the gap site beneath
the castle. Each of the four studios is an
inspirational space and number three
particularly so. Stand in the south east
corner, look up at the small skylight and
amidst the criss-cross of concrete
structural supports you will see the flag on
top of the castle flapping in the breeze.
See Sport.
www.dancebase.co.uk

Scottish Parliament
Old Town, Map 2 J5
Holyrood, 0131 348 5000
We have heard the price repeated so
frequently that we have almost forgotten
how many hospitals we could have built
with £400m. Now we simply want to see
what its designer Miralles and early
guarantor Donald Dewar have bequeathed
to us. The auguries are tantalising. Like
Gaudi – another Catalan architect before
him – Miralles knew how to create the
sublime of the natural world, using
modern engineering. An extremely
intricate interplay of organic forms in the
reception areas is contrasted with the
corridors of power in the MSPs' cloisters.
The debating chamber, with massive
views of Arthur's Seat, is the building's
heart. Here it is clear that Miralles would
have Scotland's legislators dwell upon
their insignificance beneath the enduring
hulk of Arthur's Seat.
www.scottish.parliament.uk

The Tun
Old Town, Map 2 J6
Holyrood Road, 0131 226 3997
Open by arrangement
This one will take Edinburgh's citizens a
little while to get used to. In the
revitalised north Holyrood area the tubby
Tun looks at first like the fat,

uncomfortable kid around classical looking neighbours. The bar downstairs is overly sleek with too much glass and chrome but the tidy, light-filled upper floors are magnificent. Of particular note are the European Parliament offices. Managing to be both intimate and dramatic; ostentatious yet urbanely Edinburgh, the glass fronted office, opened in 2001, has arguably the best view in the city. It will become even more of a centre when its other prestigious clients such as the BBC and Commission for Racial Equality are interacting with the adjacent Parliament.
the-tun.co.uk

Event

Doors Open Day
Citywide
0131 557 8686
25 Sep 2004
This is an annual event not to be missed. Since 1991, a selection of unique and distinguished Edinburgh buildings, normally closed to the public, have opened their doors to at least 15,000 visitors, for just one day. If all goes well, the new Scottish Parliament is predicted to be top of every curious visitors' must-see list.
www.doorsopendays.org.uk

Pause for thought at The Tun

areas

Edinburgh was established as a fortress; a city that preserved its power from a hilltop position strengthened by man-made defences. Only after peace with England was achieved in the 18th century was the city able to expand. As a result, the villages it quickly swallowed up retain a highly individual atmosphere and appearance. The areas in this section are among the most characterful today.

Bruntsfield

In 1827 a bill was passed in Westminister permitting the building of a bridge from Lawnmarket south across the Cowgate, opening up the whole of south-west Edinburgh for development. But in that same piece of legislation, all building was forbidden on the Meadows and Bruntsfield Links. In one act, the unique character of Bruntsfield was created. Where regiments had drilled during the Napoleonic wars and where the populace of the city could play a game of golf, green space was preserved in perpetuity. Given the vital role that the Links has played in the recreational life of the city, it is understandable that the area to its south should retain an atmosphere best described as easy. Cafés, boutiques and well appointed tenements abound.

Grange

After Newington, the Grange was the next area of the countryside to be colonised by the city. This time the builders and property speculators aimed at customers with greater financial clout. While the various phases of the New Town still put a premium on public co-existence with your neighbours, the Grange was all about privacy. Massive stone walls divided the gardens of semi-detached houses. Similarly solid edifices prevented the passing pedestrian from prying. In the mid-19th century, wealthy professionals could imagine themselves as rural aristocrats after they had handed their coach and horses over to the stableman. Today the stable block may be a granny flat or the au pair's pad, but the effect is much the same.

Leith

There were three major consequences of the Protestant siege of Leith in 1560. The Auld Alliance between Scotland and France effectively came to an end, Protestant England secured the Reformation in Scotland and Leith lost its independence from Edinburgh. Since that date, the capital has been encroaching on its port, and the former dockland area is now of vital importance to the city's claim to international standing. Leith's more recent past – when it was a sluice gate for cheap heroin into Scotland – gave Edinburgh the cult that is *Trainspotting* and the city's sole claim to being cool. Indeed, the yuppification of the docklands has led to a nostalgia for those halcyon days.

Marchmont

If you study in Edinburgh the odds are that for at least one year, you will live in a flat in Marchmont. Your friends from school will visit, look in awed wonder at the high ceilings and say that they don't have flats like that in London/Sheffield/Auchterarder. Street after street of four storey baronial tenements, all with tall bay windows, could be a monotonous sight. However, in Marchmont, builders were allowed to put up only a couple of tenements at a time. As a result the flats are as varied as the villas of Newington, with individual forms of decoration such as turrets or pediments. Away from the high street giants, small, independent retailers and cafés still thrive at their feet.

Morningside

Morningside is a state of mind as well as a geographical place. Although today it seems like a fairly conventional, ever so slightly genteel suburb, Morningside is still a byword for public respectability concealing private vice. Thus it recognises no geographic borders. The Morningside accent, with its famous flattened vowels, is known throughout the world, largely thanks to Dame Maggie Smith, who played the eponymous anti-heroine in the film adaptation of Muriel Spark's *The Prime of Miss Jean Brodie*. The suburb and accents were simultaneously established in the late 19th century when tradesmen moved out of the city centre and colonised the village which, at the time, was little more than a row of thatched cottages and a blacksmith's forge. Just as their new villas mimicked the grand houses of the New Town so did the new Morningside accent mimick posh vowels.

New Town

'An attempt to enlarge and beautify this metropolis will now at length be deemed necessary,' declared the pamphleteer and city grandee Sir George Elliott in 1752. Twelve years later, James Craig's design beat five unknown finalists to become the masterplan for the New Town. Although lacking any real ingenuity in its layout, his New Town has since become a UNESCO World Heritage site, thanks in no small part to its uniformity. Ironically its most famous address, Princes Street, has long since lost its pristine geometry. In the more northerly areas, the New Town is still complete in its rational elegance. Alongside the private galleries and exclusive town houses, however, lives a refined melancholy caused by the lack of poverty and bustle that brings change.

Newhaven

Newhaven was originally built in the early 16th century as a royal dockyard. James IV, desperate to compete in the boat-building race led by the English monarchy, built the doomed Great Michael here, a massive ship said to have used all the trees of Fife in its construction. By the 19th century the area had become the main fish market for Edinburgh, specialising in oysters first and herring later. Much is known of this era thanks to extensive documentary work by photography pioneers David Hill (1802–70) and Robert Adamson (1821–48), who made a unique record of the village which has lost much of its spirit. Perhaps this is just as well. Newhaven fishwives were renowned in Victorian Edinburgh for their fiery militancy. Even today you have to watch which pub you wander into.

Newington

Of course, it was not going to be to everyone's liking. 'If the population of Edinburgh were a living autonomous body, it would arise like one man and make the night hideous with arson,' wrote Robert Louis Stevenson in response to the new villas in Newington. In the early 19th century the area was at sufficient remove from the town centre to merit being called the country. Builders and architects provided smaller versions of aristocratic country houses that still stood within a short drive of Edinburgh at the time. The tranquil atmosphere has changed since Clerk Street also became known as the A7, lined with student-friendly shopping and close to the Royal Commonwealth Pool.

Old Town

Daniel Defoe called it 'the largest, longest and finest Street for Buildings and Number of Inhabitants, not in Britain only but in the World'. For although the cramped conditions of the High Street had by the 18th century prompted the need for expansion, the body of the Old Town around this spine was still an architectural wonder. For centuries well-to-do families lived in rooms, sandwiched between the homes of poorer ones in eight storey buildings on tiny closes which, at one time, numbered well over 100. These towering edifices remain in part, but it wasn't until the 1950s that the Old Town reached acceptable modern standards of hygiene. Today, with the addition of the Scottish Parliament at its foot, this area can return to its medieval claim that it is the cockpit of Scotland rather than just the relic of it.

Stockbridge

Stockbridge was the first of the outlying villages to be subsumed by the rapid expansion Edinburgh experienced after the New Town was built. Originally a small hamlet based at a fording point across the Water of Leith, it now boasts some of the most sought after addresses in Scotland. Built upon the original site of the Raeburn Estate, Ann Street, Danube Street and Carlton Street were all given what was an amazing novelty in 19th century Edinburgh – gardens. Typical of the whole area, these houses impress not through their scale but through the intimacy and refinement of their detail. After a period in the 1960s and 70s in which it was rather groovy, an atmosphere of gentility has returned, though a good clutch of boutique-style shops, delis and cafés remain.

University

Where the Old Quad now stands, Mary Queen of Scots' second husband, Lord Darnley, was murdered. And so Kirk O'Fields, as the university district was known in the 16th century, has witnessed the extremes of both light and dark in Edinburgh's history. But it wasn't until Robert Adam and William Playfair rebuilt the Old Quad that the university developed its impressive international reputation. 'At the peak of the Enlightenment, Edinburgh might best be considered a city-scaled university,' says the architectural historian Charles McKean. In the years since its hey-day, the university has come to represent another division. The buildings around George Square reflect the tension between the university's tradition for innovation as well as its respect for its past. With extremely mixed results.

MY FAVOURITE ESCAPE

Arthur's Seat

'My favourite escape Arthur's Seat I have fond memories of Arthur's Seat and it's a place I would always go to get away from it all.'
Chris Patterson, captain, Scotland Rugby

books

Edinburgh is a literary city. At one time a major publishing centre, it has associations with authors, philosophers, major reference publishers and continues to nurture writers like Ian Rankin and publishers like Canongate. The small selection of books below are some of the more important volumes with Edinburgh connections. *The List* magazine publishes up-to-date book reviews and events every fortnight.

The Waverley Novels
Walter Scott
EUP (1814)
The Great Unknown and The Wizard of the North may not be the catchiest nicknames you've ever heard in your life, but these were attached to Walter Scott after the anonymous publication of *Waverley*, his debut novel in a series which brought some fame and a little fortune for this advocate. Set in 1745, this first book follows the adventures of Edward Waverley, a British Army officer posted in Scotland who becomes attached to the ideals of the Jacobites. Unsurprisingly, this doesn't go down too well with his bosses. If nothing else, the novel admirably reveals Scott's concerns with the complexities and contradictions of Scottish history.

Private Memoirs and Confessions of a Justified Sinner
James Hogg
(1824)
The so-called Ettrick Shepherd turned his back on a life of swill for a career with the quill after an encounter with Sir Walter Scott which led to a life-long acquaintanceship. His most famous work, written in 1824 and told in three parts, is quite simply a classic of 19th century Scots literature, taking on notions of evil, religion and duality, it is deemed to have been an inspiration to Robert Louis Stevenson for his notorious split personality tale. Hogg's story, which he published anonymously, was disregarded at the time and only became a cult classic after his death in 1835.

Edinburgh: Picturesque Notes
Robert Louis Stevenson
Pallas Athene (1879)
While his Dr Jekyll/Mr Hyde tale was heavily inspired by his home city (the split personality of Edinburgh and an individual, the thieving locksmith Deacon Brodie, were quoted as being direct influences) RLS produced a literary rough guide to the capital. Dubbed as nationalist, romantic, realist and bohemian, his *Picturesque Notes* tell it like it was, with backstreet criminals, the alcoholic underclass and society scandals lending an authentic air to proceedings whenever it gets too 'touristy'.

The Prime of Miss Jean Brodie
Muriel Spark
Penguin (1961)
The daughter of an Edinburgh engineer, Muriel Spark based her most famous novel on her days (the best of her life?) at James Gillespie's School for Girls. Written in 1961, just a few years after the author's conversion to Catholicism, the story is read as a penetrating analysis of Calvinist doctrines. And as this is an Edinburgh novel, our 'heroine' is a positively contradictory character holding some fairly dubious views about education and fascism. Still, it all ends up OK, with the protégée bringing about the monster's downfall.

Body Politic
Paul Johnston
Hodder & Stoughton (1993)
Perhaps the newest arrival to the Edinburgh crime scene (literary department) is Paul Johnston, whose efforts have helped him scoop the prestigious John Creasey Memorial Dagger Award. His most renowned work with his reluctant rozzer Quint Dalrymple is *Body Politic*, which hurtles us into the year 2020 and an independent Edinburgh which is maintained by tourism and some festival or other. When a spate of nasty killings threatens to put paid to all that lovely cash, our hero steps in.

Complicity
Iain Banks
Scribner (1993)
So, which do you prefer: Iain Banks with an M or without? This distinctly non sci-fi tale sees an Edinburgh journo Cameron Colley going about his freewheeling hack way thinking he's Hunter S Thompson when he stumbles upon a real scoop over some brutal killings. Colley almost has a fondness for the avenging angel behind the slayings and the poetic justice inherent in the tale may be his route to fame and fortune. Didn't half make a duff film out of it, though.

Trainspotting
Irvine Welsh
Minerva (1993)
The soundtrack and the poster of the film of the book may have overtaken the original impact of Irvine Welsh's 1993 debut novel, but the effect which this manic urban drama had on the Scottish literary scene and a new generation of writers cannot be underestimated. There are many who prefer delving into his *Maribou Stork Nightmares* or chilling in *The Acid House*. And there's at least one person who thinks *Filth* is the

Welsh peak. The fact that the 'sequel' *Porno* was so heavily anticipated is an indicator of the *Trainspotting* myth.

Inspector Rebus – Black and Blue, The Hanging Garden (1998)
Ian Rankin
Orion (1997)

JK Rowling may have penned her fantasy tales from the safety of an Edinburgh café, but Ian Rankin's writing lives and breathes the city, in all its g(l)ory. John Rebus is a hard-bitten cop whose loathing for his superiors is almost as strong as his taste for Scotch. Rankin's stories bring out the complexities and contradictions of an investigator on the edge and a city split in two. Particularly recommended are the war criminal fable, *The Hanging Garden*, and his 'Bible John' tale *Black and Blue*, which became the first televised adaptation with John Hannah as Rebus. But you're better off with the books, believe it.

The Sopranos
Alan Warner
Vintage (1998)

If there was ever a place that Alan Warner's literature is inextricably linked with, then it is his home of Oban. But in *The Sopranos*, his most accessible novel to date, he allowed his crew of Catholic choirgirls from Our Lady of Perpetual Succour to venture into the big city for a day and early evening of boozing, shopping, piercing and flirting, all under the auspices of appearing at a singing competition. They may not have quite made the event, but the girls and their hedonistic adventures helped make Warner a literary star and the proposed movie version should cement that reputation even further.

Born Free
Laura Hird
Rebel Inc (1999)

Having already established herself as a damn fine short story writer (with a collection called *Nail* and her contributions to the Rebel Inc Albion Rovers line-ups), Laura Hird had us gasping with anticipation for her full-length debut. And *Born Free*, a gritty, tender and very funny story about an ordinary Edinburgh family and their dreams of something better, was well worth the wait. The fact that *Born Free* was pipped to the Whitbread First Novel Award post by Zadie Smith's *White Teeth* may be one indication of how far Hird came in such a short time.

Edinburgh on a Plate
Editor, Ferrier Richardson
Black and White (2000)

There's only one thing better than eating delicious grub. And that's looking at and reading about it. This compilation of recipes from 21 restaurants in the capital concentrate on the best of Scottish produce, namely fish, beef, game and venison, but are varied enough to include the Chinese and Indian representatives who have always been strong in the city. Fear not, though, for the sweet-toothed among you, puddings do not miss out. Probably best not to read if you're feeling even mildly peckish.

The Fanatic
James Robertson
Fourth Estate (2000)

A ghost is needed for the Tours of Old Edinburgh, and in this novel by James Robertson, Andrew Carlin is the perfect candidate. So with cape, stick, and plastic rat, he scares the tourists, pretending to be the spirit of Colonel Weir, a religious extremist burned at the stake in 1670. Carlin's research draws him into the past and, in particular, to James Mitchel, imprisoned in 1674 for the attempted assassination of the Archbishop of St Andrews. So, what's The Fanatic really about? Not much really – apart from history, betrayal, witch hunts, exile, smuggled journeys and disguised identities.

The 'picturesque' city, inspiration for Stevenson's Picturesque Notes

city tours

Rain or shine, the open-top double-deckers are pounding the streets and the ghost trip story-tellers turning on the terror down in the vaults. Whatever the weather, just pay the money and be entertained.

Britannia & Edinburgh Tours
City Centre, Map 2 G5
Waverley Bridge, 0131 220 0770
Check website or phone for times
Adult £8.50, conc from £2.50
Tour in old style double deckers. Britannia will take you all the way to Leith via the New Town. The Edinburgh tour takes in all the sights and can be joined at Lothian Road, Grassmarket, Royal Mile and Princes Street. Tickets on the bus or from the Tourist Information Office on top of Princes Mall.
www.lothianbuses.co.uk

city5s
GHOSTBUSTERS

■ **Adam Lyal** Hanged in the Grassmarket on 27 March 1811 for highway robbery, this spectre now heads up the popular Witchery Tours.

■ **Foule Clenger** Plague victim collector, fumigator and mass burial arranger — one of the Real Mary King's Close characters (see Attractions).

■ **Anges Fynnie** This seller of green groceries was strangled and burnt on Castlehill in 1641 for witchcraft.

■ **William Burke** Half of the infamous bodysnatching duo, his body was given to science after execution in 1829: the skeleton can be viewed today at Edinburgh University's Medical School.

■ **Deacon Brodie** This city councillor's secret life as a burgular led him to the gallows in 1788. A crowd of 40,000 looked on as the gibbet he designed took three goes to do its job.

MacTours
City Centre, Map 2 G5
Waverley Bridge, 0131 220 0770
Tours: Mon–Sun 9.40am–5.40pm every 15 mins in summer, 30 mins in winter
Adult £8.50, child £7.50, family £19.50
Another fleet of open top double deckers on a picturesque tour that covers Edinburgh Castle, Royal Mile, Palace of Holyroodhouse and the Georgian New Town. On this hour long trip live commentary is part of the deal. Multi-lingual scripts are available in seven languages and there are 24 or 48 hour ticket options. Tickets come with a 10% discount for Edinburgh Castle and Dynamic Earth.
www.mactours.co.uk

Mercat Tours
Old Town, Map 2 H7
Mercat House, Niddry Street South, 0131 557 6464
Tours: Mon–Sun 10.30am–10.30pm
Adult £6
The daddy of them all, Mercat remains hugely popular. Daytime keeps it clean with historical tours but at night, ghosts and ghouls are brought to life by well-primed guides who really know their cloak and dagger stuff. Tours leave from the Mercat Cross (next to St Giles Cathedral). Secrets of the Royal Mile 10.30am daily; the Vault Tour May–Sep on the hour 11am–4pm; Oct–Apr noon/2pm/4pm; Ghost Hunter Trail 9.30pm daily. Check website for more.
www.mercat-tours.co.uk

Scottish Literary Pub Tours
Old Town, Map 2 F7
Suite 2, 97b West Bow, 0131 226 6665
Tours: Mon–Sun 7.30pm
Adult from £7, conc from £5
Enjoy a tipple as you brush up on your knowledge of Scottish literature. Tours depart from the Beehive Inn in the Grassmarket. Tickets from the bar or book online.
www.scot-lit-tour.co.uk

Witchery Tours
Old Town, Map 2 G6
84 West Bow, 0131 225 6745
Check website for tour details
Adult £7, conc £4
Now with its very own shop of horrors, books and videos, this little company started in 1984 and its tours are among the most popular in the city. Both are headed by costumed guides, with a supporting cast of spooks who can pop up from any old alley. Skulking round Old Town haunts, Ghosts and Gore (May–Aug Mon–Sun 7.30pm) visits scenes of execution and torture, while Murder and Mystery (summer Mon–Sun 9pm, winter 7.30pm) favours death and the supernatural. Meet outside the Witchery Restaurant. Bookings only.
www.witcherytours.com

Magdalen Chapel, page 48

culture

culture

Edinburgh is Scotland's capital of art. Four major national collections are held here and the new RSA Building now makes space for the international blockbuster. A thriving commercial district in the New Town, an increasing number of artists' initiatives and a small family of public galleries complete the picture. For exhibition dates and more information on the galleries listed here, turn to the Art section of the *The List* magazine every fortnight.

Artist Run Galleries

Collective Gallery
Old Town, Map 2 G6
22–28 Cockburn Street, 0131 220 1260
Wed–Sun noon–5pm (extended during summer)
For cutting-edge art, this is *the* place to go. An independent, non profit-making artists' agency, it has two exhibition areas, project room and members' lounge in a stylish glass-fronted space converted from a Victorian shell. Shows are diverse and include the acclaimed, annual, *New Work Scotland Programme*. Christine Borland, David Shrigley and Chad McCail have all passed through in the 20 years since the gallery opened. Visit now and you might be seeing the stars of the future.
www.collectivegallery.net

Out of the Blue
Leith, Map 2 J1
The Drill Hall, 30–36 Dalmeny Street, 0131 555 7100
Currently running the Bongo Club on Holyrood Road (see Clubs), which includes a small exhibition space, the Out of the Blue organisation has great plans afoot. New artists' studios have been created in the former Territorial Army base, which, once funding is secured, will feature a workshop, exhibition space and café. If all goes well it should be open by October 2004.
www.outoftheblue.org.uk

Patriothall Gallery
New Town, Map 2 D3
WASPS, Patriothall Studios, off 48 Hamilton Place, 0131 225 1289
Opening hours vary
A converted bakery, Patriothall is a unique artist-led space below New York loft-style studios. Forming part of WASPS (Workshops and Artists Studio Provision Scotland), its two echoing rooms show work mostly by residents. Art here is for sale and every autumn, studios are open for a day, when the public can buy direct. The red brick building is tucked right behind Hamilton Place, among a cluster of newly converted, groovy flats.

Roxy Art House
Southside, Map 2 H7
2 Roxburgh Place, 0131 556 9222
Opening times vary
This former church is now home to occasional performing arts events and exhibitions. Owned by independent organisation Hope Sixteen, its director Michael Borland has been working in conjunction with Edinburgh College of Art, but is happy to talk to artists direct.

Sleeper
New Town, Map 2 D4
Reiach and Hall Architects, 6 Darnaway Street, 0131 225 8444
Mon–Fri 2–5pm
This small, no frills, minimal art space located beneath an architect's office is, quite simply, a white, windowless, subterranean room. But Sleeper is much more than that, and you never know what to expect. Exhibitions organised by Alan Johnston and Neil Gillespie are diverse and the line-up in recent years has been impressive. Bruce Nauman, Douglas Gordon, Adam Barker-Mill and Donald Urquhart have all been here.

city5s

BUY ART

■ **doggerfisher**
For cutting edge art, this is the place. Prices from £125.

■ **Patriothall Gallery**
(WASPS)
Great for picking up Scottish art works at wallet-friendly prices.

■ **Edinburgh College of Art Degree Show**
Get there in June for bargain prices before the names get known.

■ **merz**
Starter price of £15 for Turner shortlisted Simon Patterson's Great Bear poster.

■ **i2**
Prints by famous names at affordable prices in this part of the Open Eye.

Total Kunst
Southside, Map 2 G7
3 Bristo Place, 0131 220 4538
Mon–Sun noon–10pm
As any art graduate will tell you, getting
the opportunity to exhibit post-college is
not easy. With that in mind, more and
more are favouring the DIY approach,
setting up for themselves. Total Kunst has
done just that. A co-operative formed last
summer in the new, volunteer-run Forest
Café (the former Adventist Church), it
now has a room of its own as well as
making use of the building's more unusual
spaces.
www.totalkunst.com/www.theforest.org.uk

Commercial Galleries

Ingleby Gallery
City Centre, Map 2 J4
6 Carlton Terrace, 0131 556 4441
Tue–Sat 10am–5pm (extended during
Festival)
A private gallery on a residential street,
this is a fantastic space. Occupying the
ground floor of a Georgian townhouse,
two white-walled rooms show
contemporary art. Set up by Richard and
Florence Ingleby, the gallery represents
Scottish painter Alison Watt and exhibits
work by mainly established artists
including Callum Innes, Howard Hodgkin
and Thomas Joshua Cooper. Recently,
young newcomers have also been
collected under the respected Ingleby
banner.
www.inglebygallery.com

Merz
New Town, Map 2 H3
87 Broughton Street, 0131 558 8778
Wed–Sat noon–6pm (extended during the
Festival)
Halfway down Edinburgh's bohemian
Broughton Street, this wee gem of a
gallery was set up by Callum Buchanan in
2002. Work for sale is diverse – with
artists like Alan Davie and Tracey Emin
hung side by side, along with work by up-
and-comings. It holds, as Mr Buchanan
puts it, 'works by the young, the old, the

MY FAVOURITE WORK OF ART

**Major William Clunes by Raeburn at
the National Gallery of Scotland**
'It's reminiscent of a magnificent
painting by Caravaggio, *The
Conversion of St Paul* in the
church of Santa Maria del
Popolo in Rome. Both are
composed in an extraordinary
way, at odds with the aesthetic
taste of their time.'
Alison Watt, artist

dead or the unknown, known and the lost'.
The selection changes regularly and shows
are mounted four or five times a year.
www.merzart.com

Open Eye Gallery and i2
New Town, Map 2 F4
34 Abercromby Place, 0131 557 1020
Mon–Fri 10am–6pm, Sat 10am–4pm
After more than 20 successful years in
Cumberland Street, Tom Wilson's Open
Eye and sister gallery i2 have upped sticks
and moved to the heart of Edinburgh's
commercial galleryland. Both are now
under one roof. A grand entrance leads to
big white rooms which show
contemporary, often colourful art by up-
and-coming and established artists. John
Bellany is a regular. i2 retains its own
identity, showing famous-name 20th
century American and European prints.
www.openeyegallery.co.uk

Phoenix 369 Gallery
New Town, Map 2 F4
3 Dundas Street, 0131 556 6497
Tue–Sat noon–6pm (extended during summer
or by appointment)
The 369 Gallery has been around. First set
up on the Hight Street in 1978 by Andrew
Brown, it moved to the Cowgate in 1983
and then closed ten years later, after
which the building was lost to fire in
2002. Rising from the ashes in July 2003,
it's back as Phoenix 369, located in the
city's busy gallery district. A Georgian
front room hosts exhibitions devoted to
contemporary Scottish painters, with the
occasional surprise from recent graduates.

Red Door Gallery
Old Town, Map 2 G6
42 Victoria Street, 0131 477 3255
Mon–Sun 12.30–5.30pm (extended during
summer)
What happens to all those art students
after their degree shows? Some are
snapped up, some struggle to survive
and some end up showing work in the
Red Door Gallery. Set up in August
2003 by Jason Redman and Jenny
Hendra, this compact space on Victoria
Street gives a chance to new names.
Small sculpture, artists' books, paintings,
prints, jewellery and photographs all
find space here. With prices from £10 to
£800, it's a great place to start collecting
contemporary art.

Scottish Gallery
New Town, Map 2 F4
16 Dundas Street, 0131 558 1200
Mon–Fri 10am–6pm, Sat 10am–4pm
(extended during the Festival)
One of the many now clustered along the
New Town's Dundas Street, this is the
country's largest and oldest private
gallery. Its credentials are impeccable:
mananaging director, Guy Peploe, is scion

The artist run gallery Total Kunst

of the celebrated Scottish Colourist's family. Exhibitions, mostly solo shows, concentrate on 20th century and contemporary Scottish painters, both established and emerging. The basement gallery is devoted to applied art – ceramics, jewellery, glass, metalwork, wood and textiles. Outdoor art is displayed in the back garden.
www.scottish-gallery.co.uk

doggerfisher
New Town, Map 2 H3
11 Gayfield Square, 0131 558 7110
Wed–Sat 11am–6pm (extended during the Festival)
Named after the shipping forecast terms 'Dogger' and 'Fisher' (stretches of water connecting Edinburgh and mainland Europe), this gallery and art agency works with mostly new generation artists. Set up in 2001 by *The List's* former art editor, Susanna Beaumont, the minimalist space, hidden just behind Broughton Street, was converted from a tyre garage by acclaimed architect Oliver Chapman. Recent exhibitors have included Claire Barclay, Jonathan Owen and Moyna Flannigan.
www.doggerfisher.com

National Collections

Dean Gallery
West End, Map 2 A5
73 Belford Road, Dean Village, 0131 624 6200
Mon–Wed, Fri–Sun 10am–5pm, Thu 10am–7pm (extended during the Festival)
Free (charge for special exhibitions)
In 1999, this former Victorian orphanage was transformed into an atmospheric gallery of 20th century art. Permanent attractions include a renowned surrealist collection and the reconstructed studio of Leith-born Eduardo Paolozzi. Upper galleries show temporary exhibitions – Dali, the Scottish Colourists and photographer Mario Testino have all figured recently. The shop specialises in the surreal, while Café Newton does coffee and lunch (see Cafés). The Dean can be reached from the Water of Leith Walkway (see Parks) and is across from the Scottish National Gallery of Modern Art.
www.nationalgalleries.org

National Gallery of Scotland
City Centre, Map 2 F6
The Mound, 0131 624 6200
Mon–Wed/Fri–Sun 10am–5pm, Thu 10am–7pm
Free (charge for special exhibitions)
Just off Princes Street, this monumental building houses a solid gold collection of European art. Paintings by Titian, Poussin, Rembrandt, Van Dyck, Monet, Gauguin and work by Scotland's artists hang in showy, luxurious surroundings. Temporary, big name exhibitions are shown regularly and the resident Turner watercolours are aired every January. The ambitious £26m Playfair Project, opening 4 August 2004, will link this building and sister gallery, the Royal Scottish Academy Building, with underground premises full of shops and other facilities. See Architecture.
www.nationalgalleries.org

Scottish National Gallery of Modern Art
West End, Map 2 off A5
75 Belford Road, 0131 624 6200
Mon–Wed/Fri–Sun 10am–5pm, Thu
10am–7pm
Free (charge for special exhibitions)
Across the road from the Dean Gallery,
this former boys' school intimately
displays a permanent collection of 20th
century art, which includes all the
international greats past and present. Big
temporary exhibitions are held here too
with the Boyle Family and Cindy
Sherman among recent invitees. Charles
Jencks' stunning new 'landform', a
stepped, grassy hill reflected in pools of
water, makes elegant fun of the front
lawn, also a site for sculpture. The shop
sells a good selection of art books and
gifts, while the garden café (see Cafés) is
a favourite on the lunching ladies' (kids
included) circuit.
www.nationalgalleries.org

Scottish National Portrait Gallery
City Centre, Map 2 G4
1 Queen Street, 0131 624 6200
Mon–Wed/Fri–Sun 10am–5pm, Thu
10am–7pm
Free (charge for special exhibitions)
This neo-Gothic sandstone building
holds a stunning collection of historic
Scottish portraits, along with works by
great masters like Van Dyck,
Gainsborough and Rodin. Keeping
things up-to-date, the gallery also
commissions portraits of celebrated,
living Scots – artist John Bellany, actor
Sean Connery and football manager Sir
Alex Fergusson all claim posterity here.
As the Scottish National Photography
Collection is also part of this institution,
many temporary exhibitions are
photography based, with high calibre
artists like Eve Arnold, Calum Colvin
and Fay Godwin shown regularly. A
ground floor shop and popular café are
within. See Cafés.
www.nationalgalleries.org

Public Galleries

City Art Centre
Old Town, Map 2 G6
2 Market Street, 0131 529 3993
Mon–Sat 10am–5pm (extended during the
Festival)
Free (charge for special exhibitions)
Six escalator-connected floors of
municiple art gallery with a penchant for
blockbusters, this is also home to one of
the best collections of Scottish art around:
selections from the 3,500 works are
shown when space is available. Otherwise,

Talbot Rice Gallery

For information on all exhibitions please visit our website
www.trg.ed.ac.uk

or call 0131 650 2211

University of Edinburgh, Old College,
South Bridge, Edinburgh, EH8 9YL.

Tel: 0131 650 2211

E: info.talbotrice@ed.ac.uk, www.trg.ed.ac.uk

Open: Tues - Sat, 10am-5pm, ADMISSION FREE
(Open seven days during the Edinburgh Festival)

Janice McNab 2004

photo © Davidson Reid Associates

Scottish
Arts Council

The newly refurbished Royal Scottish Academy Building, page 30

it's a mixed bag, everything from solo shows by major artists to popular extravaganzas like Star Wars. Art workshops held regularly are worth booking. Café serving lunch and coffee and gift shop.
www.cac.org.uk

Edinburgh College of Art
Old Town, Map 2 F8
Lauriston Place, 0131 221 6000
Mon–Fri 10am–5pm, Sat/Sun 10am–2pm
(extended during the Festival)
Free
It goes without saying that the Edinburgh College of Art Fashion Show in May and the annual degree shows are must-sees, but ECA also runs a diverse range of exhibitions year round, with the Edinburgh International Festival slot often attracting world class acts. Most take place in the grand neo-classical Sculpture Court and the more contemporary Andrew Grant Gallery. Lectures by visiting artists and academics and art courses (sculpture to photography) are extremely popular with students and citizens alike.
www.eca.ac.uk

Edinburgh Printmakers
New Town, Map 2 H3
23 Union Street, 0131 557 2479
Tue–Sat 10am–6pm
Free
Established in 1967 by a small group of artists, this was the first open access print workshop in Britain. The two-level gallery is devoted to contemporary, original prints with a programme which showcases work

MY FAVOURITE PAINTING
Portrait Group by James Cowie, Scottish National Gallery of Modern Art
'It is a haunting picture . . . The faces of the sitters are serious, and beautiful. I could look at it for hours.'
Alexander McCall Smith, novelist

by resident artists and attracts big print-world names during the Edinburgh International Festival. The adjoining studio provides airy space for etching, lithography, screenprinting and relief painting. Practical workshops and courses are available for all.
www.edinburgh-printmakers.co.uk

The Fruitmarket Gallery
Old Town, Map 2 G6
45 Market Street
Mon–Sat 11am–5.30pm, Sun noon–5pm
(extended during the Festival)
Free
One of Scotland's leading art spaces where high profile contemporary artists like Jeff Koons, Yoko Ono and Bill Viola are shown regularly. Formerly part of the city's Victorian fruit market, the building was remodelled by Edinburgh architect Richard Murphy in 1992. More recent additions to the loft style design include Peter Fink's light installation inspired by the aurora borealis in the café (see Cafés) and a new bookshop created by Glasgow-based artist, Andrew Miller. Fiona Bradley, ex-London's Hayward Gallery, took over as director in July 2003.
www.fruitmarket.co.uk

Inverleith House
New Town, Map 2 D1
Royal Botanic Garden, 20a Inverleith Row, 0131 552 7171
Closed until summer 2004
Free
Formerly the Scottish National Gallery of Modern Art, Inverleith is a beautiful 18th century mansion on top of the hill in the Royal Botanic Garden (see Parks). Closed for upgrading, it is a favourite among gallery-goers, not only for its stunning views but also because it has something of a reputation for innovative exhibitions. Attracting internationally renowned names, it has in recent years mounted shows by Carl Andre, Lawrence Weiner, Ed Ruscha and Cy Twombly, as well as representing Scottish artists. The Terrace café is next door. See Cafés.
www.rbge.org.uk

National Trust for Scotland
City Centre, Map 2 D5
26–31 Charlotte Square, 0131 243 9300
Shop/café Mon–Sat 10am–5pm, Sun
noon–5pm. Restaurant Mon–Sat noon–4pm
Free
Four New Town houses, all given the
National Trust for Scotland's restorative,
matt-palette touch, have been shaped
into headquarters, café, restaurant and
drawing room galleries showing
selections from the Trust collection
which includes important work by 20th
century Scottish artists. To dig deeper
into the life of 18th century townies,
visit the Georgian House (see Castles
and Historic Houses) on the other side
of the square.
www.nts.org.uk

Queen's Gallery
Old Town, Map 2 K5
Palace of Holyroodhouse, 0131 556 7371
Apr–Oct Mon–Sun 9.30am–6pm; Nov–Mar
Mon–Sun 9.30am–4.30pm
Adult £4, child £2, conc £3
Opening to critical accaim in 2002, this
former church and school has been
transformed by Edinburgh architects
Benjamin Tindall into a £3m
contemporary gallery with state-of-the-
art facilities. A sweeping wooden
staircase leads to the main space, with
two smaller galleries to the rear. Here,
the Queen's treasures are exquisitely
pampered in exhibitions which have
included her fabulous collection of over
70 drawings by Leonardo da Vinci and
work by Russian jeweller Carl Fabergé.
www.royal.gov.uk

RIAS Gallery
West End, Map 2 D6
15 Rutland Square, 0131 229 7545
Mon–Fri 9am–5pm
Free
Headquarters of the Royal Incorporation
of Architects in Scotland, this place
provides information and advice to the
trade and anyone else with an interest in
buildings. Exhibitions in the small
gallery focus on architecture, art and
design, while the bookshop has quite a

MY FAVOURITE GALLERY

Scottish National Portrait Gallery
'It always seems cool and quiet
and permanent . . . It's main
attraction is, of course, the
fabulous collection – you can
gaze on Robert Louis
Stevenson, Hugh MacDiarmid
and Muriel Spark like old
friends.'
James Robertson, writer

---

reputation for its covetable selection of
titles on these subjects.
www.rias.org.uk

Royal Scottish Academy Building
City Centre, Map 2 F5
The Mound, 0131 624 6200
Opening times and charges vary
In 2001, The National Galleries of
Scotland embarked on an ambitious
restoration of this Playfair building,
home of the RSA for many years. Phase
One, unveiled in 2003, has transformed
a beautiful but tired building into a
world class venue with lots of room for
big, blockbuster shows – this year
Degas and Titian – leaving plenty of
space for organisations like the RSA to
work from. But that's not all. Phase
Two, opening in August 2004, will add
an underground link between the RSAB
and neighbouring National Gallery of
Scotland. See Architecture.
www.nationalgalleries.org

Stills
Old Town, Map 2 G6
23 Cockburn Street, 0131 622 6200
Mon–Sun 11am–6pm
Free
Set up over 20 years ago as Scotland's
first photography gallery, Stills has a
new look. A new fully equipped digital
space in the former café now
complements existing resources.
Exhibitions, accompanied by special
events, continue to cover lens or media-
based work. Stills director Deirdre
MacKenna and staff are also planning,
together with Edinburgh Printmakers
and Edinburgh College of Art, to
establish a new Centre for Photography,
Print and Digital Media in Edinburgh's
Grassmarket. Watch this space.
www.stills.org

Talbot Rice Gallery
Old Town, Map 2 H7
University of Edinburgh, Old College, South
Bridge, 0131 650 2210
Tue–Sat 10am–5pm (extended during the
Festival)
Free
Part of the Old College quad, this
enterprising gallery has three distinct
spaces. The neo-classical Torrie or Red
Gallery displays the university's
permanent collection, which includes
work by Scottish artists Joan Eardley,
William Gillies and the Scottish
Colourists. The minimalist White
Gallery shows temporary exhibitions of
work by Scottish and international
artists: recent shows include Steven
Campbell and Kenny Hunter. The
Round Room is a truly unique space for
more experimental work.
www.trg.ed.ac.uk

castles&historic houses

Everyone knows Edinburgh Castle. Lording it over the city, you can't get away from it: schmalzy associations or no, it's a magnificent centrepiece. The only real castle as fortress among them, the rest listed below are homes or meeting places which give that much coveted peek into the past and other people's lives.

Castles

Craigmillar Castle
Outskirts, Map 1
Craigmillar Castle Road. 2 miles south east of Edinburgh off A68, 0131 661 4445
Apr–Sep Mon–Sun 9.30am–6.30pm; Oct–Mar Mon–Wed/Sat 9.30am–4.30pm, Thu 9.30am–12.30pm, Sun 2pm–4.30pm (last entry half an hour before closing)
Adult £2.20, child 75p, conc £1.60
A romantic ruin near town, this 15th century tower house is best known for its connections with Mary, Queen of Scots. It was from here, in a meeting dubbed the Craigmillar Conference, that a band of Scottish nobles cooked up ways of getting rid of her husband, Lord Darnley. Murder soon followed. Today, its neighbour, the eponomous housing estate, has not been without its own notoriety, while the adjoining Craigmillar Castle Park (see Parks) with its miles of walks, offers full countryside immersion.
www.historic-scotland.gov.uk

Edinburgh Castle
Old Town, Map 2 F6
Castle Hill, 0131 225 9846
Apr–Oct Mon–Sun 9.30am–6pm; Nov–Mar Mon–Sun 9.30am–5pm (last entry 45 mins before closing)
Adult £8.50, child £2
The castle. Tourists flock and locals take it for granted. Rock concerts, the Tattoo, Festival Fireworks, BBC news, shortbread tins – all employ it in a starring role. Built into the rugged rock overlooking Princes Street Gardens, it has become a powerful national symbol. But this is no fairytale palace. A collection of military museums, grand halls and war memorials based around 19th century barracks, it has a serious, no-nonsense air. Cannons are big players here – massive Mons Meg resides

Edinburgh Castle and the fountain in West Princes Street Gardens

in the dungeons and the one o'clock gun booms across town every day. The Crown Jewels of Scotland and Stone of Destiny (brought back from Westminster in 1996) have been rather highjacked by tourism in special displays but are national treasures nonetheless. Terrific views all round, but watch out for stiletto unfriendly cobbles. Audio and guided tours. Busy café and plenty of tourist shops. (see Architecture, St Margaret's Chapel).
www.historic-scotland.gov.uk

Palace of Holyroodhouse
Old Town, Map 2 K5
Royal Mile, 0131 556 1096
Apr–Oct Mon–Sun 9.30am–6pm; Nov–Mar Mon–Sun 9.30am–4.30pm (last entry 45 minutes before closing)
Adult £7.50, child £4, family £19
Possibly best known for its annual royal garden parties, the palace has been in the thick of Scottish history since the 13th century. And with new neighbours – the Scottish Parliament (see Architecture), Our Dynamic Earth (see Attractions) and the Queen's Gallery (see Art Galleries) – it's still at the cultural epicentre. Kings, queens and enemies have come and gone – James IV and Charles II commissioned the current structure between them, Oliver Cromwell brought it down and Mary, Queen of Scots twice

married and witnessed murder here. It is now the present Queen's official residence in Scotland. When she is 'at home', the palace is closed. At open times, visitors are given access to apartments and royal collections. Combine a visit with a brisk walk up Arthur's Seat in neighbouring Holyrood Park (see Parks).
www.royal.gov.uk

Historic Houses

Dalmeny House
Out of town, Map 1
By South Queensferry. 7 miles north west of Edinburgh off A90, 0131 331 1888
July/Aug Sun–Tue 2–5.30pm
Adult £4, child £2, conc £3.50
All crenellations and fancy stonework, this palatial Tudor Gothic residence has more in common with Hampton Court than its neo-classical neighbour Hopetoun House. Ornate outside, luxurious inside, the house is stuffed with rare objects d'art, including a whole room devoted to Napolean. Goya-designed tapestries and fabulous paintings by Gainsborough and Reynolds are also part of the Earl of Rosebery's collection. Gardens open Jan/Feb especially for the snowdrop season.
www.dalmeny.co.uk

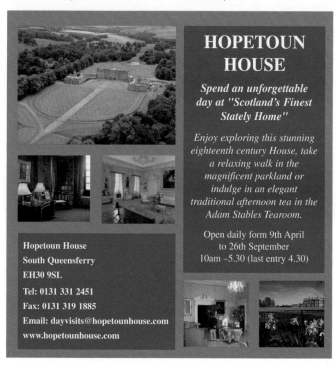

The Georgian House
City Centre, Map 2 D5
7 Charlotte Square, 0131 226 3318
Mar/Nov/Dec Mon–Sun 11am–3pm; Apr–Oct
Mon–Sun 10am–5pm
Adult £5, conc £3.75
Get a flavour of the 'upstairs-downstairs'
life of the 18th century, when masters
were more likely to be clutching a servant
than a Dyson. This is a lovely, spacious
house with a well-stocked basement
kitchen and charming reception rooms.
But it's a pity so few rooms are open.
Furnishings are mostly fine, if a little
hotch potch, and some of the warts and all
insights offered are a hoot – would you
like to be at a dinner party where a piss-
pot was handed round under the table?
More National Trust for Scotland gentility
can be sampled at No 28 Charlotte Square
(see Art Galleries).
www.nts.org.uk

Gladstone's Land
Old Town, Map 2 F6
477B Lawnmarket, 0131 226 5856
Apr–Oct Mon–Sat 10am–5pm, Sun 2–5pm.
Guided tour Sun 1–2pm
Adult £3.50, conc £2.60
Cheek by jowl living on five floors – this
was the high life before the New Town was
invented in the 18th century. Named after
merchant Thomas Gledstanes, who snapped
up this prime site in 1671, its current
interior reflects 17th century style – narrow,
turnpike stairs, cosy rooms, half-glassed
windows, a street arcade and lots of pretty
bits and bobs. A good National Trust for
Scotland place to start the Royal Mile tour.
www.nts.org.uk/gladstone.html

Hopetoun House
Out of town, Map 1
South Queensferry. 9 miles north west of
Edinburgh off A90, 0131 331 2451
Easter–Sep 10am–5.30pm (last entry 4.30pm)
Adult £6, child £3.50, family £18
The greatest of all Edinburgh's grand
houses, this elegant Adams mansion is
where the Marquis of Linlithgow hangs
his hat. The long approach through
woodland and park offers sweeping
Brideshead views and inside, there's
plenty of polished furniture and fine art to
ogle. Most lovely of all are the opulent
trompe l'oeil ceiling paintings. The house
is closed in winter, but events and
weddings are held year round. Café in
restored stables and outside, landscaped
walks, a deer park and tranquil views over
the Forth. Soul food.
www.hopetounhouse.com

John Knox House Museum
Old Town, Map 2 H6
43–45 High Street, 0131 556 9579
Closed until May 2005
Part of the new Scottish Storytelling
Centre, the museum is closed for

rebuilding until 2005. In the meantime,
above the door, look out for a wreath
flanked by the letters JM (John
Mosman) and MA (Mariota Arres), the
goldsmith and his wife who actually
lived here. (See Theatre, Comedy,
Dance).
www.scottishstorytellingcentre.co.uk

Lauriston Castle
Outskirts, Map 1
Cramond Road South, 0131 336 2060
Apr–Oct Sat–Thu, Nov–Mar Sat/Sun. Visits by
guided tour only: 11.20am, 12.20pm,
2.20pm, 3.20pm, 4.20pm. Nov/Mar at
2.20pm, 3.20pm
Adult £4.50, conc £3, grounds free
Not the most visited, and a little out of
the way, this castle/house is a patchwork
of styles, the most dominant being an
attractive blend of Scots
Baronial/Gothic, all slim-stacked
chimneys and turreted corners. Now
council-owned, the interior was given a
makeover in the Edwardian period, and
is a good example of how the movers
and shakers lived then in Auld Reekie's
suburbs. Vast grounds host annual events
which are free for all.
www.cac.org.uk

Newhailes
Outskirts, Map 1
Newhailes Road, Musselburgh. 5 miles east of
Edinburgh off A199, 0131 653 5599
Grounds Mon–Sun 10am–6pm. House
Apr–Sep Thu–Mon noon–5pm; Oct Sat/Sun
noon–5pm
Adult £7, child £5.25, family £19.
Grounds only: £2
Loved for its important 18th century
landscaping with grotto and woodland
walks (dogs allowed), the interior of this
late 17th century house also has bags of
charm. A magnificent library, described
by Dr Johnson as 'the most learned room
in Europe' and rococco interiors all have
that 'lived in' feel. Entry is by guided tour
only. There is a café and shop.
www.nts.org.uk

Trinity House
Leith, Map 3 I5
Kirkgate, 0131 554 3289
Thu eve and by appointment (phone for
details)
Adult £3, child £1
A lovely, little known time capsule almost
lost behind a shopping centre, this
Georgian building houses the complete
trappings of the Incorporation of Masters
and Mariners of Trinity House (est 1380).
In an area with an immensely influential
maritime history, the place is full to the
gunnels with souvenirs from around the
world. Visitors can peer into 16th century
vaults and the vast convening room, stuffed
with sea-faring booty and Raeburns.
www.historic-scotland.gov.uk

festivals

Edinburgh is *the* festival city. Every year during August, the Edinburgh International Festival, founded in 1947, leads a raft of organisations in a remarkable spirit of performance unlike anywhere else on the planet. During this hectic time, *The List* magazine publishes a weekly edition with all the latest reviews and comprehensive listings. Don't be an Edinburgh reveller without it.

Community

Edinburgh Mela
Leith, Map 3 G5
Pilrig Park, Pilrig Street, 0131 557 1400
3–5 Sep 2004
Free
For anyone who still hasn't shaken off the festival bug after the August marathon, the Mela is a weekend of multi-cultural music, dance, art, fashion, delicious sub-continental food and children's activities. It's a relaxed outdoors and tented event for the local community, growing in scale and popularity by the year. Not to be missed on a fine day.
www.edinburgh-mela.co.uk

Leith Festival
Leith, Map 3 J5
Leith Links, 0131 554 3062
6–13 Jun 2004
Tickets: free–£5
A week of traditional community festivities with sports, live music and children's shows, culminating in the Leith Pageant and Gala Day. Bouncy castles, pony rides, hot air balloons, bands and football pretty much keep everyone busy on the day.
www.leithfestival.org.uk

Meadows Festival
Southside, Map 2 G9
The Meadows, 0131 620 9108
7–8 Jun 2004
Free
Celebrating its 30th year next summer, this two-day community festival in the Meadows (see Parks) has 20 live bands,

> ### MY FAVOURITE FESTIVAL
> Edinburgh Fringe Festival
> 'If you remember the Edinburgh Festival you weren't really there.'
> *Mark Little, actor and comedian*

street theatre, a funfair and stalls. Highlights include performance poetry, ethnic music, skater ramps and a specially designed acoustic area. Food vans serve pancakes and tapas and there's a good lot of second hand bargains to be had.
www.meadowsfestival.co.uk

Film

Edinburgh International Film Festival
Citywide
0131 229 2550
18–29 Aug 2004
Tickets: £4.50–£10
One of the key events on the international movie festival circuit, the Film Festival has been going for nearly 60 years. It's the place to see the major arthouse releases of the forthcoming season before anyone else, as well as retrospectives of the work of world cinema's greatest names. There's a popular strand of music video screenings, as well as cartoons, documentaries, on-stage interviews and glamorous premieres with the stars. And like so many of Edinburgh's festivals, it takes place day and night.
www.edfilmfest.org.uk

Music

Edinburgh Jazz and Blues Festival
Citywide
0131 467 5200
30 Jul–8 Aug
Tickets: £6–£22.50
Nipping in just before the overkill of the August festivals, the Jazz and Blues Festival presents over 120 events in ten days from all over the world. Encompassing everything from New Orleans to the avant garde, it's a haven for lovers of low-key melodies, powerful jazz singing and contemporary interpretations.
www.jazzmusic.co.uk

Edinburgh Military Tattoo
Old Town, Map 2 E6
Edinburgh Castle, 08707 555 1188
6–28 Aug 2004
Tickets: £9–£28.50
You have to book early if you want to get into this highly popular event, which attracts punters by the coachload. Performed in front of specially erected seating on the castle esplanade, the Tattoo has arguably the most atmospheric setting of any of the many events in the city in August. It features displays of military bands and army skills from battalions around the world, and especially the tartan-clad regiments of Scotland.
www.edinburgh-tattoo.co.uk

Theatre

Children's International Theatre Festival
Citywide
0131 225 8050
25 May–2 Jun 2004
Tickets: £4
Don't feel you have to have a child in tow to enjoy this magnificent festival. Bringing together a selection of the most imaginative and provocative theatre for young people from home and abroad, it is a celebration of the kind of creative freedoms too often denied to adult audiences. Typically taking place at the Traverse, Royal Lyceum and Theatre Workshop, the festival is organised by Imaginate, a body that champions children's theatre in Scotland throughout the year.
www.imaginate.org.uk

Edinburgh Festival Fringe
Citywide
0131 226 0000
8–30 Aug 2004
Tickets: £1–£15
Even without the other festivals that run in parallel, the Fringe is single-handedly the world's biggest arts festival. It takes place in conventional theatres, church halls, lecture rooms, broom cupboards, on the streets, in moving vehicles . . . and it transforms the city like no other. Being open to anyone who wants to perform, the Fringe varies in quality from the abysmal to the cathartic, and part of the fun is seeking out the unexpected hits before anyone else. Each year, there is a crop of well known faces chancing their luck alongside regulars and first-timers, creating an air of excitement and adventure. All art forms are represented, but theatre and comedy are especially prevalent.
www.edfringe.com

Edinburgh International Festival
Citywide
0131 473 2001
15 Aug–4 Sep 2004
Tickets: £5–£50
Created in 1947, in a spirit of post-war optimism, the EIF inspired the creation of the Fringe and eventually prompted the array of festivals that turn Edinburgh into such a remarkable cultural hotspot. Participation in the 'official' Festival requires an invitation, so this is where you'll see the world's great orchestras, choirs, dance companies and theatre troupes, usually presenting British or world premieres. It's certainly more up-market than some of the rough and ready entertainment you'll find elsewhere, but it's equally partial to adventurousness and risk, and the work is almost always of an exemplary quality. Ironically, prices are sometimes cheaper than you'll find on the Fringe.
www.eif.co.uk

city5s

FESTIVAL FACTS

■ **Edinburgh Fringe Festival** 207 venues, 1541 events, 1,184,738 tickets

■ **Edinburgh International Festival** 11 venues, 170 events, over 400,000 tickets

■ **Edinburgh Military Tattoo** One venue, one event, 217,000 tickets

■ **Edinburgh International Science Festival** 19 venues, 122 events, 126, 937 tickets

■ **Edinburgh Hogmanay Royal Bank Street Party** 2 venues, 2 events, 100,000 tickets

Puppet and Animation Festival
Citywide
0131 557 5724
22 Mar–24 Apr 2004
Tickets: £3/£4
This annual celebration of puppetry began life in Edinburgh but quickly spread out across the whole of Scotland. It's pitched almost exclusively at children and includes many schools' performances as well as public events. Companies are primarily from the UK, many from Scotland, and the programme has sometimes included film as well as the usual varieties of marionettes.

Scottish International Storytelling Festival
Citywide
0131 557 5724
22–31 Oct 2004
Tickets: from £5
A celebration of storytelling traditions featuring the music, legends, myths and tales of Scottish and international cultures. Public events, workshops, guest speakers, and school visits at various venues around the city. See Theatre, Comedy, Dance.
www.scottishstorytellingcentre.co.uk

Check out the City Calendar on pages 6/7 for more events & exhibitions

The Rest

Beltane Fire Festival
City Centre, Map 2 I4
Calton Hill
30 April 2004
Free
In 1988 a group of artists and performers took it upon themselves to revive Beltane, the pagan festival marking the arrival of summer. It involved a night time procession up to a bonfire on the top of Calton Hill, accompanied by primal drumming and elaborately costumed figures. It had a thrillingly subversive edge. Word got out and, by 2002, up to 14,000 people were joining in. The costs of controlling so many people led to its cancellation in 2003, but it's back.
www.beltane.org

Capital Christmas and Hogmanay
Citywide
0131 559 4310, 0131 473 2000 (tickets)
25 Nov 2004–9 Jan 2005
Many free events, some tickets
The big winter festival in Scotland has traditionally been Hogmanay (New Year) rather than Christmas. Edinburgh was the first city to capitalise on this, packing the days at the end of the year with a busy programme of events including concerts, a torchlight procession, triathlon, street theatre and massive outdoor party with live bands. The fun also includes skating, a ferris wheel and a German market in Princes Street Gardens. It's hugely enjoyable for the whole family, which is why the city has become one of the world's most popular winter holiday destinations.
www.edinburghshogmanay.org and www.edinburghscapitalchristmas.org

Edinburgh International Book Festival
City Centre, Map 2 D5
Charlotte Square Gardens, 0131 624 5050
14–30 Aug 2004
Tickets: £3–£8
The world's biggest book festival manages to be both a non-stop procession of literary giants and an oasis of civility and calm in the middle of the various Edinburgh festivals. Taking place in a tented village in the middle of elegant Charlotte Square, the two-week event features readings, debates and discussions from morning till night. The biggest names in literature routinely make visits here and you'll also find the cream of Scottish letters, the leading authors for children and many of the most influential thinkers of the day.
www.edbookfest.co.uk

Edinburgh International Science Festival
Citywide
0131 558 7666
2–13 Apr 2004
Tickets: free–£7
A fantastic festival pitched at all levels and ages, ranging from hands-on children's activities to challenging talks from some of the world's leading scientists. Every branch of the sciences is covered, from botany to geology, astronomy to physics, all packaged in an accessible way for anyone with an enquiring mind. Without diminishing the significance of the ideas, the festival treats its subject with a healthy sense of fun, making you wish your time in the school laboratory had been like this.
www.sciencefestival.co.uk

Royal Highland Show
Outskirts, Map 1
Royal Highland Centre, Ingliston. 4 miles west of Edinburgh on A8, 0131 335 6200
24–27 Jun 2004
Adult £15, child free, conc £10
A large-scale agricultural show featuring choreographed tractor displays, more than 5,000 animals, a Scottish food exhibition, flower show and a large area devoted to crafts. The foremost event of its kind in Scotland, it attracts 140,000 visitors and 2,000 exhibitors and is the largest trade exhibition of agricultural machinery in Great Britain.
www.royalhighlandshow.org

Edinburgh Festival Fringe Society, page 35

film

Since Edinburgh was discovered in the 90's as a fabulous location for historical drama (*Jude*, 1996) as well as tough contemporary pictures (*Trainspotting*, 1995), it's not unusual to find a film crew on its streets. As far as cinemas themselves are concerned, the city has the oldest Film Festival in the world, the art-house devoted Filmhouse, the family-owned Dominion and a choice of brand new multiplexes. For the most comprehensive coverage of what's on in the city, get *The List* magazine every fortnight.

Cameo

Southside, Map 2 E8
38 Home Street, 0131 228 4141
Screenings: £1–£5.20
Built early last century, this cinema oozes character and charm, from its impressive main auditorium to its friendly, knowledgable staff. Playing a mix of arthouse, cult, classic and mainstream crossover films (*Trainspotting* and *Pulp Fiction* both premiered here), the programme also features short films, Sunday double bills and is a major venue for August's Edinburgh International Film Festival. There are regular personal appearances by filmmakers, a tradition kicked off by no less a luminary than Orson Welles back in the 1950s.
www.picturehouses.co.uk

Dominion

Southside, Map 2 off D10
18 Newbattle Terrace, 0131 447 4771
Screenings: £3.80–£11.90
One of the few family-run cinemas left in the country, this beautiful old-fashioned picture palace caters for families and a good night out. Programming avoids overtly violent and/or sexually explicit films, but lots of blockbusters and most period dramas play here. You can pay a little more for the comfy Pullman seats or watch in the lap of luxury in the newly installed electric seats which come with a free drink. Traditional style restaurant on the premises.
www.dominioncinema.com

Filmhouse

West End, Map 2 D7
88 Lothian Road, 0131 228 2688
Screenings: £1.20–£5.50
The UK's most renowned regional film theatre and the hub of the Edinburgh International Film Festival each August. It plays everything from foreign language and arthouse films to obscurities, classics, film seasons and retrospectives. Smaller festivals (French, Italian, horror, lesbian and gay, to name a few), personal appearances by filmmakers and study days find their way into a busy programme. The café/bar has a life of its own with a late license and modestly priced meals, filling to capacity every second Sunday of the month with a film quiz for buffs and boozers alike.
www.filmhousecinema.com

Odeon

West End, Map 2 D7
118 Lothian Road, 0131 221 1477
Screenings: £4.20–5.80
Edinburgh's new Odeon, opened in 2003, used to be the capital's crumbling ABC until it closed a few years ago. After a total makeover, the result is a far smaller ground floor cinema nestling into a supermarket. Inside, it has a clean feel despite the old fascia and although it may not engender the kind of nostalgia that the old picture palace on Clerk Street did, it is at least comfortable.
www.odeon.co.uk

Odeon Wester Hailes

Outskirts, Map 1
Westside Plaza, 120 Wester Hailes Road, 0870 5050 007
Screenings: £3.20–£5.20
The Odeon chain recently took over the running of this multiplex. For a time it was the largest cinema of its kind in Edinburgh, although it has since been out-screened by newer ones. Nevertheless, all new releases, with an emphasis on blockbusters, are screened here, and being out of town it serves a particular geographical audience.
www.odeon.co.uk

Ster Century

Leith, Map 3 G2
Ocean Terminal, Ocean Drive, 0131 553 0700
Screenings: £3–£5.50
If the arrival of this South African owned multiplex has brought nothing new to Edinburgh in terms of programming (it's mainstrean blockbusters all the way), Ster does provide the now redeveloped Leith waterfront area with a much-needed cinema. Located within Ocean Terminal mall, the style bar/restaurant Zinc, with its views of the Forth, makes for a fine post-screening venue.
www.stercentury.com

UCI

Outskirts, Map 1
Kinnaird Park, Newcraighall Road, 0131 669 0777
Screenings: £3.65–£5.25
From the edge of the city, the UCI offers popcorn movie-lovers all the latest blockbusters. Once out there (bus services are regular and there's plenty of parking space), Kinnaird Park's other facilities –

Warner Village in the Omni Centre

bowling, restaurants, bars – make for a whole night's entertainment.
www.uci-cinemas.co.uk

UGC
West End, Map 2 B9
Fountainpark, Dundee Street, 0870 902 0417
Screenings: £2.75–£5.30
A short walk from Lothian Road, this is one of Edinburgh's largest multiplexes. Unlike other cinemas of its type, however, the French-owned UGC programmes foreign, arthouse and cult films alongside the standard blockbusters. Furthermore, it also hosts screenings during August's Edinburgh International Film Festival. The UGC boasts a giant IMAX-type screen,

Iwerks, and the Premier Screen, which offers luxury seating and at seat service.
www.ugccinemas.co.uk

Warner Village
City Centre
Omni, Greenside Place, 08702 406020
Screenings: £3.80–£5.60
Edinburgh's newest multiplex provides the city centre with enough screens to play all the new blockbuster releases. Gold Class offers luxury seating and at seat service. There's a bar in the cinema, although the surrounding area is full of great pubs and style bars for those all-important post-screening discussions.
www.warnervillage.co.uk

libraries&publicrecords

Before you start trawling round the bookshops checking out the three for two bargains, spare a thought for the humble library. Free internet, CD loan and any book you desire are yours for nothing at the 23 Edinburgh City Libraries. If it's specialist research or the family secrets you're after, the university and national libraries and public record offices below will also help you out.

Central Library
Old Town, Map 2 G6
George IV Bridge, 0131 242 8000
Mon–Thu 10am–8pm, Fri 10am–5pm, Sat 9am–1pm
Free
A friendly Victorian pile with general lending on the ground floor and a warren of specialist libraries throughout; Edinburgh room (0131 242 8030); Reference library (0131 242 8060), a wood-panelled floor at the top with extensive study space and free internet access; Scottish library (0131 242 8070) includes a large genealogical resource; Music and Dance library (0131 242 8050); Children's library (0131 242 8027) and Fine Art library (0131 242 8040). That's a lot of books, newspapers, periodicals, CD Rom databases, sheet music, videos, press cuttings, journals and maps.
www.edinburgh.gov.uk/libraries

General Register of Scotland
City Centre, Map 2 G5
New Register House, West Register Street, 0131 334 0380
Mon–Fri 9am–4.30pm
Search fees: from £10

A vast archive of Scottish births, marriages and deaths which began with a humble baptism in 1553. If you want to check out your roots, this is the place to come. A day's search costs £17, a half-day £10. Summer is the time most people start sleuthing into their pasts, so it's best to book your search time then. For reservations call 0131 314 4449 or 4450.
www.gro-scotland.gov.uk

National Archives of Scotland
City Centre, Map 2 G5
General Register House, 2 Princes Street, 0131 535 1314
Mon–Fri 9am–4.45pm
Search fees: prices on application
Currently undergoing a £10m refurbishment, work began on this serious building at the east end of Princes Street in 1774 but due to financial problems and the death of architect Robert Adam was not completed until the 1820s. Now holding law and government records and important family and business documents, the archive itself stretches back to 1127 when land was granted to the city's first parish church, St Cuthbert's. Copies of documents can be arranged – prices on application. A tiny shop sells postcards and publications.
www.nas.gov.uk

National Library of Scotland
Old Town, Map 2 G6
George IV Bridge, 0131 226 4531
Library Mon/Tue, Thu/Fri 9.30am–8.30pm, Wed 10am–8.30pm, Sat 9.30am–1pm. Closed Sun. Exhibitions June–Oct Mon–Sat 10am–5pm, Sun 2–5pm (during the Festival 10am–8pm)
Exhibitions: free. Research: on application only
Behind this grave stone facade is one of Britain's few deposit libraries – a copy of every work published in the UK and Ireland ends up here. Seven floors of shelf space drop below street level under

Fine architecture at the Scottish Poetry Library, page 40

George IV Bridge and there is an annex at Causewayside. Just as well – around 350,000 publications, including books, periodicals, maps and music are added every year. Reading rooms are open for reference and research but admission is strictly by application only. Book-based exhibitions open to the public are mounted every summer.
www.nls.uk

National Library of Scotland, Map Collections
Southside, Map 2 I10
Causewayside Building, 33 Salisbury Place, 0131 446 3813
Mon/Tues/Thurs/Fri 9.30am–5pm, Wed 10am–5pm, Sat 9.30am–1pm
Maps: prices on application
Behind the distinctive glass frontage of this building is stored the largest collection of maps in Scotland, holding over two million cartographic items for public perusal. Over 15,000 atlases, 250,000 digital maps and 1.5 million sheet maps cover various parts of the globe and go back 700 years. The library also offers a reasonably priced copying service.
www.nsl.uk

Scottish Poetry Library
Old Town, Map 2 I6
5 Crichton's Close, Canongate, 0131 557 2876
Mon–Fri 11am–6pm, Sat noon–4pm
Browsing and borrowing: free
You could live in this library. Hidden down a close (not easy to spot, so ask) near the bottom of the Royal Mile, this bright building by architect Malcolm Fraser, has a joyful intimacy (see Architecture). Set up 20 years ago , the organisation moved here five years ago. The collection concentrates on 20th century Scottish and international poetry, but includes some historic titles and a children's library. Remarkably, for all this, there is no charge for borrowing, browsing or for research enquiries, inquiries@spl.org.uk.
www.spl.org.uk

University of Edinburgh Main Library
Southside, Map 2 G8
George Square, 0131 650 3384
Term times Mon–Sun 9am–10pm. Holiday times Mon–Sun 9am–5pm
Research charges: from £5 per day
Designed by Sir Basil Spence in the 60s, this modern block is open to all student card holders and graduates of Edinburgh University. Non-students can also use the library for research purposes for £5 per day or £15 per week and have access to main departmental libraries on application to this address. Check website for details.
www.lib.ed.ac.uk

museums

The Museum of Scotland and adjoining Royal Museum of Scotland are the big players. Taking up nearly the whole south side of Chambers Street, they pull in thousands of visitors each year and between them hold a lion's share of the nation's treasures. The smaller museums listed here range from the U-rated Museum of Childhood to the X-rated Museum of Pathology and Anatomy.

City Collections

Museum of Edinburgh
Old Town, Map 2 J5
142 Canongate, Royal Mile, 0131 529 4143
Mon–Sat 10am–5pm (Sun during the Festival)
Free
A traditional, no nonsense museum telling Edinburgh's story, from the squalid overcrowding of the High Street to the dazzling heyday of the Scottish enlightenment. A warren of small rooms houses an impressive collection of Scottish silver ware, pottery and glass. The museum remains open during refurbishments in 2004.
www.cac.org.uk

Newhaven Heritage Museum
Leith, Map 3 D1
Pier Place, Newhaven Harbour, 0131 551 4165
Mon–Sun noon–4.45pm
Free
Facing the boats of Newhaven Harbour, this little museum takes a snapshot look at 19th century fishing life. Net mending, fish gutting and much bandaged digits are faithfully recreated. Moody, Victorian photographs, including the famous fisherfolk portraits by Hill and Adamson, capture faces of the time: kids are encouraged to dress up just like them. The popular Ye Olde Peacock Inn close by on the main road (open daily noon–9.45pm, 0131 552 8707) offers a different kettle of fish, being the kind of place which serves it battered in three sizes – ladies, large and whale.
www.cac.org.uk

> **MY FAVOURITE GARDEN**
> **Royal Botanic Garden**
> 'I love the Botanic Gardens, the hot houses in winter, the Victorian lilies and the new Chinese Garden. I'm particularly fond of oak trees and there's a fabulous collection of oaks on the west side of the Botanic Gardens.'
> *Robin Harper, MSP, Green Party*

Discover
a Sense of
Scotland
www.nms.ac.uk

'Magnificent'
Time Magazine

'Pure dead brilliant'
The Herald

Museum
of Scotland

part of the National Museums of Scotland

**Chambers Street, Edinburgh
Telephone 0131 247 4422**

Admission Free

The People's Story
Old Town, Map 2 I5
Canongate Tolbooth, Royal Mile, 0131 529 4057
Mon–Sat 10am–5pm (Sun during the Festival 2–5pm)
Free
Filled with the sights and sounds of city living, this museum in a tolbooth shows the harsh realities of city life in the 18th to late 20th century. Employing models in true-to-life settings, the museum emphasises the lot of ordinary people, their grinding poverty and exploitation. The promise of a better future comes at the end with a section on the National Health Service and rise of the trade unions.
www.cac.org.uk

National Collections

Royal Museum and Museum of Scotland
Old Town, Map 2 G7
Chambers Street, 0131 247 4219
Mon/Wed–Sat 10am–5pm, Tue 10am–8pm, Sun noon–5pm
Free
The older part of this double building, the Royal Museum (see Architecture) is a favourite haunt. Galleries filled with the world's precious objects radiate from this serene milling place. Design, geology, space, costume, ceramics all have 'best bits', but it's natural history and the vast halls of stuffed animals that kids always head for. The acclaimed extension houses the Museum of Scotland (see Architecture) and links effortlessly to its older sister building. This massive collection presents with some bravura, the history of our country from BC to Kirsty Wark's SAAB. The Tower Restaurant (see Eating and Drinking) is a chic joint with fab views.
www.nms.ac.uk

Public Museums

Edinburgh University Collection of Historical Musical Instruments
Southside, Map 2 H7
Reid Concert Hall, Bristo Square, 0131 650 2423
Wed 3–5pm, Sat 10am–1pm (2–5pm during the Festival)
Free
For those of us whose musical careers ended with the recorder, this collection of instruments from around the world is quite staggering. The hundreds of bassoons, clarinets and oboes are to be expected. But what sort of sounds are produced by flageolets, sousaphones and ocarinas? The aptly named black serpents look slightly threatening even behind glass; please heed

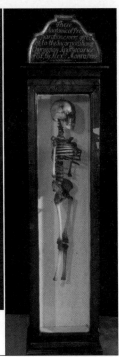

Museum of Scotland

the notice not to feed them.
www.music.ed.ac.uk/euchmi

Museum of Childhood
Old Town, Map 2 H6
42 High Street, 0131 529 4142
Mon–Sat 10am–5pm
Free
Half way down the Royal Mile, this straightforward museum is stuffed with toys from long ago. Teddies, china dolls, Victorian dolls' houses, Meccano, Hornby trainsets and all things that belong in the attic have found a final resting place here. Begun in 1953, the collection is forever expanding. A mock-up of a Victorian schoolroom gets kids thanking their lucky stars they're alive today, and there are slots for pennies in the nickelodeon. There's a good toyshop inside and cafés nearby.
cac.org.uk

Museum of Pathology & Anatomy
Southside, Map 2 H7
Playfair Hall, Royal College of Surgeons of Edinburgh, 18 Nicholson Street, 0131 527 1649
Open by appointment, groups only
Prices on application
Human disease meets classical splendour in this frighteningly enlightening museum. At the heart of a 19th century Playfair building, the clinical, gruesome collection is large and displays serried ranks of body parts riddled with disease, abnormality and deformity in the name of science. To spare the faint-hearted and preserve the integrity of this harrowing hall, you are required to book in advance. Under 15s are simply not allowed. This museum is linked to the Sir Jules Thorne Exhibition.
www.rcsed.ac.uk

Royal Observatory
Southside, Map 2 off F10
Blackford Hill, 0131 668 8404
Mon–Sat 10am–5pm, Sun noon–5pm
Adult £2.60, conc £1.85, family £6
This Victorian observatory, built in 1894, contains one of Scotland's largest telescopes, a good size at 36 inches. Keeping abreast with astronomical developments, a computer room for CD-rom exploration is now in place. Most of the action happens in winter when this northern city is at its darkest: there are Tuesday lectures on astronomy and night sky observation on Fridays from October to March. Phone for details. During the day, the historic technology, stunning views over Edinburgh, small shop and great location on Blackford Hill make a visit worthwhile.
www.roe.ac.uk/vc

Russell Collection of Early Keyboard Instruments
Old Town, Map 2 H6
St Cecilia's Hall, Niddry Street, 0131 667 1011
Check times before visiting
Adult £3
Harpsichords, chamber organs and virginals illustrate the history of keyboard music in this stunning purpose-built concert hall (Scotland's oldest), designed by Robert Mylne in 1763 for the Edinburgh Musical Society. The large collection of over 50 instruments includes pieces from the 16th

century. Musical events (sometimes using the collection) are held throughout the year in St Cecilia's Hall (see Music).

The Scottish Mining Museum
Outskirts, Map 1
Lady Victoria Colliery, Newtongrange, Midlothian, 0131 663 7519
Mid Feb–Oct Mon–Sun 10am–5pm; Nov–mid Feb 10am–4pm (last entry two hours before closing)
Adult £4, child £2.20
Exchange your numbered cage token for a miner's helmet and a tour with bone fide miners who once worked at the pit – they have their old cage numbers off by heart. The massive winding engine that hauled coal and men to the surface still works but the coalface has been reconstructed. Nevertheless, a sense of dust and sweat is all-pervading. Claustrophobes beware. Outdoor clothes and sensible shoes advised. Allow at least two hours for the exhibition, tour and café.
www.scottishminingmuseum.com

Sir Jules Thorn Exhibition of the History of Surgery
Southside, Map 2 H7
9 Hill Square, 0131 527 1649
Mon–Fri noon–4pm (except during special exhibitions)
Free
A surprising little museum which unplugs the history of surgery and its beginnings in Edinburgh in 1505. James Sime was big on amputations in the 18th century, while James Young Simpson invented chloroform to save patients from the pain of the knife. Another local, Lister, gave the world antiseptics. Robert Knox, anatomist and receiver of cadavers fresh-dug by Burke and Hare, was the first curator of this museum, one of Edinburgh's oldest. Upstairs, the slightly less fascinating history of dentistry is revealed.
www.rcsed.ac.uk

The Writer's Museum
Old Town, Map 2 G6
Lady Stair's House, Lady Stair's Close, Royal Mile, 0131 529 4901
Mon–Sat 10am–5pm (extended during the Festival)
Free
Busts of Burns, Scott and Stevenson greet you at the door and it's hushed tones and heads down from then on. Set out like a private study, this collection of manuscripts, first editions and portraits is complemented by personal items owned by the great Scottish men of letters. Burns' ink-stained writing desk and Scott's much-loved chessboard are there: Stevenson's childhood kaleidoscope looks like a prop from *Treasure Island*. Don't miss the engraved flagstones that celebrate centuries of Scottish writing on the way out.
www.cac.org.uk

music

Not a lot of big-time indigenous music in town, but plenty comes to visit. Big bands like the Stones and Chili Peppers turn up at Murrayfield Stadium: the Queen's Hall, Usher Hall and Liquid Room put big names in more intimate surroundings. The Scottish Chamber Orchestra is based in Edinburgh and the Edinburgh International Festival attracts the world's greatest classical musicians. Jazz and folk pop up in the smaller venues and bars around the city. For all the latest dates and reviews for rock, jazz, folk and classical, check out *The List* magazine every fortnight.

Bars

Bannermans Bar
Old Town, Map 2 H6
212 Cowgate, 0131 556 3254
Mon–Sat noon–1am, Sun 12.30pm–1am
This busy Cowgate boozer is a great place to catch up-and-coming local and touring bands striving to get noticed. Experience various styles of alternative live music most nights for a few quid. Popular with local students and young Edinburgh 'scenesters', the live music doesn't necessarily involve old guys with beards.

Bar Java
Leith, Map 3 I5
48/52 Constitution Street, 0131 553 2020
Mon–Sun 8am–1am
A bit of a style bar, this place continues to be a popular haunt with locals due to a homely, inviting atmosphere. Local bands stir things up two or three nights a week and there are nine comfy bedrooms upstairs for those who just don't wanna go home.
www.hotelbarjava.com

Henry's Jazz Bar
West End, Map 2 C7
8 Morrison Street, 0131 538 7385
Tue–Sun 8.30pm–3am
Entry: £5–£10
Ever wondered what hip hop/jazz fusion sounds like? Now you can find out, because this small but well formed Tollcross venue (occasionally known as the Jazz Joint or Henry's Cellar Bar) plays host to live jazz in all its myriad forms – trad, vocal, be-bop, or newer funkier fusions with a different flavour every night of the week.

Royal Oak
Old Town, Map 2 H6
1 Infirmary Street, 0131 557 2976
Mon–Sat 9am–2am, Sun 12.30pm–2am

The antidote to Edinburgh's numerous flash style bars, this is an honest, traditional pub, which hosts popular live folk nights in the basement. The upstairs bar is pretty small, so ten folk make the place seem like it's positively heaving. The basement is three times bigger. Friendly staff serve reasonably priced drinks, and the pub's folk jamming sessions are infamous.

Sandy Bells
Southside, Map 2 G7
25 Forrest Road, 0131 225 2751
Mon–Sat 11.30am–1am, Sun
12.30pm–11.30pm
A small, traditional Scottish pub known as one of Edinburgh's best venues for folk and traditional music. Residencies or one off appearances from touring musicians entertain drinkers most evenings, with sessions starting from 9pm. This friendly, atmospheric, faff-free venue can get very busy at the weekend due to its legendary reputation.

The Scotsman Lounge
Old Town, Map 2 G6
73 Cockburn Street, 0131 225 7726
Mon–Sat 6am–1am, Sun 11.30am–1am
Known by locals as the premier place to get a pint at 6am, this rough'n'ready traditional bar also offers free live folk music each day. Look out for Andy Chung.

The Shore Bar
Leith, Map 3 I3
3 The Shore, 0131 553 5080
Mon–Sat 11am–midnight, Sun 12.30–11pm
A traditional pub and acclaimed seafood restaurant sit side by side down at this enviable waterfront location. The wood-panelled, candlelit bar is cosy and comfortable, and hosts regular live folky and jazzy sessions (usually Wed and Sat) with musicians tucked away in the corner next to the fire.

Whistlebinkies
Old Town, Map 2 H6
4 South Bridge, 0131 557 5114
Mon–Thu 7pm–3am, Fri–Sun 5pm–3am
Treated by many as just another late night bar, this basement venue also features decent live music till 3am every night of the week, with acoustic, folk and rock bands all on the menu. It's taken a while, but this place has definitely managed to establish a reputation for some pretty decent bands of various flavours even if it ocassionally becomes a haven for the 'just-one-for-the-road' brigade.

Concerts

Edinburgh Corn Exchange
West End, Map 2 off A9
11 New Market Road, 0131 477 3500
Opened in 1999 as Edinburgh's equivalent to Glasgow's Barrowland, this 3000

capacity venue has proved a welcome and satisfyingly noisy addition to the music scene, playing host to acts like Blur, Supergrass and Gorillaz. Justin Timberlake even made an appearance on stage post 2003 MTV Europe awards. Although criticised for having the atmosphere of a school canteen, it's still one of Edinburgh's best venues for catching big names in music.
www.ece.uk.com

The Liquid Room
Old Town, Map 2 G6
9c Victoria Street, 0131 225 2564
This popular club and live music venue holds around 800 punters and is a good place to see both local bands and bigger names play. Travis, Public Enemy, Coldplay and the Smashing Pumpkins have all performed here. See Clubs.
www.liquidroom.com

McEwan Hall
Southside, Map 2 G7
University of Edinburgh, Teviot Place, 0131 650 2427
Used for one-off classical events, this impressive, circular building is over 100 years old, and slap bang in the middle of the main university area. Most events have a link to the university, who also use the place for graduation ceremonies and exams. More sedate concerts are also held at the adjacent Reid Hall.

Queen's Hall
Southside, Map 2 I9
South Clerk Street, 0131 668 2019
Converted from a church for the Queen's jubilee in 1977, this intimate concert hall retains a reputation as a restful, atmospheric haven for classical music and for those rock acts who think they are a little bit classy. John Cale and David Byrne have both laid their arty world rock fedoras here in the past, and while the hall is usually all seated, occasionally (as when American rock surrealists the Flaming Lips played in 2002) they'll take the pews out.
www.queenshalledinburgh.co.uk

Reid Concert Hall
Southside, Map 2 G7
Edinburgh University, Teviot Place, 0131 650 2427

The performance home of the Edinburgh University School of Music, this is a purpose-built concert hall, tucked away in a corner of Bristo Square. Tending towards the more intimate end of acoustic and semi-acoustic performances, the hall is used for folk, traditional and classical. Seating a cosy 300, this is one of the most beautiful and atmospheric live music venues in the city, and is somewhat underused.

Ross Theatre
City Centre, Map 2 E6
Princes Street Gardens, 0131 220 4351
Jun–Aug
During the summer months this 2000 seater outdoor theatre within Princes Street Gardens springs to life. Edinburgh Council owned, the Ross Theatre hosts musical performances, between June and August. The annual Bank of Scotland's firework extravaganza is centred on a concert here and there are occasional Scottish country dance evenings.
www.edinburgh.gov.uk

St Cecilia's Hall
Old Town, Map 2 H6
University of Edinburgh, Niddry Street, 0131 650 1000
Another old building owned by Edinburgh University, this central venue

hosts occasional organ and guitar recitals, as well as choral and orchestral performances of various kinds. The building also holds the intriguing and renowned Russell collection of early keyboard instruments. See Museums.

Usher Hall
West End, Map 2 D7
Lothian Road, 0131 228 1155
This seriously magnificent concert hall showcases a range of top end classical concerts as well as the occasional dalliance with the worlds of jazz, world music, country, blues and even the odd rock and pop gig when the fancy takes them. Travis and Ryan Adams played recently. The stalls area has removable seats for the latter, but no matte how they lay it out these are pretty sumptuous surroundings for any live event.
www.usherhall.co.uk

Tickets

Ripping Records
Old Town, Map 2 H6
91 South Bridge, 0131 226 7010
Mon–Wed/Fri/Sat 9.30am–6pm, Thu 9.30am–7pm, Sun noon–5.30pm
Ripping is a vital part of Edinburgh's music scene because it acts as pretty much *the* place to buy gig tickets in the capital – check the regularly updated website.
www.rippingrecords.com

Ticket Scotland
City Centre, Map 2
127 Rose St, 0131 220 3234
Mon–Wed/Fri/Sat 9am–6pm, Thu 9am–7pm, Sun noon–5pm
An essential shop for gig goers. Whether you're after hot tickets for Justin Timberlake at the SECC or the local indie intelligentsia playing a small venue, the briefs are available here. It also issues tickets for gigs across Scotland.
www.ticket-scotland.com

places of worship

There is a church on nearly every street corner in Edinburgh. Sometimes two. Many have been taken out of the fold – Belford is a hostel, the Tron is a tourist information point and both the Queen's Hall and the Edinburgh Festival's Hub, have conscripted holy places into new cultural services. A good congregation of them however, are still doing what they were built for: read all about them below.

Graveyards

Canongate Graveyard
Old Town, Map 2 I5
153 Canongate
Economical with city space, Old Town graveyards like this one tended to grow up against living quarters. In use since 1691, notable residents here include Adam Smith, author of *The Wealth of Nations*, and the poet Robert Fergusson, who died in 1774, and whose pauper's grave lay unmarked until Robert Burns ordered a memorial stone.

Cramond Kirk Graveyard
Outskirts, Map 1
Cramond Glebe Road
Although this compact, pretty little graveyard is still in use, there are plenty of graves from centuries before, including altar-style ones, and even an iron grave-marker. Several have clear examples of funerary art, such as the garlands borrowed from Roman customs, extinguished torches, and carved memento mori skulls. Walled and planted with fragrant bushes near benches, it provides a meditative spot away from the noise of the city.

SCOTTISH VIEWPOINT

Usher Hall

Graveyard of the Parish Church of St Cuthbert

West End, Map 2 D6

5 Lothian Road. Access also via Princes Street and Princes Street Gardens
Sunken and overhung with trees, this gloomy graveyard is full of noteworthy inhabitants – John Napier, inventor of logarithms, lies here, as does George Meikle Kemp, architect of the Scott Monument and Thomas De Quincey, author of *Confessions of an English Opium Eater*. A great place for reflection, a hideaway lunch or an old fashioned tryst.

Greyfriar's Kirk Graveyard

Old Town, Map 2 G7

Greyfriars Place
Arguably one of the city's most historically notorious graveyards, Greyfriars always seems to generate a chill. Burials commenced here in 1562, so there are centuries worth of mausoleums and headstones. There are also the remains of mortis safes, used to protect the dead from the robbers who provided the anatomists' tables with fresh corpses. Around 1200 Covenanters were confined here in 1679: they are remembered by the Martyrs' Memorial. On a more gentle note, both John Gray and his faithful dog, Greyfriars Bobby, rest here.

Places of Worship

Central Mosque of Edinburgh

Southside, Map 2 H7

50 Potterow, Edinburgh, 0131 667 1777
Mon–Sun, phone or check website for times of prayer, tours by appointment
Opened in 1998, the minaret of this mosque heralds a welcome addition to Edinburgh's ecclesiastical skyline. Housing both mosque and Islamic Centre with its library of Arabic and English texts, this impressive building provides a centrally-located hub for the city's Muslim community. The principal prayer room accommodates 750 worshippers.
www.edmosque.com

Church of St John the Evangelist

West End, Map 2 D6

Princes Street, 0131 229 7565
Services Mon–Fri/Sun, phone for details
Rising from the west corner of Princes Street, this is one of Edinburgh's most prominent churches. Episcopalian in faith, its interior includes 19th century stained glass and an intricate, plaster ceiling. But it is best known for its exterior – thought-provoking and often bluntly political murals give this church strong contemporary credentials. A shop and café operate daily until 4pm.
www.stjohns-edinburgh.org.uk

Cramond Kirk, Church of Scotland

Outskirts, Map 1

Cramond Glebe Road, 0131 336 2036
Services Sep–Jun 9.30/11am, Jul/Aug 10am
One of Edinburgh's most historic kirks, arguably with the prettiest location. Built on the site of a Roman encampment (signposted), most of current building can be dated to 1656. Inside, the vaulted wooden roof and galleries offer a glimpse of privileged life in church. That, coupled with beautiful stained glass (three designed by Edward Burne-Jones), make it a favourite for weddings.
www.cramondkirk.org.uk

Greyfriars Tolbooth & Highland Kirk

Old Town, Map 2 G7

Greyfriars Place, 0131 226 5429
Apr–Oct Mon–Fri 10.30am–4.30pm, Sat 10.30am–2.30pm; Nov–Mar Thu 1.30–3.30pm. Other times by arrangement. Gaelic Services Sun 11am and 12.30am
Restored now to former glory, this is one of Edinburgh's most famous churches. Its association with Greyfriars Bobby, the Skye terrier who kept vigil by his master's grave might have something to do with it – his statue sits across from the main gates. Popular legend aside, there's over 400 years of history to contend with here, including the signing of the National Covenant in 1638. Different forms of services (Gaelic included) and also frequent musical events are held here.
www.greyfriarskirk.com

Magdalen Chapel

Old Town, Map 2 G7

41 Cowgate, 0131 220 1450
Mon–Fri 9.30am–4pm, or by arrangement with Rev A Sinclair Horne
Free
This small charismatic chapel is fabulously historical. Dating back to 1541, it was the vision of an Edinburgh merchant and his wife and doubled as a guildhall for the Incorporation of Hammerman. Currently the headquarters of the Scottish Reformation Society, the chapel was restored in 1993 and features the only pre-Reformation stained glass windows still intact in Scotland.

Mansfield Traquair Centre

New Town, Map 2 G3

Mansfield Place, East London Street
Check website for details
No longer a consecrated site, this centre still plays an important part in Edinburgh's ecclesiastical history. Built in 1872, the church itself is impressive, but it's the murals within that are so special. Phoebe Anna Traquair, Edinburgh's premier exponent of the arts and crafts style, painted the rich toned Celtic beasts and stylised foliage between 1893 and

1901. It's well worth taking the time to view these scintillating works of art in situ, especially against their modern backdrop of open-plan offices.
www.mansfieldtraquair.org.uk

Parish Church of St Cuthbert
West End, Map 2 D6
5 Lothian Road, 0131 229 1142
Apr–Aug Mon–Sat 10am–4pm
Built on the site of at least six churches, there has been a place of worship here for centuries: the current building dates from 1894. It's solid rather than towering, and the cupolas suggest renaissance rather than gothic influences: inside, there is a distinctly Florentine air to the curved apse. Well worth a visit for the architecture alone.
www.st-cuthberts.net

Rosslyn Chapel
Outskirts, Map 1
Rosslyn. 7 miles south of Edinburgh off A701, 0131 440 2159 (Custodian)
Mon–Sat 10am–5pm, Sun noon–4.45pm.
Family eucharist Sun 10.30am, evensong Sun 5pm
A perplexing place of worship, which contains more representations of the Green Man than any other building in Britain. The chapel, founded in the 1400s and still a working Episcopalian church, boasts Knights Templar and Masonic connections – and there is the enduring mystery of who or what lies below the floor. Many aspects of the architecture are unique – look out for the ornate Apprentice Pillar and examine the roof's intricate designs.
www.rosslynchapel.org.uk

St Giles' Cathedral
Old Town, Map 2 G6
High Street, 0131 225 9442
May–Sep Mon–Fri 9am–7pm, Sat 9am–5pm, Sun 1–5pm; Oct–Apr Mon–Sat 9am–5pm, Sat 9am–5pm, Sun 1–5pm. Services: Sun 8am, 10am, 11am, 8pm. Musical recitals Sun 6pm
Free: donations welcome
There has been a church on the site of St Giles' for over 1000 years, during which time it has seen a lot of action – executions and riots on the doorstep, the looting of its treasures and 12 years under the ministrations of one John Knox. Today, the atmosphere is calmer, but just as busy, with frequent services and continuing a long-established musical tradition, regular recitals. There's a souvenir shop in the church, and the good basement café keeps advocates from the nearby courtrooms nourished. See Architecture.
www.stgiles.net

St Mary's Episcopalian Cathedral
West End, Map 2 B6
Palmerston Place, 0131 225 6293
Sep–Apr Mon–Sun 7.15am–6pm; May–Aug Mon–Sun 7.15am–9pm. Sung eucharist Sun 10.30am, Thu 5.30pm, choral evensong Sun 3.30pm, Mon/Tue/Wed/ Fri 5.30pm
St Mary's occupies a unique place in

Central Mosque of Edinburgh

live scottish and international comedy

THE STAND

COMEDY

COMEDY CLUB

5 York Place
Edinburgh
0131 558 7272
Open 7 Nights and
all day Sunday

www.**thestand.co.uk**

Scotland's religious culture, maintaining daily sung services. Its towering 90m spire and ornate gothic architecture pay homage to the fact that it is the largest church ever built in Scotland since the Reformation. The cathedral is used throughout the year for concerts, particularly at Christmas.

St Mary's RC Cathedral
City Centre, Map 2 H4
York Place, 0131 556 1798/0027
Phone for details
Impressively situated, looking down Leith Walk and at the meeting points of three main thoroughfares, St Mary's is the Cathedral Church of the Archdiocese of St Andrews and Edinburgh. St Mary's hosts the annual Solemn Mass, which marks the opening of the Edinburgh International Festival. Mass is held daily.
www.stmaryscathedral.co.uk

Synagogue Chambers, Edinburgh Hebrew Congregation
Southside, Map 2 J10
4 Salisbury Rd, 0131 667 3144
Phone for details of service
Constucted in 1932 by famous Glaswegian architect James Miller, this two-storey synagogue is the focus of a range of activities for the Jewish community, with a community centre on the ground floor and a 500 seat synagogue above. Visitors are welcome, but are advised to call in advance as service times vary.

MY FAVOURITE PLACE

Greyfriar's Kirk Graveyard
'I've always loved the story of that poor Skye terrier. loss, death, abandonment and grief are themes that have touched me since childhood.'
Rhona Cameron, comedian

---

theatre**comedy**dance

When the world leaves Edinburgh after festival time in August, the city takes a breather. But make no mistake – the performing arts are by no means resting. Theatre is set for a boost in 2004 with a National Theatre for Scotland, dance is a popular visitor to the Festival Theatre and comedy now has two venues all of its own. Up-to-the-minute programme details are published every fortnight in *The List* magazine.

Comedy

Jongleurs Comedy Club
City Centre, Map 2 H4
Omni Leisure Development, Greenside Place, 0870 787 0707
Thu–Sat 7.30pm–3am
Tickets: from £4
Opened last year, this London-based set-up promotes its own stable of stand-ups including Stephen K Amos, Adam Bloom, Tony Woods and Junior Simpson, round 16 countrywide venues. Have a laugh from 8–10pm, then dance the night away to a 70s-style disco. Drinks on tap, food served and dancing till 3am.
www.jongleurs.com

The Stand
City Centre, Map 2 G4
5 York Place, 0131 558 7272
Box office Mon–Sun 10am–7pm. Club Mon–Sun 7.30pm–12.45am
Tickets: £1–£8
Thanks primarily to the efforts of the Stand, which also has a branch in Glasgow, a genuine year round Scottish comedy circuit has emerged. This popular basement dive is cramped, low-ceilinged and awkwardly shaped – just the ingredients you need for an atmospheric

The graveyard at Greyfriers Tollbooth & Highland Kirk, page 48

Headquarters of the Edinburgh International Festival, The Hub, page 55

stand-up gig. It's open every night, and newer acts start the week, while bigger draws commandeer weekends – you'd be wise to book in advance. As well as a bar, extras include good, very inexpensive food. Sunday brunch with free comedy on the side is especially recommended. *www.thestand.co.uk*

Dance

Dance Base
Old Town, Map 2 F7
14–16 Grassmarket, 0131 225 5525
Mon–Fri 8am–9.30pm, Sat 10am–5.30pm
American choreographer and Dance Base patron Mark Morris, loves this beautifully designed building which runs a massive programme of classes and workshops, both amateur and professional and opens for performances during August. Check website for details. See Sport.
www.dancebase.co.uk

Theatre

Brunton Theatre
Outskirts, Map 1
Ladywell Way, Musselburgh. 6 miles east of Edinburgh on A199, 0131 226 0000/0131 665 2240
Box office Mon–Sat 10am–7.30pm
Tickets: £4–£12
No longer the magnet it was when it maintained its own producing theatre

company – now sadly defunct – this pleasant East Lothian theatre is nonetheless worth the occasional visit for its programme of touring drama and dance. Don't be put off by its civic centre appearance – on the inside, the medium-scale auditorium is comfortable and democratic, creating an intimate relationship between audience and performer.

Edinburgh Festival Theatre
Southside, Map 2 H7
13/29 Nicolson Street, 0131 529 6000
Box office Mon–Sat 10am–6pm (8pm on performance nights)
Tickets: £5–£45
Boasting one of Britain's biggest stages, the 1900-seat venue was re-opened in 1994, kitted out in the art nouveau, beaux arts and neo-classical style of its 1928 heyday. Providing a magnificent setting for dance, classical music and opera, it is the place to see Scottish Opera and Scottish Ballet as well as major touring productions from home and abroad. As its name suggests, it's a key part of the programme for the Edinburgh International Festival in August. It's one of the most popular venues, so advanced booking is advisable. The street level café is open daily 10am–6pm, while interval bars make the most of the spacious, glass-fronted modern architecture.
www.eft.co.uk

Looking for a more exciting time in Edinburgh?

There is nothing like the thrill of live theatre. To see star studded casts and world famous touring companies perform drama, ballet, opera, dance and musicals, log on to eft.co.uk or call the box office on 0131 529 6000. After all, you haven't seen Edinburgh until you've seen a show.

EDINBURGH FESTIVAL THEATRE

KING'S EDINBURGH

brian cox
john byrne
steven duffy
siobhan redmond
joe mcfadden
liz lochhead
peter arnot kathryn howden

jennifer black

alex hassell gabriel quigley
eileen mccallum
zinnie harris billy boyd

see it. feel it. hear it.

Live it live with some of the hottest names
in theatre. Talks, tours, events, bars,
workshops, exhibitions, conferences,
parties, costume hire

More than just a theatre...

Box Office: 0131 248 4848
Costume Hire: 0131 337 1997
Education: 0131 248 4838
General Enquiries: 0131 248 4800

Have a look inside – visit the website:
www.lyceum.org.uk

Royal
Lyceum
Theatre
Company
EDINBURGH

**ONE OF SCOTLAND'S
PREMIER PRODUCING
THEATRE COMPANIES**

Scottish
Arts Council

·EDINBVRGH·
THE CITY OF EDINBURGH COUNCIL

Images: Douglas Robertson; Douglas McBride; Marc Marnie

Traverse Theatre

Edinburgh Playhouse
City Centre, Map 2 H4
18–22 Greenside Place, 0870 606 3424
Box office Mon–Sat 10am–6pm (8pm on
performance nights)
Tickets: £8–£35
Britain's biggest theatre is an ungainly
former cinema that packs them in for the
most popular mainstream entertainment.
Most typically it hosts long running
musicals of the *Miss Saigon* variety, but
also finds space for big name rock and
pop acts and some comedians. Things get
a tad more esoteric during the Edinburgh
International Festival in August when it is
often used for contemporary dance. Lots
of inexpensive, bustling eateries, across
the road, are open late.
www.edinburgh-playhouse.co.uk

The Hub
Old Town, Map 2 F6
Castlehill, Royal Mile, 0131 473 2001
Box office Mon–Sat 10am–5pm
Phone for ticket prices
The administrative home of the Edinburgh
International Festival is an attractively
converted church just down the hill from
the castle. It's used for talks and events
throughout the year – upstairs in the
vibrantly decorated Main Hall or in the

more intimate Dunard Library.
Downstairs, you can buy tickets for
various events, including the Edinburgh
International Jazz and Blues Festival, and
browse the classier than average shop. The
restaurant (with outdoor terrace) is a
recommended haven for coffee, lunch or
dinner. See Eating & Drinking.
www.eif.co.uk/thehub

King's Theatre
West End, Map 2 E9
2 Leven Street, 0131 529 6000
Box office 10am–6pm (8pm on performance
nights)
Tickets: £5–£20
Nearly 100 years old, this 1300-capacity
traditional theatre is the city's main port
of call for large-scale touring drama
productions. It's the place to see pre and
post-West End musicals, thrillers and
comedies, and if the National Theatre is
on tour, this is where you'll find it.
Scotland is proud of its pantomime
tradition and the King's provides one of
the most lavish and raucous spectaculars,
running through December and January.
There are plenty of neighbouring
restaurants and cafés, with Café Favorit
open till 1am.
www.eft.co.uk

Edinburgh Festival Theatre, page 52

Royal Lyceum Theatre
West End, Map 2 E7
Grindlay Street, 0131 248 4848
Box office Mon–Sat 10am–6pm
Tickets: £1–£18
The city's foremost producing house
presents a high quality season of drama
from September to May. New artistic
director David Mark Thomson plans to
build on his predecessor's popular
programme of Shakespeare, 20th century
classics, translations and new Scottish
plays, featuring many of Scotland's best
actors. The beautifully ornate theatre,
with its massive chandelier, is also an
important venue for the Edinburgh
International Festival in August. The
Marque Central, Traverse Bar Café and
Bleu, all next door, offer good pre and
post- theatre food.
www.lyceum.org.uk

Scottish Storytelling Centre
Old Town, Map 2 H6
Netherbow, 43–45 High Street, 0131 556
2647
Box office 9.30am–4.30pm
Tickets: £5–£7
The city's cutest theatre (formerly known
as the Netherbow Arts Centre) is closed
until 2005 while architect Malcolm Fraser
rings the changes. A new bell tower, 100
seat theatre, garden and library will
upgrade this popular venue, providing a
hub for national and international
storytelling activities. In the meantime,

MY FAVOURITE PERSONALITY

Dada Artist, Andy Anderson
'This visionary one toothed
genius occasionally wanders
around Stockbridge. Stop him
for rare pearls of wisdom'
Toby Gough, playwright

---

the newly branded centre is operating
from a shop next door, while
performances continue to be mounted in
venues city wide.
www.scottishstorytellingcentre.org.uk

Theatre Workshop
New Town, Map 2 D3
34 Hamilton Place, 0131 225 7942
Box office Mon–Fri 9.30am–5.30pm
Tickets: £3–£7
Once a lively touring venue, this
Stockbridge theatre has been quieter since
artistic director Robert Rae focused his
energies on developing a resident company
for professional actors with physical
disabilities. As well as the company's
politically charged work, you're likely to
see large-scale community shows – for
which the theatre has a long history – and
an alternative Christmas show.
www.theatre-workshop.com

Traverse Theatre
West End, Map 2 E7
10 Cambridge Steet, 0131 228 1404
Box office Mon–Sat 10am–6pm, Sun
(performance days only) 4–8pm
Tickets: £4–£14
For 40 years, the 'Trav' has been at the
forefront of playwriting in Scotland,
providing a platform for many notable
names such as John Byrne, Liz Lochhead
and David Greig, while introducing us to
acting talent of the calibre of Alan
Cumming, Tilda Swinton and Robbie
Coltrane. The company has been in its
purpose-built basement for a decade,
creating an artistic hub not just during the
Edinburgh Fringe in August, when it is at its
most vibrant, but year round. There are two
flexible performance spaces, one of 250
seats, the other fitting 100 on its bench-style
seating. The public bar/café, serves
wonderful food until midnight and is one of
the city's most fashionable hang-outs.
www.traverse.co.uk

Omni Centre, page 38

out&about

out&about

What family has NOT taken the little ones to Butterfly World and who hasn't watched the Penguin Parade at Edinburgh Zoo? Whether you fancy something educational or just good ol' afternoon fun, this list should keep you out of the house/hotel. And if you think we've missed Edinburgh Castle, just turn to the Castles and Historic Houses section, where it has pride of place.

Bird of Prey Centre
Outskirts, Map 1
Dobbies Garden World. 8 miles south of Edinburgh off A7, 0790 449 5708
Feb–Oct Mon–Sun 10.30am–5.30pm
Adult £2.50, conc £1.25
A pretty majestic, screechy bunch of birds – around 30 species, including hawk, eagle and owl – are housed in this collection of huts next door to Dobbies garden centre. If you fancy more than just a peek at them on their perches (close-up, mind you) you can take the Hawk Walk or try your hand at falconry. Flying displays take off daily at 1.30pm and 3pm. A must for all Potter fans. Butterfly & Insect World is on the same site.
www.birdsofprey.org.uk

Brass Rubbing Centre
Old Town, Map 2 H6
Chalmers Close, off Royal Mile, 0131 556 4364
Apr–Sep Mon–Sat 10am–4.45pm
Free
Brass rubbing is a peaceful activity offering a cool, calm escape from the hustle of the city. Wander in just to look at the airy church itself or choose a brass plaque, pick up some paper and wax crayons and get working (rubbings cost from £1.20 a shot). Designs range from small and simple to large, intricate all-day jobs.
www.cac.org.uk

Butterfly & Insect World
Outskirts, Map 1
Dobbies Garden World. 8 miles south of Edinburgh off A7, 0131 663 4932
Summer Mon–Sun 9.30am–5.30pm. Winter Mon–Sun 10am–5pm
Adult £4.70, child £3.60, family £15
It's hot, it's steamy and if you're lucky a painted lady will land on your shoulder. A boiling mud pool, Koi carp, snake petting and some highly poisonous funsters in the back make this a greenhouse paradise for the whole family. Though fraying ever so slightly at the edges these days, this much-visited place is still a favourite. Bird of Prey Centre and Dobbie's garden centre (café) next door.
www.edinburgh-butterfly-world.co.uk

Caledonian Brewery
West End, Map 2 off A9
42 Slateford Road, 0131 228 5688, 0131 337 1286 (tours)
Tour: adult £6 (must book)
Until recently, the Edinburgh air was thick with the smell of hops. With two breweries surviving into the 21st century, you have to live in Gorgie or Fountainbridge now to get a real whiff of it. Opened in 1869, this one takes tours round its premises, with a tasty draft or two all part of the package. The company also hosts Saturday ceilidhs in its Festival Hall, a beautifully converted old barley store which opens tardis-like into a space with long bar, trestle tables and room to Strip the Willow to a live band. The Caledonian Beer Festival, attracting 3,500 beer-lovers, is held here early June.
www.caledonian-brewery.co.uk

Camera Obscura
Old Town, Map 2 F6
Outlook Tower, Castlehill, Royal Mile, 0131 226 3709
Mon–Sun 10am–5pm
Adult £5.95, child £3.70, conc £4.60
Next to the Castle, this little show is as magical now as it was when it opened in the 19th century. At the top of a tower, it presents a living image of the city projected onto a large concave disc in a tiny, dark room – brilliant low technology. Powerful telescopes on the roof offer fabulous views and eccentric displays on magic and holograms fill the lower floors. But make no mistake – the camera's the star.
www.camera-obscura.co.uk

Deep Sea World
Out of town, Map 1
North Queensferry, Fife, 01383 411 411
Apr–Oct 10am–6pm; Nov–Mar 11am–5pm
Adult £7.90, child £5.75, family £24
Set in a seafront quarry, this award-winner is a fishy subterranean experience with electric eels and sharks taking starring roles alongside less exciting, but decidedly more tasty types. Try and time your visit with feeding times. There's a touchy feely rock pool on ground level (watch out for the lobsters) and an optional shark dive lasting two hours (a scary £100). Whizzing remote control boats round the lagoon offer a cheaper thrill. Café and shop on your way out.
www.deepseaworld.com

Best UK Attraction 2003 runner-up

The Royal Yacht *Britannia*

- Award-winning Five Star Visitor Experience

- Unique insight into life on board

- Five magnificent decks to discover

- Personal audio tour included in admission price

- Next to Ocean Terminal shopping centre

Edinburgh Crystal
Outskirts, Map 1
Eastfield, Penicuik. 10 miles south of
Edinburgh off A701, 01968 675128
Mon–Sat 10am–5pm, Sun 11am–5pm
Adult £3.50, family £9.50, conc £2.50
Watch the professionals blow and cut
glass. Established in 1867, this famous
brand company offers a tour of its works,
including a VIP package (£10) which
offers a shot at glass blowing. Firsts and
seconds from massive stocks are on sale
in the refurbished shop, recently expanded
into a destination shopping centre for
homeware goods. Wedding list heaven? A
large restaurant serves meals and snacks.
www.edinburgh-crystal.com

Edinburgh Dungeon
Old Town, Map 2 G6
31 Market Street, 0131 240 1000
Apr–Jun Mon–Sun 10am–5pm; Jul–Aug
Mon–Sun 10am–7pm; Sep–Oct Mon–Sun
10am–5pm; Nov–Mar Mon–Fri 11am–4pm,
Sat/Sun 10.30am–4.30pm
Adult £8.95, child £4.95, conc £7.95
Cruel methods of torture, pestilence-
ridden streets, grave-robbers, prostitutes
and cannibals – this gruesome attraction
attempts a spine-chilling tour of the
deepest, darkest chapters of Scottish
history. Next door to Waverley Station,
these 15th century vaults, 1,600 metres of
them, have been converted to house
ghastly artefacts, a nerve-jangling boat
tour and all manner of unmentionable
graphic re-enactments.
www.thedungeons.com

**Find Edinburgh Castle on page 31
and the Georgian House on page 33**

Edinburgh Zoo
Outskirts, Map 2 off A7
Corstorphine Road, 0131 314 0300
Apr–Sept Mon–Sun 9am–6pm; Oct/Mar
Mon–Sun 9am–5pm; Nov–Feb Mon–Sun
9am–4.30pm
Adult £8, child £5, family £24
Still a grand day out, even for the most
cynical, this much-loved no, adored, zoo
might be 90 years old, but has moved with
these conservationist times. Babies are
everywhere, with hippos, tigers, meercats
and otters all highly prolific. Don't miss
the famous penguin parade, just outside
their architect-designed enclosure, held (if
the penguins feel like it, which they
usually do) daily at 2.15pm in summer
and at 12.30pm in winter. Note the zoo is
all uphill – a free Hilltop Safari bus runs
all day for lazy types. The café is basic, so
take a packed lunch.
www.edinburghzoo.org.uk

Our Dynamic Earth
Old Town, Map 2 J6
Holyrood Road, 0131 550 7800
Apr–Oct Mon–Sun 10am–6pm; Nov–Mar
Wed–Sun 10am–5pm
Adult £8.95, child £5.45, family £16
Bang next door to the new Scottish
Parliament, this tent-like structure looks
every bit the modern visitor attraction.
Basic cafés and box office upstairs offer
views of Arthur's Seat, a real volcanic
peak. Ticket holders are plummeted via
time capsule lifts down into an
underground 'science-is-fun' journey
which following our planet's lifespan,
complete with virtual earth tremors and a
touchy feely iceberg. A family affair, it's
best for kids of school age but does have
that 'one trip wonder' feel.
www.dynamicearth.co.uk

Camera Obscura, page 59

The Real Mary King's Close
Old Town, Map 2 G6
2 Warriston's Close, Writers' Court, Royal Mile,
08702 430 160
May–Oct Mon–Sun 10am–9pm; Nov–Apr
Mon–Sun 10am–4pm
Adult £7, child £5, conc £6
Cunningly hidden under the Royal Mile is an exciting warren of concealed streets where, centuries ago, people lived, worked and died. This tour tells their story from within dark closes, transporting visitors back in time. A grave-digger's family stricken with plague, a grand 16th century townhouse and a small 'laigh', or poor house, are all described by characters from the past, including a maidservant, a foulis clenger (cleaner), and the daughter of Mary King herself. Note that children under five are not allowed on this tour.
www.realmarykingsclose.com

Royal Yacht Britannia
Leith, Map 3 G1
Western Harbour, Leith Docks, 0131 555 5566
Apr–Sep Mon–Sun 9.30am–4.30pm; Oct–Mar
10am–3.30pm
Adult £8, child £4, family £20
Celebrating its half century last year with a final total of 968 voyages in the log, the Queen's private yacht now lies permanently docked outside Ocean Terminal shopping mall. Opened as an attraction in 1998, the ship's five decks are just as she left them. Scrupulously polished brass and post-war decor offer a glimpse of royal life at sea which can be savoured to the full (if you have the booty) by hiring the facilities for special/corporate occasions. This grand dame now takes about one and a half hours to circumnavigate and is boarded from the second floor of the mall, where a shop and visitor centre attempt to put you in nautical mood.
www.royalyachtbritannia.co.uk

Scottish Whisky Heritage Centre
Old Town, Map 2 F6
354 Castlehill, Royal Mile, 0131 220 0441
May–Sep Mon–Sun 9.30am–6.30pm; Oct–Apr
Mon–Sun 10am–5pm
Adult £7.50, child £3.95, family £17
Scotland's national drink has been poured into this 15-year-old commercial attraction. A trip on the barrel ride takes you back 300 years to the beginnings of whisky making. Audio-visuals and models explain all while the blender's ghost advises on what to do if you don't want malt. A restaurant, bar and shop selling a variety of whiskies, has the tourist in mind. Courses on whisky tasting and selling – phone for details.
www.whisky-heritage.co.uk

clubs

Clubbing in Edinburgh has taken a fair old battering over the last year or so (mainly due to the Old Town fire taking out a couple of key venues), but it's back on track. We've got the lot – deep dub to chart and party classics and the full gamut of dance music. From down and dirty to full-on glitz, you're gonna find something that suits you and your bank balance in this list.

Berlin Beirhaus
West End, Map 2 D6
3 Queensferry Street Lane, 0131 467 7125
Thu–Sun 10.30pm–3am
Entry: free–£10
Low ceilings give this club an intimate vibe and the classy house selection adds to the feeling of sociability. The fantastically monikered Huggy Burger Queen hosts two of the best nights in town. Mocha Rocka! combines house beats from Tokyoblu with disco and funk from the Spaceface crew. And not forgetting Funkeymagic and their Hoffbeat nights, offering the deepest tunes around to the always appreciative crowds.

The Bongo Club
Old Town, Map 2 I6
Moray House, 37 Holyrood Road, 0131 558 7604
Mon–Sun 10pm–3am (approx)
Entry: free–£8
One of the capital's most unassuming venues has moved to this larger, swankier venue. But it hasn't changed the music policy in the slightest: some of the most eclectic and interesting nights in town are based at the Bongo. There's the terminally funky Headspin; the experimental soundclash of Pogo Vogue and, of course, the Messenger Sound System, offering the deepest dub cuts and reggae platters. Add to this a few more nights that you'd never expect, a suitably relaxed environment and good bar prices and you have one of the most chilled clubs around.
www.outoftheblue.org.uk

Cabaret Voltaire
Old Town, Map 2 H6
36–38 Blair Street, 0131 220 6176
Mon–Sun 10.30pm–3am
Entry: free–£12
Cabaret Voltaire is a new player on the club scene in the capital and is settling in very nicely indeed. Its roster changes on a regular basis, keeping things fresh, but Ultragroove (real deal house with guests aplenty) has to be one of its mainstays. It also hosts some of the most unique and diverse clubs around, from the 'anything goes' attitude of Dfrnt Drum to the Brazilian party that is Say Samba! Open nearly every night with something for everyone's tastes – however unique they might be.

CC Blooms
City Centre, Map 2 H4
23–24 Greenside Place, 0131 556 9331
Mon–Sun 6pm–3am (approx)
Free (charge for special nights)
Camp as Christmas, CC Blooms has been the centre of Edinburgh's gay club scene for what seems like aeons, playing a mix of Hi-NRG dance and disco, combined with pop and cheesy classics (often played a double speed to increase the beats). See Gay Life.

The Citrus Club
West End, Map 2 E7
40–42 Grindlay Street, 0131 622 7086
Thu–Mon, times vary
Entry: free–£5
A real student hangout which clings to its indie banner with pride and still has the knock around vibe of your old student union, but welomes anyone like an old friend. With Tease Age, Planet Earth and more offering the best in indie, 80s, electro and ska. Small, intimate and perfect for a good jump around on the dance floor – you won't feel self-conscious if you do that here.

city5s

FAVE RAVES

■ **Manga at the Honeycomb** The ultimate in drum & bass; big guests and monster sounds tear the place apart.

■ **Joy at the Venue** Gay clubbing institution how hosting Alan and Maggie Joy's appropriately named club.

■ **Vegas at Ego** A real List favourite. Topping our readers' polls, it's a swing and sleazy listening shindig.

■ **Tackno at Massa** Queen of kitsch Trendy Wendy presides over the most up-front and fun night of madness.

■ **Colours at the Liquid Room** Big name house your bag? Then you cannae do better than our very own super club.

The Commplex
Leith, Map 3 H3
139–40 Commercial Street, 0131 555 5622
Times vary
Entry: free–£10
While this may be down in deepest, darkest Leith, there's no good reason not to sample the pleasures of the Commplex. Housed in an old church, this really is a luxurious venue – with plenty of seating and swish decor, it's well worth the cab fare down – and some of the clubs even reimburse that!

Ego
New Town, Map 2 H3
Picardy Place, 0131 478 7434
Mon–Sun, times vary
Entry: £2–£12
Housed in an old casino this is all faded glamour and glitz and surely the only club with a fish tank on the dance floor. One of the most diverse venues in town, it often splits into two floors of separate mayhem. Home to some of the capital's best loved nights out – the scintillating swing of *List* favourite Vegas; hot steamy disco action from Disco Inferno; the ecstatic gay frolics of Wiggle and the house sounds of Tokyoblu. And they're just the tip of the iceberg with nights nearly every day of the week.

The Honeycomb
Old Town, Map 2 H6
15–17 Niddry Street, 0131 530 5540
Times vary
Entry: free–£15
This place reeks of class, from its padded walls to its steel bar. It houses some of the city's top house nights, such as the soulful sounds of Audio Deluxe, a favourite with Master at Work Kenny 'Dope' Gonzales and the monster drum & bass sounds of the jungle masters Manga, who get all the big names from Roni Size to Goldie. And of course the best in funk from consistently jumping Motherfunk every Tuesday – and it's free.

The Liquid Room
Old Town, Map 2 G6
9c Victoria Street, 0131 225 2564
Tue–Sun 10.30pm–3am
Entry: £3–£18
The Liquid Room's stature as a main player on the Edinburgh scene keeps growing. Not only does it host some of the best live acts in town, this underground warren is also one of the busiest clubs around. The mighty Evol, every Friday, is the capital's longest running and arguably best indie night. On Saturdays, there's a mixed bag of big name talent. It is the official Edinburgh residence of Scotland's very own super club Colours (everyone from X-Press 2 to Roger Sanchez) and also

hosts Progression – housey but with a progressive slant, the saucy Luvely, the retro Rewind and the magnificent gay friendly Taste every Sunday. Does this place ever close?
www.liquidroom.com

Massa
Old Town, Map 2 G6
36–39 Market Street, 0131 226 4224
Thu–Sun, times vary
Entry: free–£10
Glamorous and flamboyant Massa (formerly Club Mercado) is the setting for some of Edinburgh's most decadent nights. Dress up or dress swish and you'll feel right at home. Highlights include the vocal garage and up front house of Flaunt and Eye Candy. But perhaps its biggest draw and one of the most entertaining nights in town is the anything goes spectacular that is Tackno hosted by the queen of kitsch herself Trendy Wendy (monthly Sundays).

Opium
Old Town, Map 2 H6
71 Cowgate, 0131 225 8382
Mon–Sun 11pm–3am
Free
When rockers' pub Legends closed its doors, many a biker was seen to shed a tear. But lo and behold, it got a full refit and a proper dance floor area added. Fortunately it didn't change its music policy, sticking to a heady brew of rock, nu metal, thrash, hardcore indie and more rock, but it's all just that bit classier these days, attracting indie kids, skate punks, students and just plain old dyed-in-the-wool metalers.

Po Na Na
City Centre, Map 2 E5
43b Frederick Street, 0131 226 2224
Sat–Mon, Wed/Thu 10pm–3am, Tue/Fri 9pm–3am
Entry: free–£5
Just off Princes Street, this is one of the better centrally located clubs. Classy and intimate, with Moroccan styling, Po Na Na is part of a national chain but feels local, thanks to its DJ talent. While offering a mix of funk, hip hop and house, disco and 80s classics, the low ceilings and a small dance floor may put off those after a serious boogie.
www.ponana.co.uk

Revolution
West End, Map 2 D7
31 Lothian Road, 0131 229 7670
Mon/Thu–Sun 10pm–3am (approx)
Entry: £4–£7
As you walk down Lothian Road you just can't miss Revolution and its usual queue of scantily clad girls and Pringle-

ESPI⊕NAGE

1 CLUB 4 BARS NO CHARGE

unique
bar & club
complex
open
7 nights
until 3am

sporting lads. Cheap and cheerful on a massive scale (with a 1500 capacity), this is your Magaluf holiday experience brought back to sunny Edinburgh. Offering a selection of pop, cheese and chart dance sounds to keep the stilettoed masses moving, plus plenty of drinks promos to keep 'em well watered and suitably drunk.

Studio 24

City Centre, Map 2 I5
24–26 Calton Road, 0131 558 3758
Thu–Sun 10.30pm–3am
Entry: £1–£10
Now this is the real deal underground clubbing experience, down and dirty, just the way we like it. Most famous for the weekly metal and goth nights such as the Mission, Nexus, DKY and Asylum. Saturdays are usually a full on mix of tuff techno (Dogma with guests such as Surgeon and DJ Rush) and gay friendly twisted trance night Mingin'.

The Subway

Old Town, Map 2 H6
69 Cowgate, 0131 225 6766
Mon–Sun 7pm–3am
Phone for prices
The Subway has been packing them in for many a year. It's not fancy by any stretch of the imagination but it plays out the chart classics and a dash of indie nearly every night, fuelled by various drinks promos and the chance of copping off. Central as you can get, it attracts the plain old drunk.

The Venue

City Centre, Map 2 H5
17–21 Calton Road, 0131 557 3073
Thu–Sun 10.30pm–3am
Entry: £3–£12
There have been plenty of ups and downs on the Venue roller-coaster in recent years, but after a recent refurbishment things are definitely back on track. This Edinburgh institution (old home to Pure and Tribal Funktion) has a mixed bag of clubbing treats. Still most at home with techno (the massive Pressure v Bugged Out with excellent guest rosters) and house (Majestica again, no stranger to big name DJs), it offers a few other delights. Every Friday, 3D puts three different clubs on each floor, so in one night you can go from funk to house to drum & bass as the mood takes you (with everyone from Rogue State and No Strings Attached to Optimo involved). Monthly special Super Saturday showcases local legends and Edinburgh's biggest gay night, Joy, has made the Venue its new home. Whatever you choose, every event's a top night of unpretentious fun.
www.edinvenue.com

gay life

Whether you're into pink and fluffy or steel and leathery, Edinburgh has a burgeoning gay scene to suit most tastes. New clubs, venues and organisations are springing up all the time, and the perennial favourites such as CC Blooms are still going strong. So whether you're Arthur, Martha, or not quite sure, there are plenty of opportunities for you to get out in Edinburgh. Here's a rough guide to some of the best.

Accommodation

Ardmor House

Leith, Map 3 F5
74 Pilrig Street, 0131 554 4944
Double room: from £55
This gay-owned but straight-friendly establishment has a reputation for quality and comfort. Five four star ensuite rooms are available, with traditional Scottish, continental or veggie breakfasts on offer. Free parking a plus at this central location and smoking is strictly forbidden throughout.
www.ardmorhouse.com

Garlands Guest House

Leith, Map 3 offF5
48 Pilrig Street, 0131 554 4205
Double room: from £40
Garland's – named after guess who? This is a cosy, home-run establishment in a pleasant Georgian terrace close to town, but away from the bustle. With six ensuite rooms at attractive rates, and a friendly atmosphere, this is the place to relax after a hard day's sightseeing. Check the website for more info and a taste of the owners' sense of humour.
www.garlands.demon.co.uk

Mansfield House

New Town, Map 2 G3
57 Dublin Street, 0131 556 7980
Double room: from £40
You won't get much closer to the heart of Edinburgh than Dublin Street, where this guest house is located. Nine rooms are available, from standards and ensuites to superior king-size, all of them equipped with extras. Self-serve continental breakfast available until midday and no smoking restrictions. Check the website for photos and booking.
www.mansfieldguesthouse.com

For more accomodation, turn to the Staying Over section, page 157

Bars and Cafes

Blue Moon Café
New Town, Map 2 G3
36 Broughton Street, 0131 556 2788
Mon–Fri 11am–1am, Sat/Sun 10am–1am
Down boho Broughton Street this fully
licensed haven is a sedate and convenient
place to chill out and meet friends, or
even strangers, for coffee or a quality
meal. They've a log fire in the winter,
friendly, welcoming staff, tanks of happy-
looking fish and eclectic background
music. Whether your appetite is big or
birdlike, there will be something on the
well-priced menu to suit. Food served till
midnight.

The Claremont Bar & Restaurant
New Town, Map 2 G1
133–135 East Claremont Street, 0131 556
5662
Mon–Sat 11am–1am, Sun 12.30–11pm
A gay-owned, gay-friendly bar and
restaurant that deals in fresh, home-made
food – nothing cooked from frozen,
according to the menu. With popular men-
only nights on the first and third Saturday
of every month, pub quizzes every
Wednesday, special meetings for Dr Who
fans every Monday night and a monthly
meeting for the local Fortean Society this
is by no means an ordinary bar . . .

Habana
City Centre, Map 2 H4
22 Greenside Place, 0131 558 1270
Mon–Sun 1.30pm–1am
Another highly popular haunt among the
city's gay crowd. All chrome, mirrors and
bare boards, it has a slightly
cosmopolitan feel. Secrete yourself in the
downstairs snuggery or strike a pose on
the balcony overlooking the bar – at
Habana you can both see and be seen.
Live guests and DJs at weekends and

weekly 'Quizoke' competition on
Thursdays. Outdoor tables appear in good
weather and it is only a door away from
CC's.

Newtown Bar
New Town, Map 2 G4
26b Dublin Street, 0131 538 7775
Mon–Thu noon–1am, Fri/Sat noon–2am, Sun
12.30pm–1am
You know pretty much by the name where
to find this sophisticated watering hole,
popular with Edinburgh's more mature,
cruisey gay crowd. An established haunt,
it recently celebrated its 10th birthday
with a Bollywood theme night. At the
weekend, resident DJs ply the downstairs
bar and dancefloor from 10pm–2am.

Planet Out
New Town, Map 2 H4
6 Baxter's Place, 0131 524 0061
Mon–Sun 4pm–1am
With its colourful, comfortable interior
and friendly atmosphere, this is a bustling
venue which plays host to regular live
DJs, quiz and bingo nights and themed
evenings. One of the central meeting
points for Edinburgh's gay scene, Planet
attracts a mixed crowd from across the
spectrum. It's a great place to chill with a
few drinks by day, while at night it
becomes a perfect pre-club place, with CC
Bloom's just doors away. A local
favourite, understandably so.

The Laughing Duck
New Town, Map 2 E4
24 Howe Street, 0131 220 2376
Sun–Thu noon–midnight, Fri/Sat noon–1am
Deep in the heart of the New Town is the
intriguingly named Laughing Duck. We're
told it's not rhyming slang for anything,
but we're not so sure. For sports fans, the
Duck sponsors a local rugby team, the
Caledonian Thebans, while for those with
a more intellectual bent there's the

Garlands Guest House

fortnightly quiz every second Sunday. Good bar meals are served all day and a function room can be hired. Just the place to meet and greet old friends and former and potential partners.
www.thelaughingduck.co.uk

Clubs

CC Blooms
City Centre, Map 2 H4
23–24 Greenside Place, 0131 556 9331
Mon–Sun 10.30pm–3am
Free
Edinburgh's oldest and best-known club is still the hive-like home to the city's queen bees. More often than not packed to the gunnels with its free admission policy, CC's is one of the first ports of call for many newcomers to the scene, and a Mecca for visitors – such as the boys from the cast of whatever extravaganza is currently on at the Playhouse. Dance into the early hours any night of the week to music which ranges from camp classics to Hi-NRG house. See Clubs.

Joy
City Centre, Map 2 H3
Club Ego, Picardy Place, 0131 478 7434
Monthly Sats 11pm–3am
Entry: from £8
One of Edinburgh's longest running club nights, Joy celebrated its 10th birthday in 2003. Centrally located at Ego, across the road from CC's, the night attracts a strong, regular fan base to its two floors of tunes – from the titular house masters Alan and Maggie Joy on the main stage upstairs to Trendy Wendy and Co's mix of kitsch and chart in the downstairs suite.
2 H3

Luvely
Old Town, Map 2 G6
The Liquid Room, Victoria Street, 0131 225 2564
Monthly Sats 10.30pm–3am
Entry: from £10
Another stalwart of the Edinburgh club scene, Luvely exists solely to help you dance your way out of one month and into the next. Being centrally located just a short step from the Grassmarket makes this a great venue to get to (from a pre-club pub of your choice) and from (taxis from George IV Bridge and the Royal Mile).

Tackno
Old Town, Map 2 G6
Massa, 36–39 Market Street, 0131 226 4224
Monthly Suns 10.30pm–3am
Entry: from £6
Arguably Edinburgh's gayest 'theme' club night, look out for posters and flyers for the dress code of the latest Tackno. Resident DJ Trendy Wendy, whose own

mix of tunes runs from hard cheese to way beyond cheddar, has become something of a cult figure on the scene, so you know you're in good hands in this dressed-up, ever-popular party night. Work on Monday morning is the downside.

Wiggle
New Town, Map 2 H3
Club Ego, Picardy Place, 0131 478 7434
Monthly Sats 10.30pm–3am
Entry: from £8
From the people who brought you Joy comes Wiggle, the new kid on the gay club circuit. Penny Pornstar personally welcomes you in, with Trendy Wendy dominating the main room with her blend of chart and camp classics, and a mix of R&B, hip hop and indie tunes downstairs. Wiggle kicks off with a pre-club session in nearby Planet Out – so that's your night sorted.

Information

LGB Community Resources
New Town, Map 2 G3
Sala Café Bar, Broughton Street, 0131 478 7069
As with any city with a thriving gay scene, Edinburgh has a strong support network of community resources. The LGB Centre, connected to the Sala Café Bar, is a useful base for a range of community gatherings, such as the Gay Dads' group and the bisexuality support group, both monthly, and the weekly women's group drop-in. Contact the centre by phone or stop by for more information. The Lothian Gay and Lesbian Switchboard (0131 556 4049, Mon–Sun, 7.30–10pm) and the Lesbian Line (0131 557 0751, Mon–Thu, 7.30–10pm) always have friendly voices on hand to offer information and support, in confidence.

Waverley Care Solas HIV Support Centre
City Centre, Map 2 K4
2/4 Abbeymount, 0131 661 0982
Café Mon/Fri 11am–4pm, Tue/Thu 11am–6.30pm
Extending its supporting arms beyond the gay and lesbian community is the Waverley Care Solas organisation. Since opening in 1991, it has offered a range of specialist advice, counselling and information groups for all people living with HIV and AIDS. These include Juice (Fridays), for gay and bisexual men and the Isis Women's Group. The Solas café, meanwhile, is staffed by volunteers and provides a great range of refreshments, from drinks and snacks to full meals. Contact the centre direct or check out its website for more information.
www.waverleycare.org

kids

This city has paying attractions, soft play centres and places to spend pocket money. But perhaps best of all are the green places, many of which are hilly and wild and just made to roll down. After reading through this lot, check out Parks, Castles and Historic Houses, Attractions, Sports and Activities and Days Out, all in this publication. No wee blighter can claim there's nothing to do.

Craft

The Art Club
New Town, Map 2 E2
19 Brandon Terrace, 0131 556 3408
Tue–Sat 11am–5pm
A brand new hangout for kids. In this cute little shop, they can design a T-shirt, paint a plate or draw the hours away. Small birthday parties are catered for, but it's the regular workshops and classes (phone for details) that make this place buzz. The back room is where it all happens and creative persuits for all ages are organised by arty owner Jenny Reynolds throughout the week. Booking advisable during school holidays.

The Ceramic Experience
Leith, Map 2 H2
8 Hopetoun Street, 0131 556 0070
Mon–Sun 10.30am–5.30pm
Ceramics: from £4.99
Opened in 2002, this unassuming building, a little off the beaten track, houses a cheery, sunny space where children and adults can paint ceramic models fresh from the kiln. There's a café and a small free ball pond which can be used regardless of whether painting pots is your thing. If it is, there's a wide range to choose from – plates, mugs, cups and cats – each one to be paid for individually. After firing (you may have to wait a couple of days), they're yours to take home. Evening and holiday classes.
www.ceramicx.biz

Doodles
Southside, Map 2 G9
29 Marchmont Crescent, 0131 229 1399
Tue–Thu 11am–9pm, Fri/Sat 10am–6pm, Sun noon–6pm
Studio fee: £5 plus price of ceramics
This cosy little studio in relaxed, studenty Marchmont is proving highly popular – it's best to book at weekends. Choose from a vast selection of ceramics including fridge magnets, animal shapes, tiles and teapots. Caters for all ages from very young artists just daubing their hand or foot print on a tile, to grown-ups, who often come armed with a bottle of wine in the evening, painting through a new set of kitchen crockery.
www.doodlesscotland.co.uk

Indoor Play

Brewsters Fun Factory
Leith, Map 3 D1
51–53 Newhaven Place, 0131 555 1570
Mon–Sun 11am–9pm (restaurant/bar until 10pm)
Child £2
Lodged within Brewsters, a 'chicken nuggets and chips' type family restaurant, this indoor play space, formerly known as Charlie Chalk's, provides ball pond, rope bridge and multi-layered entertainment for kids between 3ft and 4ft 9inches. It's basic but not bad value for money and being situated on Newhaven harbour, you can combine a visit with a walk round the boats or a trip to Newhaven Museum (see Museums) next door.
www.brewsterthebear.co.uk

city5s

ICE CREAM

■ **Café Gelataria**
Royal Botanic Gardens (West Gate), Arboretum Place
This trailer sells ices Mar–Oct, noon–5pm. Love the raspberry sauce.

■ **Espresso Bar**
East Princes Street Gardens
Cold in summer, hot in winter – this ice cream/coffee window is open year round.

■ **Piazza Espresso Bar**
West Princes Street Gardens
Next to the children's playground? Perfect. Open, with seating, Apr–Oct.

■ **Luca's**
16 Morningside Road 0131 448 0233
Irn Bru and choc ginger ice cream brought to you by the famous ice-cream firm.

■ **Marcantonio**
28 Granton Road 0131 552 4641
This splendid family-owned sweet shop next to the Water of Leith has made fresh dairy ice cream on the premises since the 60s.

Clambers at the Commonwealth
Southside, Map 2 J10
Royal Commonwealth Pool, Dalkeith Road,
0131 667 7211
Ages 3–8 Mon–Fri 10am–6pm, Sat/Sun
10am–5pm
Ages 0–3 Mon–Thu 10am–6pm, Fri
10am–1pm, Sat/Sun 10am–noon
Child £1.80
One of the city's first indoor play places.
Built quite high, which can be daunting
for all but very boisterous little ones, it has
three levels of slides, tunnels, rope
bridges, soft play and ball ponds all
geared to working up a sweat. It's all in
well-used, but respectable condition with
friendly staff on hand to help. Under
threes will need accompanying and are
not admitted during school holidays
because of the crowds. For more on the
Royal Commonwealth Pool, see Sport.
www.edinburghleisure.co.uk

Jelly Club
Outskirts, Map 1
10b King's Haugh, Peffermill Industrial Estate,
Peffermill Road, 0131 652 0212
Mon–Sun 10.30am–6.30pm
Child £3.50–£4.50
The Jelly Club provides a warehouse-style
venue for different zones; Jelly Village,
with 60 mini cars to razz about in; the
Inflatable Space Adventure, a bouncy,
starry heaven; Jelly Jungle, a multi-
levelled adventure space with ball ponds
and big curvy slides; and Wobbly Jellies,
a soft play area for under threes. There's a
friendly atmosphere and despite, or maybe
because of, the air-hanger feel, it is light
and airy with a café for the adults to sit
back and relax.
www.jellyclub.co.uk

Laserquest
West End, Map 2 B8
56 Dalry Road, 0131 346 1919
Mon–Sat 11am–11pm, Sun 11am–8pm
Game: £3.50–£9
There's no age restriction on running
around and shooting people with laser
guns, but there is a height one. Three and
a half feet is the minimum stature
required, but beyond that you can run
about the smoke filled chambers, hiding
and shooting to your heart's content. In
these recently opened premises, boasting
the 'new' laserquest, you enter a derelict
starship with over 5,000 square feet of
tunnels, ramps, catwalks and towers and
only your wits for protection. It's the
same principal as every other LQ, but the
formula's a winner so why mess?
www.lqx-edinburgh.co.uk

Leith Waterworld
Leith, Map 3 I5
377 Easter Road, 0131 555 6000
Fri–Sun 10am–4.45pm; school holidays
Mon–Sun 10am–4.45pm
Adult £3.40, child £2.40, family £9
Recently re-opened, Leith Waterworld is a
fantastic place to go for an afternoon and
play in the rapids, waves and fountains.
Bright and airy, it has a circular design
with different areas; a lagoon space if you
want a bit of calm; a fast flow channel if
action's more your scene; big flumes; and
a separate soft play and multi-sensory
area. Children over nine can come on their
own if they are competent swimmers.
Otherwise every fun kids must be
accompanied by one adult.
www.edinburghleisure.co.uk

The Old Children's Bookshop
Old Town, Map 2 I5
175 Canongate, 0131 558 3411
Mon–Fri 10.30am–5pm, Sat 10am–5pm
Not a Harry Potter in sight, this is a little
temple to 50s dreams: chalet school
romps, orphans cum ballerinas, adventures
with four children and a dog line the
shelves. It's almost disappointing not to
find a flask of ginger beer nestling in the
corner. There are, nonetheless, lots of treats
to be had including old Beanos, Eagles
annuals and prints.

Outdoor Adventure

Almond Valley
Out of town, Map 1
Millfield, Livingston. 18 miles west of
Edinburgh off A705, 01506 414957
Mon–Sun 10am–5pm
Adult £3, child £2, family £10
This is a good bet at any time of the year.
With farmyard animals to meet – and if
you're lucky, feed – a miniature railway to
chug along on, soft play for the under
fives, an adventure zone located in a
derelict oilworks, riverside walks and
picnic areas, you can't really go wrong.
www.almondvalley.co.uk

Dalkeith Country Park
Outskirts, Map 1
Dalkeith. 7 miles south east of Edinburgh off
A68, 0131 654 1666
Apr–Sep Mon–Sun 10am–5.30pm
Adult/child £2
Check out the Parks section for open
spaces in town, but if it's high action
you're after, the best place to go is this
custom built adventure playground in the
woods with excitingly big swings, flying
foxes and tree-top bridges and slides.
www.dalkeithcountrypark.co.uk

Gorgie City Farm
West End, Map 2 off A9
51 Gorgie Road, 0131 337 4202
Apr–Sep 9.30am–4.30pm; Oct–Mar
9.30am–4pm
Free: donations welcome
With a Sesame Street kind of idealism,

A splash of fun at Leith Waterworld

Gorgie City Farm puts all that's fluffy, clucky and hairy centre stage. This easy-going, much-loved rough diamond of a place has pigs, sheep, cows, ducks, hens and ponies all living in traditional stables and sties. Cuddly pets such as rabbits also lollop about. A play park is on hand for additional energy release and Jemima's Pantry serves tea and snacks. Parking is tricky and on street only.

Theatre and Film

The Big Scream
Southside, Map 2 E8
The Cameo, 38 Home Street, 0131 228 4141
Fortnightly screenings
Adult plus baby £3.50
A new and wildly successful event which brings parents and their babies together under one cinema roof. Screenings are every two weeks and range from latest releases to classic films. Ticket price is for parent and baby (under 12 months) and includes free tea/coffee, baby changing, bottle warming and buggy parking facilities. In a twist of

---

MY FAVOURITE BRIDGE

The Perspex-sided one over Princes Street Gardens
'I love the way toddlers gather here to wave at the train drivers (they toot back).'
John Fardell, cartoonist

---

certification fate, babies under one year can be exposed to any film rating – so it's *The Exorcist* next week, little Tommy.
www.picturehouses.co.uk

Biggar Puppets
Out of town, Map 1
Puppet Tree House, Broughton Road, Biggar. 29 miles south west of Edinburgh on A702, 01899 220631
Check website or phone for programme details
Adult £5, child £4, family £23–£36
Check out the Theatre, Comedy, Dance section for theatres that cater for kids (Scottish Storytelling Centre particularly) and Festivals for events specially for them. Not far from Edinburgh, there is also a little treasure worth making the half hour journey for. International Purves Puppets has its own mini mock-Victorian theatre and puts on shows several times a week. Ice cream in the cute café and a runabout in the playpark outside is all part of the fun.
www.purvespuppets.com

Royal Lyceum Theatre Company Youth Theatre
West End, Map 2 E7
30b Grindlay Street, 0131 248 4838
Here's your chance to learn in a real theatre. Workshops for young people aged 5-22 run all year round. The Youth Theatre produce and present a number of exciting, contemporary productions.
www.lyceum.org.uk

sports&activities

Read on and get off the couch. While this city of hills lends joggers a golden opportunity for tough marathon training, it also has excellent sailing, waterskiing, pony-trekking, mountain biking and hiking facilities, all within easy reach. The more confined pursuits of football, cricket, yoga, tennis, indoor climbing and bowling, are all within the city limits. This taster of the best of them should get you going. *The List*'s new *Adventure Sports Guide to Scotland*, published May 2004 (£4.95) will take you even further down the track.

Adventure

The Adventure Centre – Ratho
Outskirts, Map 1
South Platt Hill, Ratho. 5 miles west of Edinburgh off M8, 0131 333 6333
Mon–Sun 10am–10.30pm
Climbing wall: all day access £10/£7. Equipment: from £3. Other activities: check website for details
The centrepiece of this ambitious development, which opened in 2003, is the National Rock Climbing Centre, which features four indoor climbing walls (including the largest in Europe), teaching walls, vicious overhangs, three free standing boulders, the SkyRide – a huge suspended assault course, due to open in March 2004 – and a number of outdoor rock climbs. The venue also houses the centre for Judo Scotland, conferencing facilities and a gym. Mountain bike trails and sub aqua facilities are expected to open in spring 2004.
www.adventurescotland.com

Alien Rock
Leith, Map 3 D2
Old St Andrews Church, 8 Pier Place, Newhaven, 0131 552 7211
Mon–Fri noon–10pm (winter 11pm), Sat/Sun noon–7pm
Unlimited climbing: from £4
Alien Rock 1 features 180 different routes and a higher, more challenging wall where beginners must be accompanied, while Alien Rock 2 (37 West Bowling Green Street, Leith, 0131 555 3650, open from 4pm) is a bouldering wall with no ropes and lots of crash mats. Equipment is available for hire, and the team arranges climbing trips to Europe and the Highlands.
www.alienrock.co.uk

Glentress Forest
Out of town, Map 1
Glentress Forest, Peebles. 23 miles south of Edinburgh on A72, 0172 172 1736
Open at all times
Free
Part of the Forestry Commission's mission to encourage mountain biking, this is fast becoming a red hot destination, boasting some of the best singletrack anywhere in the UK. Routes are graded according to difficulty, from beginners to tough trails requiring suspension, padding and experience. The Hub café (Mon–Fri 10am–6pm, Sat/Sun 9am–7pm) is a useful place for route maps, advice, bike hire and spares, really good grub and a post-ride hose down.
www.hubintheforest.co.uk

Midlothian Ski Centre
Outskirts, Map 1
Hillend, Biggar Road. 5 miles south of Edinburgh on A702, 0131 445 4433
Mon–Fri 9.30am–9pm, Sat/Sun 9.30am–7pm
Skiing: £7.50 per hour, including hire
Can't wait till winter or stomach the trek to the mountains? Europe's longest artificial ski slope, known in the trade as 'Hillend', stretches most of the way up a Pentland hill, and features a drag lift, a chair lift and a selection of jumps as well as a learning area. Dry slopes have their detractors – snowboarding in particular is rather easier on the real stuff – but you'd be foolish not to use a resource this close to town. And there's free tobogganing on surrounding slopes when there's snow. Scotland's five main areas (Cairngorm, Glencoe, Glenshee, the Lecht and Nevis Range) are only a few hours away and enjoy variable snow cover between Dec and Apr. Check www.ski.visitscotland.com for forecasts and information.
www.ski.midlothian.gov.uk

The Scottish Gliding Centre
Out of town, Map 1
Portmoak Airfield, Scotlandwell, Kinross. 28 miles north of Edinburgh off M90, 0131 840 543
Apr–Sep Mon–Sun, Oct–Mar Tue/Wed/Fri–Sun
Gliding: £50 for 20 minutes
One of the best and busiest gliding clubs in the country, this place offers 20 minute trial flights as well as evening classes and day and holiday training sessions. Pilots can expect to go solo after about 70 flights. After their first such flight they are awarded an 'A' badge, after which they can further progress through 'B' bronze, silver and gold BGA approved awards. Check out www.gliding.co.uk, the British Gliding Association's website.
www.scottishglidingcentre.co.uk

The climbing wall at The Adventure Centre - Ratho

Entertainment

Bedlam Paintball Games
Out of town, Map 1
Near Kirkliston, South Queensferry. 9 miles
north east of Edinburgh off A90, 0131 558 1919
Check website for opening times and prices
With up to 120 people on site at any time,
Bedlam is luminous carnage.
Thunderflashes and smoke bombs will
assault your senses, while a single paint
grenade becomes a vibrant Jackson
Pollock of death. Fully insured and
following strict safety guidelines, Bedlam
caters for corporate events as well as
handling other activities like stag dos, clay
pigeon shooting and giant scalextric. There
are several packages available – book
online and find out the full range of games
and prices.
www.bedlam.co.uk

Diane's Pool Hall
West End, Map 2 C7
242 Morrison Street, 0131 228 1156
Mon–Sun 8am–1am
Game price: 20p
With nine tables and two league teams, this
is the busiest pool hall in Edinburgh. There
are no snooker facilities and no coaching is
available, but the bargain prices should
ensure that practice makes perfect.

Knockhill Karting
Out of town, Map 1
Knockhill Racing Circuit, by Dunfermline, Fife.
22 miles northwest of Edinburgh on A823,
01383 620 748
Mon–Sun 10am–6pm
Karting: from £10
You can go up to 50mph in one of
Knockhill's Honda Prokarts on this 500m
floodlit outdoor track, located just north of
the Forth. Booking is essential, and you get
ten minutes cruising for £10. They also
offer paintballing, just in case scooting
about with your bum inches from the floor
isn't enough to sate you.
www.knockhillkarting.co.uk

The Leith State Snooker Club
Leith, Map 3 H4
200 Great Junction Street, 0131 553 1113
Mon–Fri 11am–midnight, Sat/Sun
noon–11pm
Table: £4 per hour
Built in 1939, this purpose-built snooker
hall has 13 tables and an adjoining
lounge bar. Staging club tournaments, as
well as qualifiers for the Scottish
championships, the two floor venue
welcomes all ages and abilities, from
kids to pensioners. A qualified coach
plies his trade here and can be sought out
for lessons.

Megabowl
West End, Map 2 B9
Fountain Park, Fountainbridge, Dundee St,
0131 478 3000
Sun–Thu noon–midnight, Fri/Sat 10am–1am
Bowling: adult £4.95, shoe hire £1
This 18 lane bowling centre is housed
alongside a cinema, health club and a few
theme restaurants within the Fountain
Park development. What it lacks in
subtlety it makes up for in convenience.
There are various deals for students and
the under 16s, as well as a decent
selection of arcade games, American pool
tables and a bar with regular drinks
promos. The window opening onto the
next door McDonald's is a dubious gift
for lazy eaters.
www.megabowl.com

Murrayfield Ice Rink
West End, Map 2 off A7
Riversdale Crescent, 0131 337 6933
Sessions: Mon 2.30–4.30pm/5–9pm,
Tue/Thu 2.30–4.30pm/7–9pm, Fri
2.30–4.30pm/5–7pm/7.30–10.30pm, Sat
10am–noon/2.30–4.30pm/7.30–10.30pm,
Sun noon–1.45pm/2.30–4.30pm
Skating: £3–£5 including hire
This large (200ft by 90ft) rink hosts ice
hockey games (it's the Edinburgh
Capitals' base; check www.edinburgh-

capitals.com) and has a seating capacity of 3,500. Tuesday and Thursday evenings are family nights, Friday and Saturday nights are set aside for the ice disco, Wednesday evenings are for group tuition and UK Skate's instruction programme takes place noon–1.45pm on Sundays. The curling rink (under different ownership) is open between September and April – call 0131 346 4477 for info.

Raceland
Out of town, Map 1
Upper Diamond, Gladsmuir. 14 miles east of Edinburgh on A199, 0131 665 6525
Mon–Fri noon–9pm, Sat/Sun 9am–10pm
Check website for details
Situated 25 minutes drive from Edinburgh's city centre (and on the 106 bus route), Raceland is the largest purpose-built go-karting venue in the UK, featuring a 250m indoor circuit and a 930m outdoor track. It's open for corporate events, competitions and casual drivers (children must be over eight) and different karting formats take place on various week days to accommodate all levels. Speed demons should check out the 70mph practice sessions from 7–9pm on Tuesday evenings.
www.raceland.co.uk

Fitness

Dance Base
Old Town, Map 2 F7
14–16 Grassmarket, 0131 225 5525
Classes: spring, autumn, winter terms.
Perf/workshops: spring/summer. Centre:
Mon–Fri 8am–9.30pm, Sat 10am–5.30pm
Classes: adult from £45 for ten. Drop–in yoga: £4
A national treasure, Dance Base merges beautiful environs with a continually impressive programme. The £7m centre, designed by award-winning architect Malcolm Fraser, caters for all ages and abilities, with four studios hosting over 80 classes in more than 40 different forms of dance, including breakdance, ballet, tango, ballroom and belly dance. The Base also hosts residencies and workshops for amateurs and professionals. (See Theatre, Comedy, Dance.)
www.dancebase.co.uk

Iyengar Yoga Centre
Southside, Map 2 D10
195 Bruntsfield Place, 0131 229 6000
Phone for morning and evening class times
Courses: from £5 per class, from £40 per 10 week course
Housed in spacious rooms in a Victorian tenement, this centre was established in

1980 and teaches a form of yoga developed by BKS Iyengar from Puna, focussing on individual postures. There are classes for beginner, intermediate and general levels, plus teacher training courses.

The Practice Place
Southside, Map 2 G9
1 Meadow Place, The Meadows, 0131 221 9697
Mon/Tue 9.30am–9pm, Wed 3.15–9pm, Thu 4.15–9pm, Fri 6–8pm, Sat 9.45am–1.30pm, Sun 11am–1pm
Courses: £55–£65 for block of ten
The Practice Place was founded (as the Yoga Centre) in 1996 to promote the benefits of Astanga Vinyasa yoga, and its purpose-built studios in the heart of the Meadows are the largest in Europe. Teaching the pure, original form of one of yoga's more dynamic forms, classes range from complete beginners and the self-taught Mysore style to ante-natal and children. Regular workshops with some of the world's most experienced Astanga teachers. Note that while the centre changed its name in spring 2003, the website address remains unchanged as we went to press.
www.theyogacentre.co.uk

The Salisbury Centre
Southside, Map 2 J10
2 Salisbury Road, 0131 667 5483
Mon–Fri 10am–7.30pm, Sat/Sun by workshop appointment
Courses: £50 for 10–12 weeks.
Workshops: from £30
Founded in 1973, this is Edinburgh's longest standing holistic centre for physical, emotional and spiritual well-being, offering classes and workshops aimed at promoting personal development of mind, body, and spirit. Known mostly for specialty yoga and tai chi classes, it also offers meditation sessions.
www.salisburycentre.org

Union Yoga
New Town, Map 2 F2
25 Rodney Street, 0131 558 3334
Check website for class times
Courses: £55 for 8 week course
This purpose-built 2000 foot square centre opened in October 2003, offers Ashtanga Vinyasa Yoga, an active form that encourages movement – and sweat. It's run by Brian Cooper, who has taught yoga since the early 70s, and offers 8 week beginners' courses (£55) as well as power yoga, early morning self practice classes, weekend workshops and teacher training. Most appealing to novices, though, may be the free drop-in introductory sessions, currently 6–7pm on Wednesdays.
www.unionyoga.co.uk

Horses

Harelaw Equestrian Centre
Out of town, Map 1
Harelaw Farm, Longniddry. Train to Longniddry, 15 miles east of Edinburgh on A198, 01875 853559
Horse riding: from £14 per hour
Does cantering along a beach, with the wind racing through your hair and the thud of hoof on sand tickle your fancy? Along the Firth of Forth coast, Harelaw Equestrian Centre offers beach riding for experienced riders and off-road tracks for beginners. Irish draft horses are a speciality here, but ponies are also available.

Musselburgh Racecourse
Out of town, Map 1
Linkfield Road, Musselburgh. 5 miles east of Edinburgh on A199, 0131 665 2083
Check website for race times
Admission: £10–£15
A horse racing venue since 1816, Musselburgh lies by the sea. It stages flat racing and National Hunt meetings with about 24 race days throughout the year, so there's roughly one event every couple of weeks to keep you entertained. Scottish racing (01350 723333, www.scottishracing.co.uk) is the governing body for the sport and can provide details on other courses and general information.
www.musselburgh-racecourse.co.uk

Tower Farm Riding Stables
Southside, Map 2 off D10
85 Liberton Drive, 0131 664 3375
Horse riding: from £17 per hour
Just a short bus ride from Edinburgh city centre (take the 37 or 37a from Princes Street), these accessible stables offer riding around the Braid Hills, with scenic views and no road work, plus qualified instruction to all ages and abilities in either its indoor or outdoor arenas. It is fully approved by both the Trekking and Riding Society of Scotland and the British Horse Society Scotland.

Team

The Grange Club
New Town, Map 2 C2
Portgower Place, Stockbridge, 0131 332 2148
Phone for details
Founded as a cricket club in 1832 and still boasting an antiquated wooden stand, the club now accommodates hockey, tennis and squash. But it remains a major force in Scottish cricket, being home to the Scottish Saltires, who play in the National League against the English Counties – the biggest development in Scottish cricket for many years. Tickets are

available on 0131 313 7423 and cost £10/£5 concessions. Membership costs vary according to sports played. The standard of cricket is high so new members will ideally have some playing experience. For general info check out www.cricketeurope.org/Scotland. *www.thegrangeclub.com*

Heart of Midlothian FC
West End, Map 2 off A9
Tynecastle Stadium, Gorgie Road, 0131 200 7201
Phone for details
Hearts (the name comes from a Walter Scott novel via a 19th century Royal Mile dancehall) have enjoyed some success in recent years, lifting the Scottish Cup in 1998 and finishing third in the 2002/03 season, but have rarely looked likely challengers for the Premierleague title, which has been the near-undisputed property of Glasgow rivals Celtic and Rangers since the mid 80s. Still, results such as the 1–0 away victory against Bordeaux in 2003 show that the club are far from European minnows. The website has a list of fixtures and prices.
www.heartsfc.co.uk

Check out Parks on pages 151-154

Hibernian FC
Leith, Map 2 off K2
Easter Road Stadium, 12 Albion Place, 0131 661 2159
Tickets: £17–£47
The 2002/03 season saw Hibs start slowly and end up finishing seventh in the Premierleague although, due to the complications of the split league, which sees the top six and bottom six play within their own ranks, they finished with more points than fifth placed Dunfermline. Hibs, who have their roots in Edinburgh's Irish community and historically draw their support from the north and east of the city, have finished behind local rivals Hearts in recent years, but manager Bobby Williamson will be looking to turn things round.
www.hibs.co.uk

Meadowbank Sports Centre
City Centre, Map 2 off K3
139 London Road, 0131 661 5351
Mon–Sun 9am–10pm
Meadowbank Sports Centre is a 25 acre complex, built for the 1970 Commonwealth Games. There's a wide range of facilities here, including an athletics stadium, indoor and outdoor football pitches (hire from £18), badminton and squash courts (from £3.40 an hour), table tennis (from £1.70), gym

High dive at the Royal Commonwealth Pool

and fitness training (from £3.20). Balls and rackets can be hired.
www.edinburghleisure.co.uk

Powerleague Portobello
Outskirts, Map 1
10 Westbank Street, Portobello. 5 miles east of Edinburgh off A199, 0131 669 2266
Mon–Sun 9am–11pm
Pitch hire: from £25 per hour
One of two Powerleague centres in Edinburgh, the other being in Sighthill (66 Bankhead Drive, Edinburgh, 0131 442 2000). Pitches can either be hired out by you and your mates or you can enter one of the many men's or women's leagues that Powerleague runs. The pitches are Astroturf and best suited to fives or sevens. It's worth booking well in advance, as they get a hell of a lot of use.
www.powerleague.co.uk

Water

Port Edgar Marina and Sailing School
Out of town, Map 1
Shore Road, South Queensferry. 9 miles northwest of Edinburgh off A90, 0131 331 3330
Phone for details
Conveniently located on the sheltered waters of the Forth near Edinburgh, Port Edgar is one of the best known sailing schools in Scotland. A weekend course in dinghy or keel boats is £59.65, five days £131.15. It is possible to hire boats (minimum RYA Level 2 or equivalent) from £10.70–£27.70 per boat for two hours, and there are facilities for disabled sailors. Port Edgar also runs kayaking courses for beginners and paddlers with some expeience. Courses for both adults and children available.

Portobello Swim Centre
Outskirts, Map 2 off A10
57 Promenade, Portobello, 5 miles east of Edinburgh off A199, 0131 669 6888
Mon–Fri 7am–9pm, Sat/Sun 9am–3.40pm
Check website or phone for details
The Portobello Swim Centre is prized for its Victorian Turkish baths. An impressive facility, it has three hot rooms, two rest areas, a Russian cold bath and steam room. Men and women's nights are available every week. With similarly aged swimming baths a newly installed gym, fitness classes and cafe all under the same roof, this is a deservedly popular place.
www.edinburghleisure.co.uk

Royal Commonwealth Pool
Southside, Map 2 K10
21 Dalkeith Rd, 0131 667 7211
Mon–Fri 6am–9.30pm, Sat 6am–4.30pm, Sun 10am–4.30pm
Swim: from £2.90
Built for the 1970 Commonwealth Games and used again during the 1986 games, this 50m pool on the edge of Holyrood Park is the site for many national and international competitions. Facilities also include a diving and children's pool and Clambers, a children's play gym (see Kids). Swimming programmes are offered for all abilities, including disabled athletes, and private lessons and Bronze Medallion courses are available. Leisure card holders receive discounted entry.
www.edinburghleisure.co.uk

The Scottish National Water Ski Centre
Out of town, Map 1
Town Loch, Townhill Country Park. 19 miles north west of Edinburgh off A907, 01383 620123
Apr–Oct Mon–Fri 1–9.30pm, Sat/Sun 10am–8pm
Skiing: £16 for 15 minutes, £42 annual membership
The flatwater of Scotland's lochs is ideal for waterskiing, with many water ski centres based on Loch Lomond, Loch Ken and Lochearnhead. This state of the art arena (run by waterskiscotland, the sport's national body) is rather closer to Edinburgh, and hosts both national and international competitions. It also offers 'come and try' ski sessions for £10 (15 mins), and runs regular training for all levels in various disciplines.
www.waterskiscotland.co.uk

Warrender Swim Centre
Southside, Map 2 off F10
55 Thirlestane Road, 0131 447 0052
Phone for times and prices
This small, attractive Victorian pool in
Marchmont, not far from the city centre,
includes a Pulse gym and sauna. Classes,
including aqua fit, are available in the
afternoon and evening. Hours vary
somewhat; while the pool is open
Mon–Fri 8am–10pm; Sat–Sun
9am–3.40pm, public bathing hours are
eaten into by lessons, coaching and the
swim club. Bathing with lanes is
guaranteed Mon–Fri 8am–9am,
12pm–1.40pm and 5–5.45pm. Phone for
other times.
www.edinburghleisure.co.uk

The Rest

Bruntsfield Links
Southside, Map 2 E9
Wright's Houses, Barclay Place, Bruntsfield
The original Bruntsfield Links (not to be
confused with the larger private course at
Cramond) was the first golf course in
Edinburgh and is still one of the city's
busiest, and a splendid resource. Access
to the short hole course (holes 30–40
yards) is free, and clubs and balls can be
hired in the hut by the Golf Tavern, on the
west side. During winter, a small course
operates but in summer 36 holes are on
offer. Flags are removed before dusk,
although you can play at any time, but do
bear in mind that this course is an integral
part of a large city park with all the bustle
that entails.
Opening

Craiglockhart Tennis and Sports Centre
Southside, Map 2 off A10
177 Colinton Road, 0131 444 1969
Mon–Fri 9am–11pm, Sat–Sun 9am–10.30pm
Court hire: from £14.30 per hour
The most comprehensive tennis centre in
Scotland has six indoor courts and eight
American outdoor fast-dry clay courts
available for hire (booking advisable). It
offers comprehensive coaching
programmes for all ages and abilities and
is the home of the organising body,
Tennis Scotland (0131 444 1984,
www.tennisscotland.org), to boot.
International competitions, star names
included, occasionally occupy the centre.
www.edinburghleisure.co.uk

The Edinburgh Marathon 2004
Citywide
01620 890444
13 June 2004
This major charity event is set to attract
well over 6000 runners this year, in part
due to the new Team Relay scheme
which allows teams of 4 to tackle the 26
miles together. The route – starting and
ending at Meadowbank Stadium, taking
in Arthur's Seat, Princes Street and
Ocean Terminal – is not a fast one, but
should be enough to inspire even the
most fatigued of runners. Also this year,
Picnic in the Park at Holyrood, will
create a bumper party atmosphere for
spectators. Book your place by phone or
on the web now.
www.edinburgh-marathon.co.uk

The Meadows Tennis Courts
Southside, Map 2 H9
Meadow Lane, 0131 444 1969
Apr–Sep Mon–Fri 9am–9pm, Sat–Sun
9am–6pm
Court hire: from £3.50
Set in the leafy Meadows, this council-
run facility offers 16 good quality tar
courts. Leisure card holders get
discounts, and be prepared to either book
or wait on hot summer days. Note that
courts are (legally) accessible outside
opening hours in summer – which means
you can play for free. Weekend opening
in the winter months is dependendent on
weather.
www.edinburghleisure.co.uk

Pentland Hills Regional Park
Outskirts, Map 1
7 miles south west of Edinburgh off A702,
0131 445 3383
The Pentland hills combine great views of
Edinburgh to the north and the Borders to
the south with easy walking just a few
minutes drive from the city centre.
Caerketton and Allermuir hills are best
reached from the Midlothian Ski Centre
(see entry in this section), while a better
base for Carnethy and Turnhouse hills is
the Flotterstone Visitor Centre, also just
off the A702. The area is covered by OS
Landranger map 66.
www.ski.midlothian.gov.uk

Water of Leith Walkway
Citywide
Visitor Centre, 24 Lanark Road, Wester
Hailes, 0131 455 7367
Visitor Centre: Apr–Sep Mon–Sun
10am–4pm; Oct–Mar Wed–Sun 10am–4pm
Centre admission: £2
You could live for years in Edinburgh
and never discover this hidden jewel – a
35km stretch of water that starts in the
Pentland Hills and flows down through
the villages of Balerno, Juniper Green
and then into the heart of Edinburgh. One
of the most attractive stretches, accessible
from the city, takes you from Stockbridge
along a wooded path to Dean Village,
under the massive arches of the Dean
Bridge. The new architect-designed
Visitor Centre has exhibitions on the river
and sells a guide book complete with
map for £2.70.
www.waterofleith.org.uk

Mussel Inn, page 105

eating &
drinking

eating&drinking

bars&pubs

Dress up or down in Edinburgh's bars. Hours are longer than in almost any other city in the UK: you can sup till 3am in Pivo, then head off for a 5am pint at the Penny Black. During the festival season in August, hours are even longer. For those less keen on such Herculean sessions, the choice is vast – historic pubs, DJ-heavy pre-club haunts, boozy student venues and mellow hangouts are all up your street. For more *The List*'s *Bar Guide to Edinburgh & Glasgow* is now available (£4.95).

Hangouts

The Bailie Bar
New Town, Map 2 D3
2 St Stephen Street, 0131 225 4673
Mon–Thu 11am–midnight, Fri/Sat
11am–1am, Sun 12.30–11pm
Basic pint: £2.35
This ultra-relaxed basement boozer is everything a self-respecting time waster could want. With low ceilings and dark red and brown decor, the Bailie redefines the word 'cosy'. Always busy day or night, it attracts all ages and has plenty of lounging space. With real ales and above-average pub grub on offer as well, it's not easy to find a reason to leave. Food is served Monday to Thursday until 10pm and Friday, Saturday and Sunday until 5pm.

Bar Sirius
Leith, Map 3 H2
7–10 Dock Place, 0131 555 3344
Sun–Wed 11.30am–midnight, Thu–Sat
11.30am–1am
Basic pint: £2.50
Having brought in a new menu and ditched its bright colours for muted ones, Sirius has changed its spots, but has retained its laid-back vibe. The large, low-ceilinged space of the main bar sees a smattering of daytime drinkers watching the hours tick by over the papers and office types enjoying a decent lunch. Things take on an easy, pre-clubby vibe at weekends when the DJs move in. Food is served until 9pm.

The Basement
New Town, Map 2 H3
10a–12a Broughton Street, 0131 557 0097
Mon–Sun noon–1am
Basic pint: £2.40
Mature and modern with an easy confidence, the Basement is the business for many of the creative, socially active types who make up the Broughton Street crowd. OK, so it's dimly – almost dingily – lit, the decor verges on the nondescript and there is all that rather odd furniture made out of Caterpillar tracks, but these things just make regulars love it all the more. Serious food (Mexican a speciality) is served until 10.30pm daily, at plain wooden tables or less formally in the bar.
www.thebasement.org.uk

Black Bo's
Old Town, Map 2 H6
57–61 Blackfriars Street, 0131 557 6136
Mon–Sun 4pm–1am
Basic pint: £2.60
With a serving area smaller than a telephone box, it's a wonder anyone can ever get a drink here. But somehow they do, and that's just one of the mysteries of this cool, ramshackle pub. Where do they get the laid-back DJs from? How come there's an award-winning vegetarian restaurant next door? How do I get back from the downstairs toilets when drunk?

city5s
BRILLIANT BARS

■ **Black Bo's**
It's small, it's scruffy and it's got some of the best DJs in town.
■ **Café Royal Circle Bar**
Grade 'A' listed, and with good reason – superb hand-painted tiles and great seafood.
■ **Borough**
Very smart but comfortable style bar with lovely food and fine cocktails.
■ **Human Be-In**
Regular live music and DJ events distinguish this trendy hangout near Edinburgh Uni.
■ **Canny Man's**
Legendary eccentric Morningside pub (complete with beer garden and occasional dress code) cluttered with cubbyholes and ornaments.
■ **The Pond**
A favourite hideaway in darkest Leith.

Such worries leave your mind once ensconced at a tiny table in this front room of a place. But be warned – it's not always open on the dot of four.
www.blackbos.com

Eighty Queen Street
City Centre, Map 2 D5
80 Queen Street, 0131 226 5097
Mon–Wed noon–midnight, Thu–Sat noon–1am. Closed Sun
Basic pint: £2.50
Enjoy a hearty pub meal here from the comforts of a leather armchair or cosy booth. The menu is extensive and specialises in spectacular sandwiches. There's live jazz in the cellar bar downstairs at weekends.
www.eighty-queen-street.com

The Golf Tavern
Southside, Map 2 E9
30 Wrights Houses, 0131 221 5220
Mon–Sun 10am–1am
Basic pint: £2.70
Established in 1456, this pub re-opened in December 2003 after major refurbishment and now has a more modern air throughout its four floors. The course outside (the world's oldest – see Sport) makes this a popular post-game haunt but it is also a favourite of students and sporty types. Food is served until 1am.

The Great Grog Wine Bar
City Centre, Map 2 F5
43 Rose Street, 0131 225 1616
Sun–Thu 10am–11pm, Fri/Sat 10am–1am
Basic pint: £2.60
There's none of the usual Rose Street rowdiness in this bar, linked to the eponymous wine warehouse. Indeed, once past the brightly-coloured vestibule, you'd be forgiven for thinking you'd travelled through a portal and arrived at a civilised, continental taverna. There's something pleasingly jumbled about the place, from the polished floorboards to the IKEA-esque deckchairs. Attracting a wide age range, it appeals to quiet chatters and lovers of wine.

The Pond Bar
Leith, Map 3 off K4
2–4 Bath Road, 0131 467 3825
Mon–Thu 4pm–1am, Fri/Sat/sun 2pm–1am
Basic pint: £2.30
Relocate an Amsterdam brown bar to dockside Edinburgh, add a healthy dose of bartending passion and you have something approaching this remarkable pub. A goldfish pond sits in a small barbeque area round the back, while the inside is adorned with lovingly chosen second-hand furniture and eclectic memorabilia. The original bar features an old-style soda pump and an impressive range of draught German lagers plus many more bottled beers.

Star Bar
City Centre, Map 2 F4
1 Northumberland Place, 0131 539 8070
Mon–Sun noon–1am
Basic pint: £2.35
Though tiny, the Star Bar packs it in – there's a small beer garden, two big screens, darts, a jukebox, and internet access (£2 an hour). The real star, however, is quite possibly the best table football in the world – a huge, artisan glory. Folk come from all over town to chill out; twentysomethings exchange vinyl or listen to live acoustic music; others come for the Thursday night backgammon. It's a happy atmosphere whatever you're in for.
www.starbar.co.uk

Traverse Bar Café
West End, Map 2 E7
10 Cambridge Street, 0131 228 5383
Mon–Wed 10.30am–midnight, Thu–Sat 10.30am–1am, Sun 5pm–midnight
Basic pint: £2.60
An institution among Edinburgh's arty young drinkers, this subterranean delight is expansive but surprisingly cosy. Part of the Traverse Theatre complex, the 'Trav' remains an excellent place. See Cafés.
www.traverse.co.uk

Yo! Below
City Centre, Map 2 F5
66 Rose Street, 0131 220 6040
Sun–Thu 5pm–1am, Fri 3pm–1am, Sat noon–1am
Basic pint: £3
Gimmick-heaven, this bright, open-plan space under the restaurant, has beer taps on tables, smoke-removing ashtrays, karaoke bar staff, massages on request, tarot card readings, manga films on big screens and big bed areas for stretching out. Among all this is a decent bar that serves interesting and well-prepared South East Asian food alongside an array of weird and wonderful cocktails and Japanese spirits.
www.yosushi.com

Party Central

Bar Kohl
Old Town, Map 2 G6
54–55 George IV Bridge, 0131 225 6936
Mon–Sat 4pm–1am, Sun 5.30pm–1am
Basic pint: £2.70
Vodka for breakfast. Vodka for lunch. Vodka for dinner. If this sounds appealing, Bar Kohl might well be your blurry idea of heaven. This central hangout, stretched tight around a busy bar, is packed most evenings and while the R&B tunes pump into your ears, you might need a pint while deciding which of the 55 flavours of vodka to go for. Opt for a shot of bubblegum, a passion fruit milk shake, a healthy pure fruit smoothie or a pitcher of Jaffa Cake cocktail. Avoid the chilli, though. It is deadly.

THE WORLD FAMOUS
FRANKENSTEIN
1818

7 nights
until 1am
with food
served
daily from
10am

Beluga
Old Town, Map 2 G7
30a Chambers Street, 0131 624 4545
Mon–Sun 10am–1am
Basic pint: £2.70
Whether you're staying upstairs in the swank restaurant or going down to the bar, the one thing you can't help but notice is the bloody great waterfall next to the steps. Inside, it's similarly opulent – leather seating and subdued lighting mark out Beluga as another addition to the beast we know as the style bar. Daytimes are relaxed and food reasonably-priced. At weekends, DJs playing house, funk and soul make this big bar a lively – if absolutely rammed – evening haunt.
www.beluga-edinburgh.com

Espionage
Old Town, Map 2 G6
4 India Buildings, Victoria Street, 0131 477 7007
Mon–Sun 7pm–3am
Basic pint: £2.80
With a licence extending to 3am and no cover charge, this is probably the pre-eminent spot in town for young, late-night boozehounds. Over five levels, each of the bars within has a vague theme related to the sort of exotic location you might find in a *Bond*-esque thriller. It's plusher than any late licensed drinking den has a right

to be – not that you'll notice, given how drunk you'll probably be when you end up there. The bottom two floors have regularly heaving dancefloors.
www.espionage007.co.uk

Frankenstein
Old Town, Map 2 G7
26 George IV Bridge, 0131 622 1818
Mon–Sun 10am–1am
Basic pint: £2.70
Frankenstein has only been on the scene since 2001 and makes full use of a gothic façade and crypt-like interior to create a Hammer-horror vibe. The ornately carved wooden booths and ubiquitous party tunes are cheesy to the hilt, but are the very reason this pub is a popular haunt for students and weekend revellers alike.
www.frankenstein-pub.co.uk

Medina
Southside, Map 2 G7
45–47 Lothian Street, 0131 225 6313
Mon–Sun 10pm–3am
Basic pint: £2.60
Its frontage may be small, but there can't be many regular city drinkers who don't know all about this subterranean haunt (beneath sister bar, Negociants) and the distinctive seating arrangements available therein. Comfy sofas and padded seats so huge that tables float on them like glass-

The Pond, a popular Leith hangout, page 82

strewn islands, guarantee one of the most relaxing pints in town. And despite a music policy regulars say is getting cheesier every week, the dancefloor is regularly mobbed.

The Three Sisters
Old Town, Map 2 G6
139 Cowgate, 0131 622 6801
Mon–Sun 9am–1am
Basic pint: £2.70
This is a behemoth of a bar in the thick of the action. A vast, heated 150-seater beer garden (barbeques on Fridays in summer) leads to the pub proper which just keeps extending, theme-warping from style bar into Irish pub, and further back, into a dimly lit scenario resembling Castle Dracula. The clubbier upstairs with dancefloor is available for hire (free) until 10pm. Friday and Saturday nights it's a braying mêlée of stags and hens – expect to queue for bar and loos. Food is served 9am–9pm (9am–8pm on Fridays and Saturdays).
www.festival-inns.co.uk

Pre-Club

Assembly
Southside, Map 2 G7
41 Lothian Street, 0131 220 4288
Mon–Sun 9am–1am
Basic pint: £2.75
Under its previous guise as Iguana, this bar was a stomping ground for many of the city's more affluent students and, since its reinvention in 2003, the place is swanker than ever. Alterations have been effective, though it's essentially the same mix of loud house and hip-hop grooves, a bustlingly stylish clientele and an atmosphere that's vaguely exclusive yet unthreatening. An appetising food menu is available 9am–8pm (late night snacks till 1am) seven days.
www.assemblybar.co.uk

City Café
Old Town, Map 2 H6
19 Blair Street, 0131 220 0125
Mon–Sun 11am–1am

Basic pint: £2.80
Back when the world and his wife went to glam house nights, this central style bar (first of its kind and now an Edinburgh institution) was positively awash at weekends with dressed-up dancefloor-devotees. Nowadays, the clientele is less conspicuously fashionable. During the day, the upstairs bar (decked out like a 50s American diner) is good for a cheap lunch and a lazy game of pool. The pulse of this venue still races during the weekend sessions (progressive house to R&B) held at night downstairs in City Café 2.

Human Be-In
Southside, Map 2 off I10
2–8 West Crosscauseway, 0131 662 8860
Mon–Sun 11am–1am
Basic pint: £2.80
Named after the group of political and cultural rebels in Haight-Ashbury during the 60s, this bar isn't overtly 'underground'. Instead, it aims at a laid-back vibe, with pale wood and slate looks. World, funk and soul music is played by some of the city's finest DJs (weekends) and live performers (alternate Tuesday and Thursday nights). Lots of outdoor seating and superior bar menu (all day, light snacks after 9pm) have made this one of *the* places for style-conscious drinkers.
www.humanbein.co.uk

The Outhouse
New Town, Map 2 H3
12a Broughton Street Lane, 0131 557 6668
Mon–Sun 1pm–1am
Basic pint: £2.70
This hip hideaway is an ideal locale for beers, snacks and chat. The red-walled bar is backed up by a spacious upstairs function room – a regular party-central for big groups. The cosy beer garden is hugely popular in summer, although its sheltered position and patio heaters allow fresh outdoor drinking (and barbeque eating) even in Edinburgh's Baltic winters. The venue was refurbished complete with new menu in October 2003. You can access the club Ego through the rear of the bar.

the golf tavern
est 1456

food &
drinks
served
7 days
10am
till late

Pivo
City Centre, Map 2 H5
2–6 Calton Road, 0131 557 2925
Mon–Sun 4pm–3am
Basic pint: £2.70
A deserved winner of numerous 'style bar of the year' accolades, Pivo (Czech for beer) has come a long way since the rather dubious ad campaign that encouraged punters to 'Czech' the place out. This Eastern European theme bar – all dark wood dressers, plush velvet and battered leather – is now best known for its 3am licence. Queues of twentysomething trendies often stretch round the block as they seek a spot for one last drink. Local DJs supply beats afternoon and night.
www.for-you.uk.com

PopRokit
New Town, Map 2 H3
2 Picardy Place, 0131 556 4272
Mon–Sun 11am–1am
Basic pint: £2.80
Formerly known as the Catwalk Café, this is a warm, minimalist style bar with installations by local graphic artist Harry 3D. Downstairs hosts DJ sessions at weekends (hip hop, soul, disco and funk) while upstairs capitalises on the airy atmosphere created by the glass frontage. Though a popular pit-stop for next door club Ego, PopRokit is keen to push itself as a 'destination' venue for Broughton Street bohos and well-heeled workies.

Style Bars

Borough
Southside, Map 2 I10
72–80 Causewayside, 0131 668 2255
Mon–Sun 11am–1am
Basic pint: £2.65
Hidden behind an unassuming frontage, Borough is a wide-open, bizarrely retro/futurist looking place, with ultra-comfy leather sofas and chairs scattered about willy-nilly among blond wood and metal. With a classy restaurant (the hotel is upstairs) in an adjacent room, it's worth checking out the delicious bar food menu (served until 10pm, Friday and Saturdays until 11pm) as well as the range of cocktails and wines, all delectable, if a little heavy on the pocket. Possibly the best style bar in town.
www.edin-borough.co.uk

Centraal
Southside, Map 2 H8
32 West Nicolson Street, 0131 667 7355
Mon–Sat 11am–1am, Sun noon–midnight
Basic pint: £2.85
Centraal might be in one of the student boozer heartlands of the capital but it's aimed at the sort of undergrads who don't rely on a student loan to get by. Metal and leather finishings, undeniably flash (if rather distracting) flat screen TVs and soft fairy-lighting in the dining area all ooze quality. 90 varieties of bottled beers and impressive array of lagers on tap can't fail to win respect.
www.centraal.co.uk

The Dome
City Centre, Map 2 F5
14 George Street, 0131 624 8624
Sun–Wed noon–11pm, Thu noon–midnight, Fri/Sat noon–12.30am
Basic pint: £3
Maintaining high standards among the glut of recently arrived rivals, this huge place was converted from a bank. There's an ostentatious air about both the main bar and Frazer's, the saloon bar. Indeed, there's luxury everywhere, from the enormous domed ceiling to the chandeliers. While the punters might not quite live up to this sense of style, the door staff and red carpet do tend to keep the riff-raff out. Excellent food is served until 10pm, Fridays and Saturdays until 11pm.

Hurricane
City Centre, Map 2 E5
45 North Castle Street, 0131 226 0770
Mon–Sat 4pm–1am. Closed Sun
Basic pint: £2.80
Below the restaurant of the same name, this bar opened in summer 2002 but boasts the confidence of an old-timer. Grown-up cocktails, made by amiable staff, are an inspiration with a choice of champagne, classic, short/long mixed, traditional and dairy. Soothing lights, sultry red walls, leather sofas and chilled-out house music create a sophisticated environment in which to try a Mayan.
www.hurricanerestaurants.com

Indigo (yard)
City Centre, Map 2 D5
7 Charlotte Lane, 0131 220 5603
Mon–Sun 8.30am–1am
Basic pint: £2.90
Indigo's smartly-dressed clientele savour the pose factor of this bar, but that doesn't mean you'll be kicked out for wearing a T-shirt. Tricked out in multiple textures and colours, the stylish decor includes a stone floor, ultraviolet lighting and a trendy mezzanine. The kitchens offer a fine bistro menu, specialising in Thai and Chinese dishes, from 8.30am-10pm. It all comes at a price, but this slick, chic bar is unbeatable for showing off those new shades.
www.indigoyardedinburgh.co.uk

MY FAVOURITE BAR
Black Bo's
'Good tables and chairs, low key friendly vibes.'
Roddy Womble, Idlewild

Montpeliers of Bruntsfield
Southside, Map 2 D10
159–161 Bruntsfield Place, 0131 229 3115
Mon–Sun 9am–1am
Basic pint: £2.60
The Montpeliers Group is big in town, with Indigo (yard), rick's and the Opal Lounge all bright stars in their portfolio. Opened ten years ago, its oldest, eponymous member was smartened up in classic contemporary style (lots of wood, leather and comforting orange) a year ago, reaffirming its position as Bruntsfield's swankiest and most popular neighbourhood bar-bistro. The choice of drinks is vast (draught beers, wines by the glass, cocktails, smoothies etc) and reliable food is served at breakfast, lunch and dinner (until 10pm).
www.montpeliersedinburgh.co.uk

North Bridge
Old Town, Map 2 H6
20 North Bridge, 0131 622 2900
Sun–Wed 11am–midnight, Thu–Sat 11am–1am
Basic pint: £3
The Scotsman is one of Edinburgh's headline five-star hotels, full of trendy tweeds and vast views and its swanky bar/brasserie hasn't been shy about promoting itself as a glam downtown destination: certainly the interior is a must-see, with magnificent marble and outstanding plasterwork combined with shiny stainless steel. Champagne, cocktails, as well as snacks, including some of the city's best sushi are de rigeur at the bar. Or you can retire to one of the dressed tables or secretive balcony, where upmarket, trendy meals are served. Lunch from noon–2.30pm, dinner from 6.15pm–10pm.

The Opal Lounge
City Centre, Map 2 F5
51a George Street, 0131 226 2275
Mon–Sun noon–3am
Basic pint: £2.95
Since opening in 2002, the Opal Lounge has established itself as one of *the* places on George Street. Naturally, given the area, it's a style bar, but with a fair-sized dancefloor in the central room and a 3am licence it also gives plenty of opportunity to let your hair down, as well as show it off. Service is friendly and efficient and you even get your drinks on a napkin. There is a cover charge in the evenings – and things can get messy later on – but this style bar largely lives up to its reputation.
www.opallounge.co.uk

Traditional

The Abbotsford
City Centre, Map 2 F5
3 Rose Street, 0131 225 5276
Mon–Sat 11am–11pm. Closed Sun
Basic pint: £2.30
It's hard to believe this is one of the most famous pubs in Edinburgh. In the 50s and 60s this is where writers like McCaig and McDiarmid would sink a jar or several, and where Auden and Dylan Thomas visited when in town. It's still all about good service, with well drilled staff serving an interesting selection of well-prepared guest ales. Though the food is pretty drab, this is a real Rose Street pub.

The Athletic Arms
West End, Map 2 off A9
1–3 Angle Park Terrace, 0131 337 3822
Mon–Thu noon–midnight, Fri–Sat noon–1am, Sun 12.30–11pm
Basic pint: £2.10
'Not as good as it used to be.' It's a phrase people have been directing at the Athletic Arms since it was first opened over 100 years ago, but this place is still a great boozer today. Known to absolutely everybody as Diggers – there's a graveyard close by and a good number of its employees drank here – this pub serves 80/-, IPA and decent whiskies. They may have their own house cask ale now and brighter lights but the principle of unfussy quality drinking is the same as it ever was.

Bennet's Bar
Southside, Map 2 E9
8 Leven Street, 0131 229 5143
Mon–Wed 11am–12.30am, Thu–Sat 11am–1am, Sun 12.30–11.30pm
Basic pint: £2.15
Some historic pubs are more museum than boozer – not Bennet's. Off the tourist track, this compact place is the perfect example of a living, breathing, traditional bar, where friendly staff dish up excellent real ales and malt whiskies to a mostly local, older clientele. The ornate fixtures and fittings, red leather seating and humungous mirrors down one wall are a sight to behold. Well-priced food is served lunchtimes and evenings (except Sundays) in the lounge, which is less spectacular but no less welcoming.

The Bow Bar
Old Town, Map 2 G6
80 The West Bow, Victoria Street, 0131 226 7667
Mon–Sat noon–11.30pm, Sun 12.30–11pm
Basic pint: £2.25
Pubs don't come much more traditional than the Bow Bar. Basic but extremely welcoming, this little boozer is nothing fancy, concentrating instead on impeccable service, top quality whiskies and fine beer. With bolted-down tables, walls of brewery mirrors and slightly scuffed wooden fixtures and fittings, it's not going to win any style awards, but if it's a quality traditional Scottish drinking experience you're after, this is the place.

Café Royal Circle Bar
City Centre, Map 2 G5
19 West Register Street, 0131 556 1884
Mon–Wed 11am–11pm, Thu 11am–midnight,
Fri/Sat 11am–1am, Sun 12.30–11pm
Basic pint: £2.30
With one of the most impressive pub
interiors in town, this famous bar, nestled
down a back alley off Princes Street, has
remained virtually unchanged for 140
years. A 'Grade A' listed space, the bar is
decorated with unique Doulton tile
paintings and ornate plasterwork. Staff are
efficient and food (including oysters from
the excellent seafood restaurant behind the
partition wall) is reasonably priced and
served to a mix of suits and tourists until
10pm every day. A traditional drinking
environment with class.

The Canny Man's
Southside, Map 2 D10
239 Morningside Road, 0131 447 1484
Mon–Wed 11.30am–11pm, Thu–Sat
11.30am–midnight, Sun 12.30pm–11pm
Basic pint: £2.85
There's no denying the unique atmosphere
of the Canny Man's. Unchanged for 130
years, the interior of this Morningside bar
is a collection of cubbyholes and side
rooms, each decorated with a bizarre
range of ornaments and knick-knacks. The
beer garden is a little walled oasis and
excellent food is served throughout.
Populated by punters of a certain age and
certain wage bracket (both high), this pub
is in a stratum of its own.

Cloisters
West End, Map 2 E8
26 Brougham Street, 0131 221 9997
Sun–Thu noon–midnight, Fri/Sat
noon–12.30am
Basic pint: £2.40
Refurbished recently, this pub has wisely
avoided going in for that awful fake
antiquity that dogs so many new real ale
joints. A combination of wood and stone,
Cloisters is simply classic. Nine real ales
are regularly on offer, as well as great
whiskies. Staff are knowledgeable and no
music means you'll be able to hear
yourself speak.

MY FAVOURITE PUB

The Oxford Bar
'No prizes for guessing that my
favourite thing in Edinburgh is
something I share with Inspector
Rebus: namely, the Oxford Bar. It's
a no-frills pub where conversation
is prized over the clatter of
machines and jukeboxes.'
Ian Rankin, author

The Jolly Judge
Old Town, Map 2 G6
7 James Court, 0131 225 2669
Mon/Thu–Sat noon–midnight, Tue/Wed
noon–11pm, Sun 12.30–11pm
Basic pint: £2.40
Hidden in one of the city's classic Old
Town courts, the Judge has an ancient,
beamed ceiling hanging low over the red
and green interior. A blazing log fire
glows in winter, when it can get a little
over-heated especially when crowded.
Aside from the summer tourist influx
which brings on the pavement seating, this
is a pub frequented by locals who value
genial service and good single malts.
Monday nights are dominated by what is
probably the most fiendish quiz in town.
Food is served until 2pm.
www.jollyjudge.co.uk

Kay's
New Town, Map 2 E4
39 Jamaica Street West, 0131 225 1858
Mon–Thu 11am–midnight, Fri/Sat 11am–1am,
Sun 12.30–11pm
Basic pint: £2.40
The only reason we are loath to
recommend this bar is that we want to
keep it to ourselves. The front two rooms
of an old stable building, Kay's is a small,
comfy den run by owner and chief source
of entertainment, Dave McKenzie. The
range of malts is not vast, but includes all
the best, real ale is on draught and the
food is good value in an expensive area.

The King's Wark
Leith, Map 3 I3
36 The Shore, 0131 554 9260
Mon–Thu noon–11pm, Fri/Sat noon–midnight,
Sun 11am–11pm
Basic pint: £2.40
In the days when the King's Wark was but a
bairn (circa 1400), Leith was so far away
that after arriving by sea, you'd feel like
stopping for a day or two before the long
hike up to Edinburgh. Though things have
speeded up a little, comforting customers is
still the business here, with food dominating
affairs under the old ships' lamps. The
superior bar lunch menu offers fresh soups,
moules, game, swordfish and more. The
menu changes and steps up in the evenings.

The Oxford Bar
City Centre, Map 2 D5
8 Young Street, 0131 539 7119
Mon–Sat 11am–1am, Sun 12.30pm–1am
Basic pint: £2.25
Now firmly established as one of
Edinburgh's literary boozers thanks to Ian
Rankin making it Inspector Rebus' local,
this busy bar is an earthy delight in the
swanky New Town. Unassuming from the
outside, it concentrates on serving proper
ales at decent prices, and has a 'lived-in'
air. The tiny main bar can sometimes be a
little crushed – to the point where patrons

The Bailie, a busy Stockbridge pub, page 81

spill out into the street – but squeeze through to the lounge and you'll find a smattering of tables in a quiet back room.
www.oxfordbar.com

Pear Tree House
Southside, Map 2 H8
38 West Nicolson Street, 0131 667 7533
Mon–Thu 11am–midnight, Fri/Sat 11am–1am, Sun 12.30pm–midnight
Basic pint: £2.55
This pub with its big, leafy garden is arguably Edinburgh's number one outdoor drinking venue. All it takes is a glimmer of sunshine and it's packed with locals, office workers and students brandishing Snapfax. Stone walls keep the worst of the wind out. The pub's interior is a tad dingy, but the central bar creates a warm, communal ambience best experienced on Monday's quiz night. A limited menu of soup and filled rolls is on offer.
www.thepeartreehouse.co.uk

Penny Black
City Centre, Map 2 G5
15 West Register Street, 0131 556 1106
Mon–Sat 5am–noon. Closed Sun
Basic pint: £2.20
You just need to take a look at the

ungodly opening hours to understand that this is not a place for the faint-hearted drinker. Serving a wildly eclectic bunch of very late night and early morning revellers, this pub, entered through a beaten up door and up rickety stairs, has a touch of the opening scene of *Apocalypse Now*. A solid gold reputation as the place to end up, especially during the Festival.

Port o' Leith
Leith, Map 3 I4
58 Constitution Street, 0131 554 3568
Mon–Sat 8.30am–1am, Sun 12.30pm–1am
Basic pint: £2
They don't come much more potty or quasi-bohemian than this legendary pub. First there's the blistering redness of the exterior. But that's nothing to the inside – a low-ceilinged room crammed with flags, model U-boats, old diving suits and even an old ship's figurehead. This is like a working men's club run and designed by Timothy Leary, full of grit and psychedelia. The bar has a formidable selection of wheat beers, difficult enough to find in the poshest of uptown bars, as well as a good variety of lagers and spirits at decent prices.
www.ednet.co.uk/~portoleith

The Sheep Heid Inn
Outskirts, Map 2 K9
43 The Causeway, Duddingston, 0131 656
6951
Mon–Wed 11am–11pm, Thu–Sat
11am–midnight, Sun 12.30–11pm
Basic pint: £2
It wins the oldest-pub-in-town
competition (apparently 600 years and
counting) but age isn't everything.
Thankfully, this snug bar, out in the
village of Duddingston, is as friendly as
it was in the days when James IV
visited. Probably. It's a fairly no-frills
kind of place, though the presence of a
recently refurbished beer garden and an
ancient skittle alley make it an great
place to waste some quality time. Hearty
scran is offered every lunch and evening
and all day weekends.

The Starbank Inn
Leith, Map 3 B2
64 Laverockbank Road, 0131 552 4141
Mon–Wed 11am–11pm, Thu–Sat
11am–midnight, Sun 12.30–11pm
Basic pint: £2
Turned towards the Forth, this bar, part
of a Newhaven house, is a genuine
antidote to the modern waterfront
developments of Leith. With green
leather benches, brewery mirrors, dark
tables and a dining conservatory tacked
on the back, it's an unfussy, traditional
pub. Half a dozen real ales and food like
mince and tatties (served all day) takes it
into the reassuringly old-fashioned
catagory.

cafés & takeaways

The Edinburgh tearoom has almost
gone and European café style is in.
You can sip capppucino from a
pavement table in summer and get a
freshly made sandwich to eat in or
takeaway in most areas of town.
Some of the best are mentioned
below. *The List* magazine's *Eating &
Drinking Guide* includes reviews of
800 restaurants and cafés in
Edinburgh and Glasgow and is
published every May.

Arts Venues

Café Hub
Old Town, Map 2 F6
Castlehill, Royal Mile, 0131 473 2067
Sun/Mon 9.30am–6pm, Tue–Sat
9.30am–10pm
Average price two course meal: £13
Headquarters of the Edinburgh International
Festival, the Hub is centred on a spacious,
yellow café which mixes traditional dishes
with modern tastes. Pan-fried lamb's liver
comes with pancetta and bubble and squeak,
while salmon is dished up with bashed
celeriac and butter sauce. Vegetarians are
well looked after and wines and beers are as
competitively priced as the main courses.
Out of season, the place dips a little, but
never loses its friendly ambience.
www.eif.co.uk/thehub

The new and already much frequented Circus Café, page 97

Café Newton
West End, Map 2 A5
The Dean Gallery, 72 Belford Road, 0131 624 6273
Mon–Sun 10am–4.30pm
Average price two course meal: £7.50
Across the hall from Eduardo Paolozzi's reconstructed studio and named after one of his favourite subjects, this demure little café is tucked away from city hustle behind walls of modern art and grand grounds. Lunch is simple, freshly made in-house and offers soup, specials and a range of mostly Mediterranean, hearty fork-and-knife sandwiches. A cappuccino from its magnificent shiny beast of a machine goes well with the sumptuous brownies. See Art Galleries.

Filmhouse Café Bar
West End, Map 2 D7
88 Lothian Road, 0131 229 5932
Sun–Thu 10am–11.30pm, Fri/Sat 10am–12.30am
Average price two course meal: £6
Out of sight behind the box office of Edinburgh's main independent film theatre, this is an up-beat place with wide screens showing movie previews, music and a bustling bar. Half smoking, half non, it is relaxed and with film start times in mind, service is speedy and helpful. Generously portioned complete meals,

around a fiver, include veggie lasagne, salmon flan and spicy coconut chicken. Baked tatties, wraps and nachos, cakes and coffee provide snackier options. See Film.
www.filmhousecinema.com

The Gallery Café
West End, Map 2 A5
Scottish National Gallery of Modern Art, 74 Belford Road, 0131 332 8600
Mon–Sun 10am–4.30pm
Average price two course meal: £7.50
Free parking, garden tables in summer, exciting exhibitions upstairs and healthy, home-made food conspire to bring the crowds into this pleasant gallery cafe, particularly at weekends and lunch. Food is made fresh daily. Salads are the thing here, either alone or as accompaniment to most main dishes taken from an imaginative range including Morrocan chicken with tomato and saffron jam. A couple of soups always head up the blackboard menu and home-baking fills the morning and afternoon gaps.

No 28 Charlotte Square
West End, Map 2 D5
28 Charlotte Square, 0131 243 9339
Mon–Sat 9.30am–4.30pm. Closed Sun
Average price two course meal: £12.50
Part of the National Trust for Scotland conglomerate, this restaurant serves

refined lunches and teas in Georgian surroundings. It's a proper sit-down affair with contemporary dishes worked around Scottish produce: creamy chicken liver pâté matured in whisky comes with a citrus sauce. In the adjacent coffee house there are plenty of all-day snacks, including sandwiches, cream teas and homebaking, while a scrambled egg and smoked salmon roll makes a real Charlotte Square breakfast. See Art Galleries.
www.nts.org.uk

Queen Street Café
City Centre, Map 2 G4
The Scottish National Portrait Gallery, 1 Queen Street, 0131 557 2844
Mon–Sat 10am–4.30pm, Sun 11am–4.30pm
Average price two course meal: £7
Brick-walled, bright rooms in the quirky, Victorian Portrait Gallery give this café a high brow yet cosy feel. Lunchtimes can be busy though service at the self-serve counter is steady. At least four inventive salads like pear, rocket and blue cheese, two main dishes and soup, are all made fresh daily. Coffee and home-baking is available all day. See Art Galleries.

Traverse Bar Café
West End, Map 2 E7
Traverse Theatre, 10 Cambridge Street, 0131 228 5383
Mon–Wed 10.30am–midnight, Thu–Sat 10.30am–1am, Sun 5pm–midnight
Average price two course meal: £8
Since the Traverse Theatre moved from its swinging 60s roots in the Grassmarket to this architect-designed space, the bar/restaurant has taken a new turn and become a popular city centre eating/drinking venue at all times of day: bacon rolls at breakfast, cakes with coffee, lunch specials, light bites, tapas for late (after 8pm) and drinks on tap. The regular menu, all freshly made on the premises, works around bumper-sized sandwiches with extras slotted in daily. See Theatre, Comedy, Dance.
www.traverse.co.uk

the cafeteria @ the fruitmarket
Old Town, Map 2 G5
Fruitmarket Gallery, 45 Market Street, 0131 226 1843
Mon–Sat 11am–5pm, Sun noon–5pm
Average price two course meal: £7
A neat gallery/bookshop/café in a slick, sophisticated space which hosts international grade exhibitions. Next to Waverley Station, it's a busy, welcoming place for lunch. The menu is simple with soup, big sandwiches and giant, crouton-covered salads in wide white bowls. Good coffee and continental pastries are served outside lunch hours. See Art Galleries.
www.info@fruitmarket.com

Cafés

Always Sunday
Old Town, Map 2 H6
170 High Street, 0131 622 0667
Mon–Fri 8am–6pm, Sat/Sun 9am–6pm
Average price two course meal: £6
With an ever-changing specials board and food of surprising freshness and originality, this is a café you could visit every day. Offering tea and traditional breakfasts, this bright, Scandinavian-style pit stop also serves lunch, wheat-free dishes and fairtrade coffee. Soups like mackerel and green split pea or rustic salads like sweet potato and spinach are made daily. If you manage to grab the best seat in the house, a raised cubbyhole at the back, it will be even harder to get to work on time.
www.alwayssunday.co.uk

Au Gourmand
New Town, Map 2 F2
1 Brandon Terrace, 0131 624 4666
Mon–Fri 9am–10pm, Sat 8.30am–10pm, Sun 10am–6pm
Average price two course meal: £18.50
Since opening in 2002 this Canonmills establishment has quickly established itself as a very popular café and deli. There are only a handful of tables just beyond the deli counter (see Shopping), but it's a relaxed stone-walled setting. During the day, the menu is based around soups, crêpes and sandwiches. In the evening a full restaurant menu comes into play, offering formal French cuisine such as deliciously garlicky mille feuille layered with snails.
www.augourmand.co.uk

Beanscene
Old Town, Map 2 J6
67 Holyrood Road, 0131 557 6549
Mon–Sat 8am–8pm, Sun 10am–8pm
Inviting leather sofas, soothing jazz, no-smoking and low lighting combine to create a mellow ambience in both Beanscenes. In the afternoons, toys and child-friendly snack bags attract young families, particularly at the Holyrood branch, where a BYOB policy after 6pm and savoury platters of meats, cheeses and dips to share encourages a sociable atmosphere. Regular live music at 99 Nicolson Street (0131 667 8159) encourages an upbeat rhythm.
www.beanscene.co.uk

Black Medicine Coffee Company
Southside, Map 2 H7
2 Nicolson Street, 0131 622 7209
Mon–Sat 8am–6pm, Sun 10am–6pm
With its dimly-lit interior and wide windows, this café makes an ideal vantage point for coffee-sippers to watch the street life outside. Chunky hand-made furniture

gives it a quirky, rough-hewn look which complements the friendly atmosphere. Bagels, hot panini (£3.50), smoothies, soup and pastries are the main orders of the day, while dinnerplate-sized cookies are just perfect for dunking. Robust portions, both food and drink, are always served here.

Blue Moon Café
New Town, Map 2 G3
1 Barony Street, 0131 556 2788
Mon–Thu 11am–11pm, Fri/Sat
10am–11.30pm, Sun 10am–11pm
Average price two course meal: £9.50
This reliable and vibrant neighbourhood café-cum-bistro is a landmark in Edinburgh's gay scene, but unquestionably straight-friendly. It serves a full menu all day – lasagne, baked potatoes or fish and chips, with daily specials such as spicy Jamaican jerk chicken. The great British fry-up is served at weekends till 4pm, together with a Bloody Mary if absolutely necessary. See Gay Life.
www.bluemooncafe.co.uk

Café Florentin
Old Town, Map 2 G6
8 St Giles Street, 0131 225 6267
Mon–Fri 8am–6pm, Sat/Sun 9am–6pm
Average two course meal: £7.50
This bright, cheerful place with its sunflower logo brought café culture to Scotland in the late 80s. Now you can get a latte on nearly every street corner, but Florentin still manages to stay up there with the best of them. Sandwiches, croissants, big milky coffees, fancy patisserie and home-made soup are served in an easy atmosphere which encourages paper-reading and dreams of Paris.

Circus Café
New Town, Map 2 D3
15 North West Circus Place, 0131 220 0333
Mon–Sun 10am–late
Average price two course meal: £12
The owner of this new venue, Keith Murray, has been ambitious, putting a café/bar, bakery, takeaway and food hall all under one roof. The retro cum up-to-the-minute decor in this former bank is glammy but surprisingly comfy. Waiters are super friendly and the minimal, Italian-based menu uses fresh ingredients. Delicious starters include warm onion tart, while mains offer a couple of daily specials as well as regulars like chicken with buffalo mozzarella. Coffees are very, very good and the vanilla espresso martinis make a change for dessert.
www.circuscafe.co.uk

Cornerstone Café
City Centre, Map 2 D6
St John's Church, 3 Lothian Road, 0131 229 0212

Mon–Sat 9.30am–4pm. Closed Sun
Average price two course meal: £6
In the vaults of St John's Church, on one of the busiest junctions in Edinburgh, this café is high on atmosphere and usually busy. This is vegetarian country, stepping out of line only on a Friday with a fish of the day. At £3/£4, dishes like mushroom stroganoff with rice or pepper and onion bolognese are fine value and good to fill up on. Sandwiches, salads and cakes offer lighter, even cheaper options.

Elephant House
Old Town, Map 2 G7
21 George IV Bridge, 0131 220 5355
Mon–Wed 8am–10pm, Thu/Fri 8am–11pm,
Sat 9am–11pm, Sun 9am–10pm
Average price two course meal: £9
Taking the elephant theme to an extreme (ornaments, framed articles, even rocking ones for kids) and with a fine view of the castle in the large smoking section, this café has a character of its own and the food's not bad either. Counter service (sometimes slow) operates during the day – a selection of baked potatoes, panini and baguettes can be eaten in or out. After 6pm table service brings on tasty meals which range from lasagne to burgers to enchiladas.
www.elephant-house.co.uk

Favorit
Southside, Map 2 E9
30–32 Leven Street, 0131 221 1800
Mon–Sun 8am–3am
Average price two course meal: £7.25
A stylish pair of cafés (also at 20 Teviot Place, 0131 220 6880) serving food from early morning right through to the wee small hours, the Favorit formula of diner-style eating is a hit with Edinburgh's youth. Favorit relies on combining good quality deli ingredients with a minimum of preparation. Olives, tapas, chorizo and pitta bread or hummus and salad make easy sidekicks to chilled white beer. Smoothies, pastries and Ben & Jerry's ice cream satisy sweeter inclinations.

Glass & Thompson
New Town, Map 2 F4
2 Dundas Street, 0131 557 0909
Mon–Sat 8.30am–5.30pm, Sun
11am–4.30pm
Average price two course meal: £11
It's a few minutes from Princes Street and well worth the detour. Also functioning as a deli and takeaway, the modestly sized G&T is perfectly relaxing at even the busiest times. House speciality is a platter made up from the cheeses, cured meats, jars and bowls which crowd the counter. Or you might consider the pâté platter, the seafood platter, or the New York deli platter. Small but perfectly formed, this is one of Edinburgh's foodie hot spots.

Maxi's
New Town, Map 2 C3
33 Raeburn Place, 0131 343 3007
Mon–Sun 11am–1am
Average price two course meal: £14
A spick and span café right in the middle of the boutique shopping area of Stockbridge. Alongside a small selection of pre-packed foods on sale, Maxi's has a good café menu. Breakfast can be a simple croissant or muesli or sweet/savoury pancake or scrambled egg muffin topped with bacon, salmon or cheese. Lunch consists of salads, panini, sandwiches, pasta or an antipasta platter.

Metropole
Southside, Map 2 I10
33 Newington Road, 0131 668 4999
Mon–Sun 9am–10pm
Average price two course meal: £7
With a rather opulent interior decorated with art nouveau prints and dominated by the fronds of a huge potted palm, this is a relaxed place, full of hungry young people sitting at small continental-style tables or in the more private four-seater wooden booths. A long glass display counter is arranged with hot meals and cold snacks. There are no fewer than seven blackboards heralding what's on offer that day.

Monster Mash
Old Town, Map 2 G7
4A Forrest Road, 0131 225 7069
Mon–Fri 8am–10pm, Sat 9am–10pm, Sun 10am–10pm
Average price two course meal: £7
Since opening in July 2003, this retro-style café has earned a reputation for shamelessly generous portions and good prices. The menu is basic, featuring trad Scottish dishes like steak pie, fish & chips and five kinds of sausage, but all is freshly cooked. Cream coloured walls with black borders, aluminium cruet sets and tomato-shaped ketchup bottles complete the ambience. Booking recommended for

groups over five.
www.monstermashcafe.co.uk

S Luca of Musselburgh
Southside, Map 2 off D10
16 Morningside Road, 0131 446 0233
Mon–Sun 9am–10pm
Average price two course meal: £7
Like the original Musselburgh shop, this branch, despite its modern polished design, is an old-fashioned ice-cream parlour at heart. It's popular on Sunday and attracts kids from local schools on weekday afternoons. Late opening makes it a great family treat in the evenings. As well as the knickerbocker glory treats there is a good menu of favourites like baked potatoes, toasties, pizza, panini as well as an excellent brunch. Ice-cream cakes are a speciality.
www.lucasicecream.co.uk

Spoon
Old Town, Map 2 H6
15 Blackfriars Street, 0131 556 6922
Mon–Sat 8am–6pm. Closed Sun
Average price two course meal: £7
NOT the greasy spoon. This is a caff with good looks and a big heart which beats with New York style. It's a great place. In fact, we would much rather keep it secret as it is *The List's* local. Everything is fresh and bright (soups are particularly colourful) and dishes (including daily specials) are all prepared to order lovingly by the owners. Sandwiches are big but sophisticated – chicken breast with garlic, parmesan and marinated anchovies on focaccia, and coffee is superlative. A top marks kind of place.
www.spoon-cafe.co.uk

Susie's Diner
Southside, Map 2 H8
51–53 West Nicolson Street, 0131 667 8729
Mon noon–8pm, Tue–Sat noon–9pm. Closed Sun
Average price two course meal: £8
Bright and sunny, behind two large south-

Spoon, a top marks kind of place in the Old Town

facing windows, this is a place for peace and quiet, not to mention an incredibly good cup of coffee. Hot food is served from lunch onwards and you can expect to find a choice of six main courses like broccoli quiche, Spanish omelette, cashew flan or tofu stir fry. Combine a slice/portion of any of them with one or two salads and you're well fed.

Terrace Café
New Town, Map 2 C1
Royal Botanic Garden, Inverleith Row, 0131 552 0616
Winter: Mon–Sun 10am–3.30pm Summer: Mon–Sun 10am–6pm
Average price two course meal: £8
On top of the hill, in the middle of the Royal Botanic Garden, this café has panoramic views and a busy outdoor patio. Inside, the atmosphere is smart cafeteria and inevitably always full of kids. The menu these days is attractive and includes smoothies, coffee and fresh baking along with homemade soups, baked potatoes and lunch specials. A great place, especially in summer.
www.drewnorloch.co.uk

Valvona & Crolla
City Centre, Map 2 I3
19 Elm Row, 0131 556 6066
Mon–Sat 8am–6pm, Sun 11am–4.30pm
Average price two course meal: £15
The café in the world's best deli (give or take a couple in New York) is right at the back behind the mountain of wine (see Shopping). To some, this is a place of foodie worship - certainly Clarissa Dickson Wright seems to pop in a lot. Lunch (brunch on Sunday) is fuelled by frequent deliveries from artisan producers in Italy, France and Scotland. The antipasto of cured meats with roasted vegetables is exemplary, the spicy sausage is all Italian and desserts include a Valrhona chocolate tart and panna cotta. It's almost always busy, so you'd be wise to book a table.
www.valvonacrolla.com

blue bar café
West End, Map 2 E7
10 Cambridge Street, 0131 221 1222
Mon–Thu 11.30am–midnight, Fri/Sat 11.30am–1am
Average price two course meal: £15.50
Popular as ever, Blue is still as fresh as its ingredients: a benchmark in Edinburgh for up-market café-style eating. Soups, sandwiches or 'light blue' cater for smaller appetites in a menu with many influences – local black pudding with apple and pommery mustard is a favourite. You can stop there or go on to have a bigger 'main' dish too. Tender venison loin gets snappy with a peppery gravy and mellow with creamed cabbage. The menu changes six-weekly and there are daily specials.
www.bluebarcafe.com

Takeaway

L'Alba D'Oro
New Town, Map 2 E2
5/9 Henderson Row, 0131 557 2580
Sun–Wed 5pm–11pm, Tue–Sat 5pm–midnight
Owner Filippo Crolla cites fresh ingredients as the key to a good fish supper; he's used the same supplier since opening in 1975. The results speak for themselves; firm, fleshy haddock in a light batter, served with chips crispy outside, creamy within. More exotic suppers of squid, monkfish and swordfish are sometimes available. Crolla's other passion is wine – his selection is ever-improving. Next door, son Gino runs the pizza and sandwich side of the business.

Bene's
Old Town, Map 2 I5
162 Canongate, 0131 551 1092
Mon–Thu 11.30am–1.45pm, 4.30pm–midnight; Fri 11.30am–1.45pm, 4.30pm–1am; Sat 4.30pm–1am; Sun 4.30pm–midnight
Given its location, down in the heart of the Canongate, it's no surprise that Bene's fish and chip bar caters for the tourist trade, with every health minister's scourge, the deep-fried Mars Bar, advertised in the window. But it is also a popular local takeaway: some of the best chips in the capital are served from the small counter with its big friendly atmosphere. The usual menu of sausages, puddings and fish is served as well as a good selection of pizzas.

Made in France
West End, Map 2 D8
5 Lochrin Place, 0131 221 1184
Mon–Fri 9.30am–5.30pm, Sat 10am–6pm. Closed Sun
Everything here is imported from France – from the 80s music to the Coca-Cola and the flour. The baguettes (of epic length, from £2.40) are filled with mouth-watering choices; rillette du porc, jambon blanc, pâtés and cheeses. The chef's quiche, irresistible gâteaux and croissants can be teamed with a cup or bowl of coffee or chocolat chaud, while you peruse the French magazines and groceries for sale. For £3 you can even rent a raclette machine!
www.madeinfrance.co.uk

Rapido
New Town, Map 2 H3
79 Broughton Street, 0131 556 2041
Mon–Fri 11.30am–2pm, 4.30pm–1am; Sat/Sun 4.30pm–1am
This legendary chippy is always busy, and it's got everything. Fish and chips top the bill, but the menu also offers great pizzas, wraps, baked potatoes, ice creams and a selection of beer and wine. Vegetarians can now indulge in fish and chip shop fare too, as this is one of the few to offer an excellent meatless menu.

restaurants

Not that long ago, Edinburgh was hard pressed to come up with more than a handful of decent restaurants, never mind pavement cafés. So this generous selection is something of a celebration of the burgeoning number of good places to eat. If you take food really seriously, the popular annual *Eating & Drinking Guide, Edinburgh & Glasgow* (£4.95) is published by *The List* and includes reviews of over 400 restaurants in each city.

American

Bell's Diner
New Town, Map 2 D3
7 St Stephen Street, 0131 225 8116
Sun–Fri 6–10.30pm, Sat noon–10.30pm
Average price two course meal: £13
With just a handful of tables, there isn't a great deal of room in the crimson interior of Bell's: you may even be asked to share a table if you haven't booked. But this long-established burger joint never seems to tire. Pâté and toast style starters introduce meaty mains, centred around succulent, home-crafted burgers and seven generously sized cuts of steak. Vast portions of chips and salad come with everything. With ice-cream sweets for afters, a healthy appetite is a must.

Mamma's American Pizza Company
Old Town, Map 2 F7
30 Grassmarket, 0131 225 6464
Sun–Thu noon–11pm, Fri/Sat noon–midnight
Average price two course meal: £8
As the city says goodbye to the two other branches of Mamma's, this one remains and is going strong. One of the best pizzas in town, the Mamma's version is thin, fresh and comes in a size and flavour chosen by you. It's a great value place for families, students and anyone who wants to eat pizza with a little North American style. In summer, the tables outside are like gold dust.
www.mammas.co.uk

The New York Steam Packet
City Centre, Map 2 F5
31 Rose Street Lane North, 0131 220 4825
Tue–Sat 6–11pm. Closed Sun/Mon
Average price two course meal: £13
There can't be many places that offer so much for so little: for just £13 you get three courses, served in a cosy room decorated with artwork from the days of ocean-going liners. The menu is small and does not favour vegetarians. Starters include corn on the cob or potato skins, while main courses centre on the pepper steak which is probably one of the best in town.

Smoke Stack
New Town, Map 2 H3
53–55 Broughton Street, 0131 556 6032
Mon–Fri/Sun noon–2.30pm, 6–10.30pm; Sat noon–10.30pm
Average price two course meal: £15.50
Opened in 1995 by owners of the New Town's popular bar The Basement, this steak house flaunts its American influence with massive portions and meaty mains (vegetarian options available). A rich red interior and art deco lamps create a stylish but cosy mood. Check out the newly opened Smoke Stack at 19 Shore Place, Leith, 0131 476 6776.
www.smokestack.org.uk

Bistros and Brasseries

Blonde
Southside, Map 2 I9
75 St Leonards Street, 0131 668 2917
Mon 6–10pm, Tue–Sun noon–2.30pm, 6–10pm
Average price two course meal: £14
Blonde is all that's best about a neighbourhood restaurant. There's a one-sheet menu, with all mains £8 to £10 and a one-sheet wine list with six house bottles under a tenner. It is also blessed with an uncomplicated but stylish design. The resident chef, Andy Macgregor, uses ingredients in intriguing combinations – salmon in poppy seeds with black olive noodles or venison with red wine, cardamom and bitter chocolate. A dining room for the Jamie Oliver generation.

Daniel's Bistro
Leith, Map 3 H3
88 Commercial Street, 0131 553 5933
Mon–Sun 10am–10pm
Average price two course meal: £13.50
An established Leith resident, Daniel's has all-day attractions, whether it's patisserie and unlimited coffee, a sandwich from the deli, a couple of beers or a three course meal. The light beech decor belies some of the hearty offerings on the menu which is made up of French staples such as beef bourguignon and moules marinieres alongside more unusual regional offerings like the national dish of Alsace, with its variety of meats served with sauerkraut and potato.
www.edinburghrestaurants.co.uk

FAVOURITE RESTAURANT

French Corner Bistro
'It's been a favourite of mine for years. Good food, good prices, a lovely view onto Queensferry Street.'
Laura Hird, novelist

**Delicious food.
Wonderful
atmosphere.**

Looking for somewhere different to eat? Then look no further.

The Caledonian Hilton Hotel, built in 1903 and situated in the very heart of Edinburgh, offers a unique dining experience.

The dining in the **Pompadour Restaurant** is fine Scottish and International cuisine in an intimate atmosphere. The staff attentive. The wine list a delight and the panoramas breathtaking. This is undoubtedly a room with a view. The Pompadour is open for lunch Tuesday to Friday 12.30pm-2.30pm and dinner Tuesday to Saturday 7.00pm-10.00pm.

Should you wish for a less formal venue, **Chisholms Restaurant** offers a blend of Scottish and International specialities. Open for breakfast, lunch and dinner and also for a fabulous Sunday Jazz Carvery lunch. Uniquely, Chisholms incorporates the original architecture of the former Caledonian Railway Station. Open daily.

Chisholms Bar can be found at the front of the hotel. A fantastic venue to meet friends for a drink or for a light bite to eat. The Bar is open daily until 11pm. Enjoy afternoon tea in the relaxed and luxurious surroundings of the Lounge. Available daily.

For more information and to book your table, please call **0131 222 8888**.

Caledonian Hilton, Princes Street, Edinburgh EH1 2AB.

Caledonian Hilton
welcome to Hilton time
hilton.co.uk

Tables offered subject to availability. Menu subject to change at the hotel's discretion.

The Doric Tavern
Old Town, Map 2 G6
15/16 Market Street, 0131 225 1084
Mon–Sat noon–1am, Sun 12.30–midnight
Average price two course meal: £16.95
Inviting smells accompany your climb upstairs to this first floor bar and bistro, while traditional fixtures, heavy curtains and old Edinburgh prints create a convivial atmosphere appealing to regulars and tourists. Using fresh produce in a small selection of dishes, the menu changes daily. Scottish influences are given a twist so pheasant is parcelled in a samosa and comes with sweet ginger chutney. The wine list is excellent, with bin end offers.
www.thedoric.co.uk

Fenwicks
Southside, Map 2 I10
15 Salisbury Place, 0131 667 4265
Mon–Sat noon–2pm, 6pm–late; Sun 6pm–late
Average price two course meal: £17.50
Tucked among the antique shops of Causwayside, this cosy bistro has a 'fin de siècle' feel with its dark wood and art nouveau prints. Candlelight and mellow jazz complete the mood. Food is Scottish shot with gutsy influences from France, Italy and even North Africa – succulent chicken supreme with buttery polenta fritters and cider jus or a mountain of luscious mussels cooked to perfection in white wine and cream. The wine list is thoughtful and well priced.
www.fenwicks-restaurant.co.uk

The Grain Store
Old Town, Map 2 G6
30 Victoria Street, 0131 225 7635
Mon–Thu noon–2pm, 6–10pm; Fri/Sat noon–3am, 6–11pm; Sun noon–3pm, 6–10pm
Average price two course meal: £23
In vaulted store rooms with bare stone walls and mismatched tables, this unpretentious place is comfy and relaxed. Menus are imaginative, keenly priced and, in the case of lunch, commendably flexible: you can assemble a tapas-style meal or go for a more traditional main course like the fabulously fragrant plate of seared mackerel, fennel, olives and tomato. Combine this with an extensive, cool, well priced wine list and a jazzy soundtrack and it's easy to make this a perennial favourite.
www.grainstore-restaurant.co.uk

Hadrian's Brasserie
City Centre, Map 2 H5
2 North Bridge, 0131 557 5000
Mon–Sat 7–10.30am, noon–2.30pm, 6.30–10pm; Sun 7.30–11am, 12.30–3pm, 6.30–10pm
Average price two course meal: £15
Civilised, and favoured by guests of the adjoining Balmoral Hotel and locals alike, this restaurant is surprisingly affordable, with an evening set menu priced at £10.99. A mix of classic European dishes, the food is competent, unfussy and flavourful. Confit of pork with apple sauce and sage jus is delicious, while vegetarian options include baked aubergine and saffron risotto. The wine list is solid, and Hadrian's gets the simple things right with a straightforward elegance.
www.thebalmoralhotel.com

Maxies
Old Town, Map 2 G6
5b Johnston Terrace, 0131 226 7770
Mon–Sun 11am–1am
Average price two course meal: £14
With its chilled out approach to the French-style bistro, good value and great views from its garden terrace, Maxies is a popular spot (and not just with MSPs from across the road). The hot seafood platter is a particular favourite, while breast of duck with a rich Grand Marnier sauce is a definite highlight. Vegetarians will be impressed by the choice and standard of options available.
www.maxies.co.uk

The Waterfront
Leith, Map 3 H3
1c Dock Place, 0131 554 7427
Mon–Sat noon–midnight, Sun 12.30–11pm
Average price two course meal: £19
Refurbished not so long ago, one of Edinburgh's most charming and long-established bistro restaurants now has a little more space and a slightly cooler look (though the cosy booths remain). Starter and main courses, all well priced, are spiced up by a large dose of daily specials. Starters are large with pan-fried squid and chorizo and olives almost a meal in itself. Mains include Szechuan pepper tuna with mango and lychee salsa or whole lemon sole with ginger and roast red pepper butter.

Zinc Bar & Grill
Leith, Map 3 G1
Ocean Terminal, Victoria Dock, Leith, 0131 553 8070
Sun–Thu 10am–10pm, Fri/Sat 10am–1am
Average price two course meal: £19
An outpost of Terence Conran's empire, this bar and grill exploits the dramatic view over Leith docks to the full. The interior is of course impeccably designed, with chefs performing in full view of the diners. The menu is simplicity itself, with fish, chips and peas, tempura prawns, chilli squid and a special burger among its mix and match starter/main/sides style. Not your average mall haunt, you can get away from the shops for just a drink, a snack or a sit down meal.
www.conran.co.uk

Bell's Diner, a small joint with big burgers, page 100

Chinese

Jasmine Chinese Restaurant
West End, Map 2 E7
32 Grindlay Street, 0131 229 5757
Mon–Thu noon–2pm, 5–11.30pm; Fri
noon–2pm, 5pm–12.30am; Sat
2pm–12.30am; Sun 2–11.30pm
Average price two course meal: £14
Jasmine's decor is based on the look of
high-class 1940s Shanghai restaurants and
it's popular with big groups and business
lunchers. Steamed turbot with ginger and
spring onion or fried and chilli prawns are
among the many well prepared dishes,
which are headed up by starters like salty,
spicy chicken and deep-fried crab claw.
Touches, like topping up your Chinese
tea, make this place a cut above the
average.

Kweilin
New Town, Map 2 F3
19–21 Dundas Street, 0131 557 1875
Tue–Thu noon–2pm, 5–11pm; Fri/Sat
noon–2pm, 5pm–midnight; Sun 5–11pm.
Closed Mon
Average price two course meal: £19
Opened in 1984, Kweilin might be an
institution, but still leads the pack in
pursuit of fine Cantonese dining in
Edinburgh. Be sure to opt for seasonal
specials: steamed scallops in black bean
sauce are a light and delicious appetiser
and crayfish is well worth the mess. The
clay pot dishes – braised seafood and
meat cooked in a casserole with
vegetables – are adventurous, with stewed
duck feet only for the very brave. A well-
heeled clientele ensures Kweilin is both
formal and busy.
www.kweilin.co.uk

Loon Fung
New Town, Map 2 F1
2 Warriston Place, 0131 556 1781
Mon–Thu noon–11.30pm; Fri noon–12.30am;
Sat 2pm–12.30am; Sun 2–11.30pm
Average price two course meal: £12.50
Comfort food, Chinese style – this is a
real favourite among locals. Since it
opened over thirty years ago, its
reputation has never dimmed and its
barbequed spare ribs remain legendary.
Food comes steaming hot from the busy
kitchen and is always fresh. That, and a
cosy, bustling atmosphere, is a recipe
which brings customers back again and
again.

Wok and Wine
New Town, Map 2 E5
57a Frederick Street, 0131 225 2382
Mon/Wed–Sat noon–2pm, 5.30–11.30pm; Sun
5.30–11.30pm. Closed Tue
Average price two course meal: £12.50
A Chinese tapas bar-cum-restaurant, this is
the sort of place you can just have a drink,
take in a snack or have a full-blown meal.
Sofas allow full relaxation to mellow music
if you so require. The food is good: the
spicy kung bao king prawns kick without
hurting and aubergine tempura spiced with
fresh chilli is a winner. A new blackboard
menu with fresh seafood has added some
western-style steak dishes.

Far East

Izzi
West End, Map 2 D7
119 Lothian Road, 0131 466 9888
Mon–Sat noon–midnight, Sun
12.30pm–midnight
Average price two course meal: £15
Izzi is the place to go in Edinburgh if you
want to eat authentic Japanese food. The
interior is appropriately minimal with
brightly coloured Kabuki wall hangings.
Staff are gentle and helpful and the food
beautiful – you can watch it being prepared
at the city's only teppanyaki bar. Superb
octopus sushi, eel tempura and pork katsu
are hits with regulars, who are now being
tempted by the restaurant's foray into
Chinese food.
www.izzi-restaurant.co.uk

Thai Lemongrass
Southside, Map 2 D10
40–41 Bruntsfield Place, 0131 229 2225
Mon–Thu 5–11.30pm, Fri–Sun noon–11.30pm
Average price two course meal: £15
What food! This modern Thai delivers
delicacy and heat in equal proportions. Red
snapper in green mango salad is cooked to
firm perfection under a tangle of red
onions, mango strips, and an intense red
chilli paste that provides fire and flavour.
Service is swift and elegant and if you're
feeling flushed, indulge in the melon, palm
sugar and coconut milk dessert, a simple
but effective finale to your oriental dinner.

*The List's Eating & Drinking Guide,
Edinburgh & Glasgow (£4.95) reviews
over 800 restaurants*

no theme
no gimmicks
just a great bar...

owned by a couple of self-confessed...

TEUCHTERS

26 William Street, West End
EDINBURGH 0131 225 2973

Teuchters (tjuxtər,tʃuxtər) n, freq disparaging
term for a Highlander (HIELAND) esp a GAELIC-
speaker or anyone from the North, an uncouth,
countrified person.

Open 12pm - 1am Mon - Sun

a room in the town

a room in the west end

18 Howe Street
Edinburgh
0131 225 8204

26 William Street
Edinburgh
0131 226 1036
(below Teuchters)

Scottish BYOB bistros and fully licensed too
open 7 days for lunch and dinner

Thai Me Up in Edinburgh
City Centre, Map 2 H3
4 Picardy Place, 0131 558 9234
Mon–Sat 11.30am–10.30pm; Sun
12.30–2.30pm, 5.30–10.30pm
Average price two course meal: £15
What the gimmicky name belies is that
this spanking new venture has startlingly
good food. The building is a carefully
restored New Town jewel dating from
1790 and the Thai cuisine is presented
with imagination and contemporary flair.
Tight, brittle spring rolls, moo yang
(twangy honey and coriander roast pork)
and pah neng (powerful lamb shank
stewed in a thick red curry sauce) are all
fireworks to the tastebuds. So far it's a
winner.
www.tmeup.com

Thaisanuk
Southside, Map 2 G10
21 Argyle Place, 0131 228 8855
Mon–Sun 6–11pm
Average price two course meal: £14
Hidden deep in Marchmont, the excellent
Thaisanuk is smart and modern. From the
chatty menu, owner and chef Madam Ae's
passion for fresh, healthy Thai food is
immediately apparent. The Malaysian
curry with prawns is typical – huge juicy
beasts in a mild coconut-flavoured sauce
with ultra-fresh pineapple chunks and
grapes. Other Asian specialities such as
noodle dishes from Vietnam and Korea,
are also on offer. Remember to BYOB.
www.thaisanuk.com

Fish

Fishers Bistro
Leith, Map 3 I3
1 The Shore, 0131 554 5666
Mon–Sat noon–10.30pm, Sun
12.30–10.30pm
Average price two course meal: £19
While its popular new sister restaurant in
the city centre (58 Thistle Street, 0131
225 5109) goes for urban sophistication,
the original Fishers in Leith sticks to what
it knows best, providing excellent seafood
in an informal, friendly atmosphere. The
food, a successful blend of experiment
and tradition, has earned itself a great
reputation. Mackerel in pomegranate, lime
juice and tequila is served with a crunchy
fennel salad, while shellfish and steak
options round off a superb menu.
www.fishersbistro.co.uk

Mussel Inn
City Centre, Map 2 E5
61–65 Rose Street, 0131 225 5979
Mon–Thu noon–3pm, 6–10pm; Fri/Sat
noon–10pm; Sun 12.30–10pm
Average price two course meal: £16
Owned and run by shellfish farmers, it's
not really a surprise that this is just about
the best place to get the freshest, tastiest

and most succulent mussels, oysters and
scallops in town. The compact and simply
decorated space is always busy as a result,
and it can feel a little cramped. Who
cares? It's worth it. The fish is fantastic,
with the flagship dish of a kilo pot of
mussels fairly flying out of the kitchen
every few minutes.
www.mussel-inn.com

French

Café Marlayne
City Centre, Map 2 F5
76 Thistle Street, 0131 226 2230
Tue–Sat noon–2pm, 6–10pm. Closed Sun
Average price two course meal: £15
A tiny restaurant now famous for serving
very good food at low, low prices in a
charming atmosphere. Mains range from a
perfect rack of lamb with herb dressing
and Greek yoghurt to food like smoked
haddock with poached egg from the
comfort zone. Decent vegetables come
with everything. Puddings are on the
board and the wine list is all French,
reasonably priced and imaginatively
chosen. Packed to the gunnels all nights,
this is a place to book.

Le Café St Honoré
City Centre, Map 2 E4
34 North West Thistle Street Lane, 0131 226
2211
Mon–Fri noon–2.15pm, 5.30–10pm; Sat/Sun
6–10pm
Average price two course meal: £23
This little piece of Paris is hidden down a
cobbled New Town lane. Classic but
unstuffy inside, it has dark wood-panelled
mirrored walls and crisp white tablecloths.
The menu changes daily, offering half a
dozen starters such as a warm salad of
scallops with cherry tomato, catfish and
chorizo and half a dozen mains, such as
boeuf bourguignon with mash. This is
traditional brasserie food, beautifully
cooked. The set price menu (from
6–7pm) of £13.50 for two courses and £18
for three makes early dining very
tempting.

La Cuisine d'Odile
West End, Map 2 C5
Institut Francais d'Ecosse, 13 Randolph
Crescent, 0131 225 5685
Tue–Sat noon–2pm
Average price two course meal: £6.95
Neither sign nor name plate gives away
the location of one of Edinburgh's best
French cafés, a lunch only place. Two
courses are £6.75 and the menu changes
daily. Home-made soups, pâtés, delicious
savoury tartes, game and a fish dish keep
things simple. Owner Odile Petrie's
dedication to good ingredients, well
cooked, at an excellent price, ensures an
extremely loyal clientele, so it's worth
booking.

The French Corner Bistro
West End, Map 2 D6
17 Queensferry Street, 0131 226 1890
Mon–Thu noon–3pm, 5–10pm; Fri noon–3pm
5–10.30pm, Sat noon–3.30pm, 5–10.30pm.
Closed Sun
Average price two course meal: £15.50
This is a sunny, bustling place which
matches great food with delightfully low
prices. Daily changing, set lunches (from
£7.90) and dinners offer a choice for each
course with desserts and coffee extra.
Beef, game, seafood and vegetarian
options are always fresh and cooked to
order. Locals love it.
www.cornerbistro.co.uk

Petit Paris
Old Town, Map 2 F7
38–40 Grassmarket, 0131 226 2442
Mon–Sun noon–3pm, 5.30–10pm. Closed
Mon in winter
Average price two course meal: £18.90
The cobbled Grassmarket makes for good
outdoor dining on sunny days, and Petit
Paris has all the traditional ingredients of
a French bistro: gingham tablecloths,
accordion music and Pernod bottle vases.
The plat du jour offers exceptional value –
a main dish and coffee will set you back
only a fiver. Otherwise choose from
French standbys like sausages stewed with
Puy lentils and fresh fruit which arrives
ready to be dipped in chocolate fondue.
www.petitparis-restaurant.co.uk

Plaisir du Chocolat
Old Town, Map 2 I6
251–253 Canongate, 0131 556 9524
Mon–Sun 10am–6pm (later in summer)
Average price two course meal: £15
Plaisir du Chocolat is so deeply civilised a
salon du thé that the menu opens with a
quote from Baudelaire. In this case, his
paradise on earth comes in the shape of an
elegant dining room with art nouveau
mirrors and white linen. A wide range of
food is served, from croissants to eggs
Bénédicte and capers on brioche toast,
alongside ten speciality hot chocolates and
hundreds of varieties of tea. Service is
unhurried and when you finally need to
leave, you can take away exquisitely
wrapped packets of tea and jewel-like
little gateaux.
www.plaisirduchocolat.com

Indian

Kalpna
Southside, Map 2 I8
2/3 St Patrick's Square, 0131 667 9890
Mon–Sat 11am–2pm, 5.30–10.30pm. Closed
Sun
Average price two course meal: £15
There's no romance to Kalpna, but the
food is fabulous. Vegetarian only, the
Gujurati flavours blend sweet and spicy,
smooth and textured, drawing new ideas

into old recipes. From the home-made
cheese paneer to the spinach and lentil
dishes, every bite is a reminder that
vegetarians may just have a point. Quality
food, keen prices and a wine list with
Indian and European labels have made
Kalpna a winner of accolades from diners
and critics since it opened in 1982.

Namaste North Indian Frontier Cuisine
Southside, Map 2 I9
41 West Preston Street, 0131 466 7061
Mon–Sun 5.30–11pm
Average price two course meal: £14
A welcoming interior, softly-lit and gently
scented, gives this restaurant instant
karma. Away from the main drag, it dishes
up a mellifluous curry, presented with
charm and carefully spiced in both meat
and vegetarian departments. Fish tikka is
glorious and the sharply spiced signature
pudini chicken is a tangy combo of mint
and meat. If you're making a night of it,
the gulab jamun dessert, a sweet dumpling
in syrup, is worth a try.

Suruchi
Southside, Map 2 H7
14a Nicolson Street, 0131 556 6583
Mon–Sat noon–2pm, 5.30–11.30pm; Sun
5.30–11.30pm
Average price two course meal: £14.50
Across from the Festival Theatre, this is
a popular restaurant. The furniture is

city5s
BOOGIE WITH BRUNCH
■ **Plaisir du Chocolat** Silken
eggs Bénédict at this elegant
French salon du thé, half way
down the Royal Mile.
■ **King's Wark** A big, warm-
hearted Scottish breakfast with
black pudding and sausage,
served in this well-kent Leith
pub.
■ **Circus Café** Croissants and
muffins all baked on the
premises, from this delicious
new Stockbridge café.
■ **Valvona and Crolla** City
centre bacon and eggs with a
style that only a top notch
Italian café like this one can
serve.
■ **Always Sunday** Sunny
breakfasts cry out 'fresh' in this
new High Street hangout.

Indian, but the eccentric menu, with its haggis fritters (a take on pakora), might throw you to begin with. Dishes are made with fresh herbs and spices and an intelligent, confident touch. There is live jazz on Wednesdays and Fridays and other special events throughout the year. Its sister restaurant in Leith (Suruchi Too, 121 Constitution Street, Leith, 0131 554 3268) is less atmospheric but serves equally impressive food.
www.suruchirestaurant.co.uk

Zest
City Centre, Map 2 G4
15 North St Andrew Street, 0131 556 5028
Mon–Sun noon–2pm, 5.30–11.30pm
Average price two course meal: £14
Anyone needing a speedy update on trends in Indian cuisine should visit this vanguard of sub-continental gastronomy, which breaks the classical curry mould to create unique and delicious hybrids. All meat is wonderfully tender and the menu rich in earthy specialities from Assam, including the uniquely aromatic shaktora aloo gosht featuring the bitter zesty Assamese citrus fruit shaktora. Staff serve with flair and confidence in this superior curry house.

Italian

La Bruschetta
West End, Map 2 B7
13 Clifton Terrace, 0131 467 7464
Tue–Sat noon–2pm, 6–10.30pm. Closed Sun/Mon
Average price two course meal: £15.50
A cosy little restaurant serving up good, clean-cut Italian cuisine. Fish is the speciality: fresh mussels, monkfish and turbot rival plates of creamy tagliatelle, home-made lasagne and pan-fried veal. There's a more selective bistro menu at lunchtime (£7.50), featuring mainly pizza, pasta and omelettes. The decor's nothing special and the Dean Martin-esque crooners hardly original, but a happy ambience reflects the charm and authenticity of the owners, ensuring that there's rarely a spare seat in the house.
www.labruschetta.co.uk

Cosmo
City Centre, Map 2 E5
58a North Castle Street, 0131 226 6743
Mon–Fri 12.30–2.15pm, 7–10.45pm; Sat 7–10.45pm. Closed Sun
Average price two couse meal: £25
Decorated in sumptuous burgundy and green with well-spaced, intimate tables, this elegant dining room has a long-standing reputation. The menu, complemented by a connoisseurs' wine list, offers classy Italian cuisine, including filetto di manzo rustica (fillet steak with porcini) and classic saltimbocca all'Italiana. All is served immaculately. A favourite haunt of the movers and shakers

in the business community.
www.cosmo-restaurant.co.uk

Ecco Vino
Old Town, Map 2 G6
19 Cockburn Street, 0131 225 1441
Mon–Thu noon–midnight, Fri/Sat noon–1am, Sun 12.30pm–midnight
Average price two course meal: £9
This Italian-style bar and bistro, wood-panelled and warm, makes a soothing, congenial venue for inexpensive meals, drinks and snacks. A plate of char-grilled vegetables and cured meats or gooey bruschetta and mixed crostini, are both ideal for communal snacking. Mains are variations on a theme of panini or frittata and tarts, with the latter option the more enticing. The wine list stars over 50 varieties.

Gordon's Trattoria
Old Town, Map 2 G6
231 High Street, 0131 225 7992
Sun–Thu noon–midnight, Fri/Sat noon–3am
Average price two course meal: £14.50
Location, location, location. A site at the heart of the Royal Mile is a bit of a coup for this traditional little trattoria. Inside, there are comfy booths at the front where lively staff mill around the bar, with a quieter section at the back. The menu is predictable: pastas, pizzas, a decent seafood selection and some saucy meat dishes and it's not that cheap, but this is a friendly, reliable place which has been around for years and is particularly useful late at night.

Pizza Express
New Town, Map 2 D3
1 Deanhaugh Street, 0131 332 7229
Mon–Thu/Sun 11.30am–11pm, Fri/Sat 11.30am–midnight
Average price two course meal: £10.50
Edinburgh now has four branches of this London chain, all of them busy and for good reason. Stylish, light interiors in wood and chrome with original art have been carved out of great locations – none better than the Stockbridge branch on Deanhaugh Street, overlooking the Water of Leith, which covers two floors as well as outdoor dining in summer. Pizzas are thin and crusty with original toppings: pasta and meat dishes on the simple menu come second in the popularity stakes. While relatively expensive, these are reliable joints with a real knack for ambience. Other branches at 32 Queensferry Street (0131 225 8863); 23 North Bridge (0131 557 6411) and 38 The Shore (0131 554 4332).
www.pizzaexpress.co.uk

The List's **Deli & Good Food Directory to Scotland (£4.95) reviews over 300 outlets**

North Bridge Brasserie, good food in stylish surroundings, page 89

Prego
Old Town, Map 2 I6
38 St Mary's Street, 0131 557 5754
Mon–Sat noon–2pm, 5.30–10pm. Closed Sun
Average price two course meal: £16
Managed by Pasquale Pavone, whose 46
years in the business include service in
Cosmo and Rafaelli's, two legendary Italian
restaurants, Prego is a small place with a
contemporary feel. Describing itself as a
'cucina rustica Italiana' it sticks rigorously
to the concept of simple, authentic Italian
food. Tagliatelle al guanciole e asparagi is a
delicious, light and creamy mix of
asparagus, pancetta and white wine; the
Barbary duck with red wine is for
connoisseurs.
www.prego-restaurant.com

Vittoria
City Centre, Map 2 I6
113 Brunswick Street, 0131 556 6171
Mon–Sat 10am–11pm, Sun noon–11pm
Average price two course meal: £14.50
A family-owned business which just keeps
getting better. Now refurbished, with
extended premises, it's packed every night
of the week. The trattoria atmosphere, laced
with music (sometimes live) is infectiously
happy and dishes range from 30 year old
favourites like mixed grill to really good
sirloin and well presented pasta and pizza.
The senior members of the family have a
takeaway (Eatalia's) next door.

Mexican

The Blue Parrot Cantina
New Town, Map 2 D3
49 St Stephen Street, 0131 225 2941
Mon–Thu/Sun 5–11pm, Fri/Sat
11am–10pm
Average price two course meal: £15
Snuggled in a basement in Stockbridge,
this popular restaurant is small with
simple, dimly-lit decor. Serving up giant
portions and a deadly array of cocktails
to get you drooling from the start, it's a
place to be hungry in. The menu
changes frequently with dishes like taco
de cameron – prawns, chillies and
tomatoes, all fresh and spicy, or lime-
spiced sirloin teamed with sweet
potatoes.

Coconut Grove
Southside, Map 2 D8
3 Lochrin Terrace, 0131 229 1569
Mon–Sun noon–2pm, 6–11pm
Average price two course meal: £15
A stone's throw from both the Kings
Theatre and Cameo Cinema, this is a
buzzy place with colourful walls and
smiling staff. The food is among the
best Mexican to be found in the capital.
Chilli relleño combines prawns with just
enough spice to bring out the flavour,
while the beef fajita, with its generous
strips of sirloin, is one of the best.

Viva Mexico
Old Town, Map 2 G6
41 Cockburn Street, 0131 226 5145
Mon–Sat noon–2pm, 6–10.30pm; Sun
6.30–10pm
Average price two course meal: £14
A cute restaurant on two levels featuring
classic Mexican decor. Hospitable staff
dish out the usual suspects but the place
has a hot reputation. Chicken fajita is, as
the menu warns, a messy business, but it
sizzles at the table and is full of flavour.
Margueritas are served in massive
pitchers, delicious, deadly and arguably
the best in town.

Round the World

Barioja
Old Town, Map 2 H5
19 Jeffrey Street, 0131 557 3622
Mon–Sat 11am–11pm. Closed Sun
Average price two course meal: £10.50
With a central location just off the Royal
Mile, this tapas bar is handy for a bite to
eat before a night on the town or a quiet
lunch. The glass-fronted upper level
enjoys views across to Calton Hill, though
tables are rather cramped; downstairs is
roomier, with a stylishly cosy feel. Size
and quality of the tapas can vary, but there
are daily specials and a small but
interesting choice of bocadillos (rolls),
plus additional options for two to share
such, as paella or mixed grill.

Brazilian Sensation
Southside, Map 2 I9
117–119 Buccleuch Street, 0131 667 0400
Apr–Aug Mon–Sun 11am–10pm; Sep–Mar
Mon–Thu 11am–6pm, Fri/Sat 11am–10pm
Average price two course meal: £13
Given its size (four tables in front of a deli
counter) it would be easy to pass this off

as just another takeaway joint. A huge
mistake. Painted the colours of the
national flag and filled with Brazilian
music that makes you want to samba on
the spot, this family-run business is
unique and charming with it. And when
faced with such dishes as the feijoada
(black beans and mixed meats – the
football team's favourite) it's a blessing
that owner John Falconer is at hand to
guide you through the possibilities.
www.braziliansensation.co.uk

Igg's
Old Town, Map 2 H6
15 Jeffrey Street, 0131 557 8184
Mon–Sat noon–2.30pm, 6–10.30pm. Closed
Sun
Average price two course meal: £22
This award-winning Spanish restaurant is
one of the oldest in town, but its
contemporary attitude ensures it's not
overly steeped in tradition. Igg's à la carte
evening menu successfully combines
Scottish and Spanish cuisine to create
conventional dishes with some exotic
tones such as Aberdeen Angus fillet with
wild mushrooms in red wine and onion
jus, topped with jamon. It's a pricey place
with all the trimmings, including a
lengthy, carefully selected wine list
ranging from £13.50 to £150.

Nargile
City Centre, Map 2 F5
73 Hanover Street, 0131 225 5755
Mon–Thu noon–2pm, 5.30–10.30pm; Fri/Sat
noon–2pm, 5.30–11pm. Closed Sun
Average price two course meal: £14.50
Turkish and Middle Eastern mezzes are
the speciality here – around 40 different
delicious starters served tapas-style. Main
courses range far beyond 'kebab only'
expectations – hunkar begendi, a house

One of Edinburgh's top restaurants, Atrium

speciality, combines char-grilled lamb with a sophisticated yet mellow aubergine sauce. Turkish vineyards are well represented on the wine list, and black-dregged traditional coffee and Turkish delight complete the experience.
www.nargile.co.uk

Ndebele
West End, Map 2 E8
57 Home Street, 0131 221 1141
Mon–Sun 10am–9pm
Average price two course meal: £7
It is always refreshing to find somewhere as genuine and enthusiastic as this Tollcross café, named after the Ndebele tribe of southern Africa. Its menu traverses the entire continent, with vegetarian food from the north alongside tasty bean-based dishes from the central regions and fruit and meat stews out of the south. Ostrich, kudu and springbok are sometimes available and an array of unfamiliar ingredients behind the counter can be combined into sandwiches or salads.
www.ndebele.co.uk

Nile Valley
Southside, Map 2 H8
6 Chapel Street, 0131 667 8200
Mon–Sat 11am–4pm, 6–10pm. Closed Sun
Average price two course meal: £13
A colourful African café by day, popular for its chunky wraps made with khobz bread, by night it's a vibrant restaurant with an extensive menu. Traditional dishes include the salata aswad, a sleek blend of aubergine, peanut butter and garlic, while the diverse main courses include dojaj bil salsa, tender chicken in a spicy coriander sauce. Joyfully haphazard decoration, African music and friendly staff create a homely vibe.

Santorini
New Town, Map 2 G3
32c Broughton Street, 0131 557 2012
Tue–Sun noon–10.30pm, Closed Mon
Average price two course meal: £10
This exceptionally good value and charming restaurant offers authentic Greek cuisine with stews and mousakka, salads and souvlakis (grilled meats with onions, sauces, pitta bread, fries or rice). There's an excellent selection of mezedes – small dishes which are ideal for sharing, such as dolmades or bekri meze (marinated pork with peppers, shallots, mustard, brandy and yoghurt). Desserts like Greek yoghurt with honey and nuts around £2 are as satisfying as the rest.

Walima
New Town, Map 2 F4
3a, 1 Dundas Street, 0131 652 3764
Mon–Sat noon–2.30pm, 5–11pm. Closed Sun
Average price two course meal: £19
'You are now in Morocco' says the scented world of Walima, a basement decorated with pots, tea glasses, mosaics and hookahs. It's drama all the way. The menu is lengthy, so grab a glass of Moroccan wine or beer and don't get too distracted by the belly dancer nearby (Wednesday to Sunday only). Lamb, chicken and seafood dominate and are served in briwats (lightly fried filo parcels) or tajines as mashwi (char-grilled dishes).

Scottish

Atrium
West End, Map 2 E7
10 Cambridge Street, 0131 228 8882
Mon–Fri noon–2pm, 6–10pm; Sat 6–10pm. Closed Sun
Average price two–course meal: £27.50
Somewhat at odds with its highly corporate steel-and-glass surroundings, the Atrium has carved out an enviable reputation under the guidance of Andrew and Lisa Radford. The dining area is contemporary yet intimate and cosy, with gleaming candle-lit wood tables. Chef Neil Forbes combines fine Scottish produce with flair: chicken breast is stuffed with truffles and comes with artichoke and mushroom ragout. The 'sommelier's choice' menu marries wines perfectly to each course.
www.atriumrestaurant.co.uk

Café Royal Oyster Bar
City Centre, Map 2 G5
17a West Register Street, 0131 556 4124
Sun–Wed 11am–11pm, Thu 11am–midnight, Fri/Sat 11am–1am
Average price two course meal: £25
This 140-year-old oyster bar is a delight. Extravagent decor with Victorian stained-glass and tiles (as seen in the film *Chariots of Fire*) is matched by a sumptuous menu. Oysters, offered in a number of sauces and styles, dominate the list of starters. Main courses include fillet of turbot on goat's cheese champ or up-market surf and turf – a superb fillet of Scotch beef topped with grilled langoustines. Service is refreshingly informal for surroundings so posh, but no less meticulous for that.

Cardoon
Southside, Map 2 D10
The Bruntsfield Hotel, 69 Bruntsfield Place, 0131 229 1393
Mon–Sat 5.30–9.30pm, Sun 6–9.30pm
Average price two course meal: £15
With stylish stone and wood floors and a bright dining room overlooking the patio garden, Cardoon promises not to succumb to a reputation as just another hotel restaurant. A varied menu and extensive wine list offer something for every appetite – from light and delicate dishes to more hearty Scottish cuisine.

Duck's at Le Marché Noir
New Town, Map 2 F2
2–4 Eyre Place, 0131 558 1608
Tue–Fri noon–2.30pm, 7–10pm; Mon–Sat
7–10pm, Sun 7–9.30pm
Average price two course meal: £23
Forest green panelling and white
tablecloths brighten Duck's by day, while
at night, tealights make the room sparkle.
It's a great venue for romance – provided
you don't mind a soundtrack ranging from
jazz to *Hello Dolly*. An open door implies
the kitchen has nothing to hide and the
food that emerges confirms it: tender roast
pheasant is paired with celeriac purée and
a lip-smacking mustard sauce. The
extensive wine list has bottles to suit every
pocket and, eccentrically, invites bids for
the very best.
www.ducks.co.uk

Forth Floor Restaurant
City Centre, Map 2 G4
Harvey Nichols, 30–34 St Andrew Square,
0131 524 8350
Mon 10am–5.30pm, Tue–Sat 10am–midnight,
Sun noon–5.30pm
Average price two course meal: £20
Harvey Nichols arrived in Edinburgh in
the summer of 2002 and the surprisingly
friendly penthouse restaurant is now a
popular venue, particularly at lunchtimes.
Served against a stunning view of the
castle, the concise menu uses top quality,
organic Scottish ingredients. Dishes such
as roast venison with bitter chocolate
sauce and seared scallops with chilli
chutney provide colouful choice. Semi-
opaque glass screens mark the first-versus
standard-class division between restaurant
and cheaper, but no less classy, brasserie.
www.harveynichols.com

Howies
Old Town, Map 2 G6
10–14 Victoria Street, 0131 225 1721
Mon–Sun noon–2.30pm, 6–10pm
Average price two course meal: £15.50
David Howie Scott's concept of informal
dining has proved a winner, with his
empire now extending as far as Dundee
and Aberdeen. There are four Edinburgh
branches. In Stockbridge, 4–6 Glanville
Place (0131 225 5553) is your typical
lively neighbourhood brasserie. Victoria
Street has whitewashed walls and rustic
furniture bringing a hint of Provence to
the Old Town. In contrast, 29 Waterloo
Place (0131 556 5766) has a wonderful air
of grandeur – the vast oval space has
fireplaces, marble busts and Corinthian
columns. 208 Bruntsfield Place (0131 221
1777) formerly a bank, has a period feel
on a smaller scale. A typical Howies menu
shows a careful balance of meat, game,
fish and vegetarian options both at lunch
and dinner, with chefs at each location
adding a little of their own character.
www.howies.uk.com

The Marque Central
West End, Map 2 E7
30b Grindlay Street, 0131 229 9859
Tue–Thur noon–2pm, 5.30–10pm; Fri/Sat
noon–2pm, 5.30–11pm. Closed Sun/Mon
Average price two course meal: £18
A stylish restaurant, with a quirky two-
tier layout. White walls and blonde wood
keep it cool, with an outbreak of gutsy
character in the John Bellany self-
portrait which presides. The food is
outrageously tasty – roast duck breast
with shallot jam and smoky duck tart
flambée is typical. Tucked under the
wing of the Royal Lyceum Theatre, this
lovely restaurant offers pre and post-
theatre meal deals and a swift, good
value express lunch.

Martins
City Centre, Map 2 F5
70 Rose Street North Lane, 0131 225 3106
Tue–Fri noon–2pm, 7–10pm; Sat 7–10pm.
Closed Sun/Mon
Average price two course meal: £25
Surrounded by back doors and air
conditioning units, this restaurant is an
oasis of tranquillity. Flowers, pink
napkins and white tablecloths make it
summer fresh and from the welcoming
handshake offered by owner Martin
Irons, all the way to his enthusiastic
guided tour of the cheese trolley, it feels
as if you are a guest in someone's home.
Food is fairly gorgeous and goes
something like this – roasted Barbary
breast, Gressingham confit and seared
foie gras with fondant potatoes, green
beans, savoy cabbage and beetroot jus.
www.edinburghrestaurants.co.uk

The New Bell
Southside, Map 2 I10
233 Causewayside, 0131 668 2868
Tue–Sun 5.30–10pm
Average price two course meal: £18
The New Bell works hard to provide a
balance between cosiness and
sophistication, with its dark wood
surroundings, prints and mis-matched
chairs. The imaginative menu, changing
monthly, blends modern with trad.
Chicken on black olive mash or sun-
dried tomato, cream cheese and pine nuts
with a balsamic reduction are typical
dishes. Dessert here is a treat with
banana and Baileys bread and butter
pudding among other sweet classics.
www.thenewbell.com

Number One
City Centre, Map 2 G5
1 Princes Street, 0131 557 6727
Mon–Fri 12.30–2.30pm, 7–10pm; Sat/Sun
7–10pm
Average price two course meal: £35
Hotel dining as it should be and so rarely
is: elegant, opulent and impeccably
served. Number One, named for its

prime address on Princes Street is in the basement of the Balmoral Hotel (see Architecture). It's smart, not stuffy, and definitely worth dressing up for. Jeff Bland's cooking does not come cheap, but this is Michelin star territory and, on the whole, you get what you pay for – from two-course lunch for £14.50 to a six-course chef's tasting menu at £52.50. Sautéed pig's trotter with truffle madeira is a star turn as is nearly everything else. *www.rfhotels.com*

Oloroso
City Centre, Map 2 E5
33 Castle Street, 0131 226 7614
Mon–Sun 11am–1am
Average price two course meal: £23.50
The foyer and lift give few clues to what lies above: two sides of this restaurant are glass and the panorama across to Fife is just about as magnificent as the close up of the castle. Inside, smart, minimalist decor is complemented by Tony Singh's innovative menus, which include a starter of smoked salmon, red onion, sliced potatoes, capers and truffle oil, and mains such as loin of pork with chickpeas, saffron onions, baby corn and Asian pesto. The wine list has plenty to offer under £20 and reasonably priced snacks are served in the bar.
www.oloroso.co.uk

The Outsider
Old Town, Map 2 G6
15–16 George IV Bridge, 0131 226 3131
Mon–Sun noon–11pm
Average price two course meal: £14
As pretentious as you might find the name (after Albert Camus' existentialist novel), there's no denying that its owner, Malcolm Innes, has done much to inject Edinburgh's culinary scene with a sexy youth and vitality. Having helped create a runaway success at the Apartment in Bruntsfield (7–13 Barclay Place, 0131 228 6456) his new venture offers much the same menu, more cool interior design and lots more good-looking staff. Diners are encouraged to share a main dish, all of which bear strong Mediterranean and Asian influences, as a starter. Book early to secure a table at weekends.

The Reform
Old Town, Map 2 I6
267 Canongate, 0131 558 9992
Winter: Mon–Sun noon–2.30pm, 5.30–10.30pm
Summer: Tue–Sat noon–2.30pm, 6–10pm
Closed Sun/Mon
Average price two course meal: £20
An appealing and quietly successful restaurant, headed by Paul Mattison, a chef who has contemporary fusion cooking licked – ingredients come from Scotland, and flavours and combinations mainly from

THE NEW BELL
restaurant

233 causewayside, eh9 1ph
0131 668 2868
www.thenewbell.com

RICHARD CAMPBELL

Castle views from The Outsider, page 120

the Pacific rim. So scallops and monkfish are presented as tempura with wasabi crème fraiche and Aberdeen Angus sirloin comes on roast sweet potato wedges. Lunchtime prices are very reasonable.
www.reformrestaurant.com

Restaurant Martin Wishart
Leith, Map 3 I3
54 The Shore, 0131 553 3557
Tue–Fri noon–2pm, 7–10pm; Sat 7–10pm.
Closed Sun/Mon
Average price two course meal: £31.50
One of the city's two Michelin-starred chefs, Martin Wishart's cooking style, impeccably grounded in his training with the Roux brothers and Marco Pierre White, sends out a series of beautifully executed, brilliantly delicate dishes. Pot roasted pork cheek is coated with unusual spices and pineapple tarte tatin is balanced by silky fromage frais ice-cream. The five course tasting menu is £45, while lunch at £14.50 for two courses is a star buy. See Relish in Food and Drink, Shopping for details of takeaway Wishart.
www.martin-wishart.co.uk

Rhubarb
Southside, Map 2 offK10
Priestfield Road, 0131 225 7800
Mon–Sun noon–3pm, 6–11pm
Average price two course meal: £21
Part of the new regime at Prestonfield (see Accommodation), this latest James Thompson venture (he of the Witchery and the Tower) opened in November 2003. All plums and reds and silk brocade, the dining room in this historic house has been dramatically transformed and serves good Scottish contemporary cuisine.

Rogue
West End, Map 2 B7
Scottish Widows Building, 67 Morrison Street, 0131 228 2700
Mon–Sat noon–3pm, 6–11pm. Closed Sun
Average price two course meal: £12
This famously 'designed' restaurant is located incongrously in the no-man's land between Lothian Road and Haymarket. Immaculate white linen contrasts with the absolute black of surrounding furniture. Enigmatic proprietor Dave Ramsden is at home here. The menu offers options for any size of appetite: creamy gorgonzola and walnut tagliatelle can be had alone or as a starter to an extravagant fillet of beef with black truffle and foie gras butter. Rogue is much more than the sum of its parts, an outstanding outpost of stylish, fine dining.
www.rogues-uk.com

A Room in the Town
New Town, Map 2 E4
18 Howe Street, 0131 225 8204
Mon–Sun noon–2.30pm, 5.30–10pm
Average price two course meal: £18
An oasis of warm Highland hospitality, this room is cheerfully decorated, candlelit and filled with hundreds of decorative wine and whisky bottles – cosy pub meets gourmet food. The seasonal menu revels in a racy Scottishness offering dishes like spice-encrusted salmon with lime jam or pork and apple meatballs with mash and onion gravy. Vegetarians eat well and dessert whips up delights like creamy crowdie laced with 'toddy' syrup.
www.aroomin.co.uk/the town

The Shore Bar and Restaurant
Leith, Map 3 I3
3/4 The Shore, 0131 553 5080
Mon–Fri 11am–midnight, Sat/Sun 12.30–11pm
Average price two course meal: £21
A favourite of Leithers, the Shore is an institution. The bar has a wooden sea-faring atmosphere with real fire and live music several nights a week. The more formal dining room has linen-covered tables, large mirrors and lots of foliage, with a compact, changing seafood menu which trades on dishes like sautéed squid with sweet chilli sauce or tuna steak with spinach salad and cumin yoghurt. A solid reputation brings everyone here, either for special nights out, or for a pint and a plate of prawns in the bar.

Sweet Melindas
Southside, Map 2 G10
11 Roseneath Street, 0131 229 7953
Mon 7–10pm; Tue–Sat noon–2pm, 7–10pm
Closed Sun
Average price two course meal: £18
The name might be taken from Bob Dylan's *Just Like Tom Thumb's Blues*, but a couple of hours spent here are guaranteed to chase away any negative vibes. A popular neighbourhood restaurant, Sweet Melindas' reputation for fresh, interesting food at good prices has spread well beyond Marchmont. Top quality fish and seafood from Eddie's Fishmarket next door feature heavily: tuna steak teamed with tomatoes, cannellini beans and parmesan, or cod with chorizo, pak choi and oyster mushrooms are the norm. Charmingly, on Tuesday nights, customers pay only what they think the meal is worth.

The Tower
Old Town, Map 2 G7
Museum of Scotland, Chambers Street, 0131 225 3003
Mon–Sun noon–11pm
Average price two course meal: £24.50
In penthouse premises, at the top of the Museum of Scotland, the Tower is one of the swankiest restaurants in town. Guests are whisked by lift into a slick space decorated with a breathtaking view of the castle. Cuisine is contemporary Scottish with hints of the exotic: the signature dish is Aberdeen Angus fillet served with smoked garlic and shiitake mushroom broth. For figure-conscious film stars, the menu also offers 'lighter' dishes such as a subtle smoked haddock and spiced couscous salad.
www.tower-restaurant.com

The Vintners Rooms
Leith, Map 3 H4
The Vaults, 87 Giles Street, 0131 554 6767
Mon–Sat noon–2pm, 7–10.30pm. Closed Sun
Average price two course meal: £25
There can be few more splendid places to dine than this former wine merchants' auction room. The main dining room is illuminated entirely by candles, its ceiling decorated with early 18th century plasterwork. Starters include gravadlax over potato and watercress salad. Mains feature a juicy Aberdeen Angus fillet topped with foie gras, all on a heap of spinach. A beautiful setting serving up-market Scottish cuisine.
www.thevintnersrooms.demon.co.uk

The Witchery by the Castle
Old Town, Map 2 F6
Castlehill, Royal Mile, 0131 225 5613
Mon–Sun noon–4pm, 5.30–11.30pm
Average price two course meal: £26
A famous restaurant in a private portfolio which includes the hotel Prestonfield and the Tower restaurant, this 16th-century house has all the atmosphere of a gentleman's club. That's upstairs. Downstairs, the Secret Garden is all about romance, with tapestries and painted panelling making it a breathtaking venue for dining à deux. Service is formal, not snooty, and the menu features classic dishes with innovative touches. The wine list is almost 140 pages with prices running to three figures. Opulent suites above can be purchased at a price. See Accommodation.
www.thewitchery.com

Vegetarian

David Bann's Vegetarian Restaurant
Old Town, Map 2 I6
56–58 St Mary's Street, 0131 556 5888
Sun–Thu 11am–midnight, Fri/Sat 11am–12.30am
Average price two course meal: £14
Opened in 2002, this latest creation from local restaurateur David Bann, is a well-designed space with rich tones, natural woods and stylish soft lighting. Serving up to 12 hours a day, seven days a week, the menu offers an intriguing variety of global tastes with mini skewers dipping into ginger vinaigrette and Malaysian curry with butternut squash, baby corn, banana chutney and rice tantalising your palate. TLC guaranteed on every plate.
www.davidbann.com

Henderson's Salad Table
City Centre, Map 2 F4
94 Hanover Street, 0131 225 2131
Mon–Sat 7.30am–10.30pm
Average price two course meal: £9
Henderson's recently celebrated 40 years of delivering their 'eat better, live better' cooking to generations of Hanover Street diners. Not much has changed – you'll still find the self-service salad bar inviting you to follow a well-trodden path to the hot foods, salads, fruit juices and cakes. Around six daily specials, such as lentil lasagne and chickpea Thai curry, are dished up. With live music most evenings, the two and three-course table service deals (£9.25/£11.95) provide good value.
www.hendersonsofedinburgh.co.u

JENNERS

Jenners, page 127

shopping

shopping

If you don't want to buy a car, hire it. If you want to go to the movies, but don't have a babysitter, phone an agency. If you want to take a flight of fancy, phone Alba Ballooning. Hints for hiring below.

Aircraft

Air Charter Scotland Ltd
Outskirts, Map 1
Business Aviation Centre, Eastfield Avenue, Edinburgh Airport, 0131 339 8008
Mon–Fri 8.30am–5.30pm
Flights: from £550 per hour
Flights operate round the clock using company pilots. Tours over the city can be arranged.
www.aircharterscotland.com

Alba Ballooning
Southside, Map 2 I9
12 Gladstone Terrace, 0131 667 4251
Mon–Fri 9am–6pm
Flights: from £149 per person
Take off with this local company at any time of year, dawn till dusk. Flights cost £149 per person with a discount for groups. In-flight photo, champagne and a commemorative certificate are all included.
www.albaballooning.co.uk

Lothian Helicopters
Out of town, Map 1
The Vineyard Business Centre, Tynehead, Pathhead, 01875 320032
Flights: from £45 for 10 minutes
Fly over the city – but be warned, it's best to contact this company through its website.
www.lothianhelicopters.co.uk

Bike

Bike Trax Cycle Hire
West End, Map 2 D8
11 Lochrin Place, 0131 228 6333
Summer Mon–Fri 9.30am–6pm, Sat 9.30am–5.30pm, Sun 9am–5pm
An established firm close to the city centre. £100 deposit required. Helmets, locks and pumps are included in the price. Bikes can be hired from £10 per day, tandems £15. Bike trailers are also available.
www.biketrax.co.uk

Rent-a-Bike: Edinburgh Cycle Hire and Scottish Cycle Safari
Old Town, Map 2 H6
29 Blackfriars Street, 0131 556 5560

Jun–Sep Mon–Sun 9am–9pm; Oct–May Mon–Sun 10am–6pm
Just off the Royal Mile, this little shop does big business. It's the biggest credit card deposit required, but you can hire here and drop off in Inverness. Helmets, locks and repair kits are included. Bikes can be hired from £10 per day or £50 per week. Edinburgh Sightseeing Tours (from £15), as well as Highland tours, are also available.
www.cyclescotland.co.uk

Car

Car Hire
Citywide
All the usual international car hire companies have a base in Edinburgh. Here are three popular ones. Arnold Clark, West End, Lochrin Place, 0131 228 4747 www.arnoldclark.co.uk; Avis, West End, 5 West Park Place, 0131 337 6363 www.avis.co.uk (also a branch at Edinburgh Airport, 0131 344 3900); Hertz, New Town, 10 Picardy Place, 0131 337 8686, www.hertz.com. Prices vary, so best to contact the company by phone.

city5s

TOP SHOP STREETS

■ **George Street** A boulevard lined with high class, designer brand stores, with label mecca Harvey Nichols at its east end on St Andrews Square.

■ **Victoria Street** Colourful boutiques on a winding Old Town cobbled street: maps, jokes, clothes, luggage, cheese and piercing all down the same hill.

■ **Cockburn Street** A clutch of zany, independent stores. Gothic stuff, skatewear and record boutiques.

■ **William Street** A cosy community of feminine fashion shops with a touch of London style.

■ **Raeburn Place** Part of the 'village' of Stockbridge, this main street has cafés, delis, jewellery shops, charity traders and a fabulous butcher, fish shop and cheesemonger.

Edinburgh City Car Club
Citywide
31 Argyle Place, 0845 458 1784
Membership: from £11 per month
This ecologically friendly alternative form of car hire allows drivers to pay only for the time and distance they drive, following a standard annual membership fee. Operated by Smart Moves and supported by the local council, Edinburgh's City Car Club is the largest in Britain with 17 vehicles and over 200 active members and offers very reasonable rates for 24-hour short notice car access.
www.smartmoves.co.uk

Scott Frogatt, Travel Marketing
Outskirts, Map 1
4 Rothsesay Place, Musselburgh. 5 miles east of Edinburgh on A199, 0131 225 5559
If you want to get out of town in style, book one of these two to four day self-drive tours including accommodation at the Roxburgh Hotel and golfing in the Borders. Cars include Aston Martin, E-type Jag and Porche.

Childcare

Baby Baby Equipment Hire
West End, Map 2 off A7
45 Glendevon Place, 0131 337 7016
This home-run company supplies car seats, playpens, travel cots, pushchairs etc for one day up to three months. Equipment is checked, cleaned and fully serviced regularly. It's best if you pick up yourself, but delivery is available. Member of the Baby Equipment Hirers Association.

Edinburgh Childcare Information Service
Citywide
PO Box 777, 0131 529 7777
Mon– Fri 8.30am–4pm
Set up by the City of Edinburgh Council, this service provides impartial advice and information to parents and carers, including details of childminders, independent nurseries, out of school care, crèches, playchemes, and more.
www.childcarelink.gov.uk

Emergency Mums
West End, Map 2 B7
21 Lansdowne Crescent, 0131 226 3339
Offers various forms of childcare, including long and short-term placements to both parents and nurseries. Staff are fully vetted, and are available for different forms of care, including special needs. Can also provide crèches for all types of occasions.
www.emergencymums.co.uk

Nappy Days
Outskirts, Map 2 off K9
44 Bingham Broadway, 0131 669 8851
Environmentally friendly, real nappies delivered to your door weekly. Five sizes are available, professionally cleaned in hospital laundries, so the service is convenient and hygenic. One week free trial service available.

Kilts and Costume

Geoffrey (Tailor) Kilt Hire
City Centre, Map 2 H6
57–59 High Street, 0131 557 0256
Mon–Wed/Fri/Sat 9am–5.30pm, Thu 9am–7pm, Sun 10am--4pm
All descriptions of kilts from this successful company. Check out the 21st Century Kilts department. See Shopping, Scottish.
www.21stcenturykilts.com

Hector Russell
City Centre, Map 2 F5
95 Princes Street, 0131 225 3315
Mon–Fri 9am–6pm, Sat 9am–6pm, Sun 11am–6pm (extended during Summer)
Prince Charlie gear: from £44.95 per weekend
All your Highland orders from this established firm. Kilts can be hired or bought outright.
www.hector-russell.com

The Kilt Hire Co
West End, Map 2 B7
54–56 Haymarket Terrace, 0131 337 3333
Mon–Fri 9am–5.30pm, Thu until 6pm, Sat 9am–5pm, Sun noon–5pm
Prince Charlie gear: from £57 per weekend
This is a small, individual outfit near near Haymarket Station.
www.thekiltstore.com

Royal Lyceum Theatre Company Costume Hire
West End, Map 2 off A7
29 Roseburn Street, 0131 337 1997
Costumes: from £10 per day
Offers a wide range of period and contemporary costumes created for the stage. From the Cavalier excesses of doublet and hose to bodice swelling 18th century evening gowns, the Lyceum has everything you need to be who you want to be.
www.lyceum.org.uk

shops

Harvey Nichols, opened in 2002, takes the designer buzz to its most expensive extreme: if you want labels in your bag, you can have them. But don't forget to wander into the corners of town. Boutiques like Concrete Wardrobe, music shops of Drum Central's calibre and names as famous as deli royalty, Valvona and Crolla are what make Edinburgh special. Forget the out-of-town malls: stay city central for creative consumption. For more deli delights check out *The List's Deli and Good Food Directory to Scotland*, May 2004 (£4.95).

Antiques

The Bachelor Pad
New Town, Map 2 D3
36 St Stephen Street, 0131 226 6355
Tue–Sat 10am–6pm, Sun noon–6pm, Mon by appointment
In just two years, the Bachelor Pad has established itself as one of the most unique and popular of the independent shops in Edinburgh. A James Bond cave of stylish, classic furniture and nick-nacks from the 50s to 70s, its emphasis is on quality, with lighting a particular focus. Any piece would make an ideal addition to a des res pad. Mid-20th century Scandinavian jewellery and classic toy robots also pop up in this quirky shop.
www.thebachelorpad.org

Causewayside Antiques
Southside, Map 2 I10
67–189 Causewayside
Causewayside is home to a close-knit community of antiques shops. Courtyard Antiques (108 Causewayside, Mon–Sat 10am–5.30pm) is well known for furniture and curios, and also militaria, uniforms, models and film props. Clyde Antiques (Mon/Thu–Sat 11am–5pm, Sun 1–4pm) round the corner on Grange Road, stocks well-maintained furniture. General antiques can be found in Allan Jackson's shop at 67 Causewayside (Mon–Sat 9am–5pm) which has been operating for almost 30 years. Finally, specialising in furniture, Millers Antiques (Mon–Sat 10am–4.30pm phone in advance) is a relative newcomer to the antique estate.

Edinburgh Architectural Salvage Yard, EASY
Leith, Map 3 F4
31 West Bowling Green Street, 0131 554 7077
Mon–Fri 9am–5pm, Sat noon–5pm
This Leith family business has been supplying the homes of Edinburgh and beyond since 1985. Set up by Lizzie and Neil Barrass, it sells a range of architectural fittings, from church pews and banisters to art deco fittings, sinks and bathworks – about as far from IKEA as it gets. Sourced from all over Scotland, stock moves out fast, but is replaced with equal gusto.
www.easy-arch-salv.co.uk

Body and Soul

Helios Fountain
Old Town, Map 2 F7
7 Grassmarket, 0131 229 7884
Mon–Sat 10am–6pm, Sun noon–5pm
Books go with beads, toys and wholesome gifts in this quirky shop which surely contains the complete works of Rudolf Steiner. If not, then he simply has to be the busiest writer in the history of the Anthroposophical Movement. Helios also has a fine selection of books on vegetarianism, complementary therapies, Celtic art and finding out whether he's really the fella for you.
www.helios-fountain.co.uk

Second Sight
West End, Map 2 D3
52 Hamilton Place, 0131 226 3066
Mon–Sat 10am–5.30pm
People from all walks of life are attracted to the new age and spiritual books on offer in Second Sight. The company changed direction in early 2003 to become a dedicated second-hand bookstore, and now sells a range of literature on personal improvement and health development. Previously called Body & Soul, it also sells a limited selection of healing paraphernalia, such as tarot cards and music. A very relaxing environment in which to shop.
www.secondsightbookshop.com

Tribal Body Art
Old Town, Map 2 I6
248 Canongate, 0131 558 9019
Mon–Wed/Fri/Sat 11am–6pm, Thu 11am–8pm, Sun noon–5pm
Tattoo shops often get a bad press. Not Tribal Body Art. The company is firmly committed to customer service: its three trained tattoo artists offer a consultation service, there are books full of ideas, plus a photo collection of their previous work. The tattoes are carried out by appointment only, so there's no chance of inebriated stags and hens stumping up for a lasting reminder of Edinburgh.
www.tribalbodyart.co.uk

Wildwood Books
Old Town, Map 2 H6
16 High Street, 0131 557 4888
Mon–Sat 9am–6pm, Sun 11am–5pm
Wildwood Books is a mine of worldwide

Absolutely fabulous fashion at Harvey Nichols, page 127

gifts and reading matter. Specialising particularly in Celtic, Pagan and Wiccan literature, it also stocks Celtic silver jewellery, gems, drums and didgeridoos. Owned by father and son partnership Thom and Brett McCarthy, Wildwood, and its sister stores Golden (109 High Street) and Crystal Clear (52 Cockburn Street), bring New Age to the Old Town.
www.royalmile-edinburgh.com

Books

Analogue
Old Town, Map 2 G7
102 West Bow, 0131 220 0601
Mon–Sat 10am–6pm, Sun noon–4pm
Born in 2001, this lovely little shop is a book retailer that also sells mags, music, T-shirts and 'other things we like'. Clothing from egg74 and Stolen, nudge up against CDs from the likes of Venetian

Snares and Takagi Masakatsu. On the literary front, the Art of Barbie and legendary graffiti artist Banksy's Banging your Head are the norm, while subscriptions to Dot Dot Dot and Graphics International are being scribbled out as we speak.
www.analoguebooks.co.uk

Beyond Words
Old Town, Map 2 G6
42–44 Cockburn Street, 0131 226 6636
Mon–Sat 10am–6pm, Sun 1–6pm
There can't be too many bookshops in Edinburgh, or maybe even the world, that can lay claim to having been recommended in *Outdoor Photography* for its tremendous range of titles from as far afield as Germany and Scandinavia. But Beyond Books certainly has. Quite simply a must visit for a higher quality coffee table tome.
www.beyondwords.co.uk

Blackwell's
Southside, Map 2 H7
53–59 South Bridge, 0131 622 8222
Mon/Wed–Fri 9am–8pm, Tue 9.30am–8pm,
Sat 9am–6pm, Sun 11am–5pm
Having marked its 120th anniversary
from humble beginnings in 1879 in a tiny
Oxford room, it seemed less of a trauma
than expected when the legendary James
Thin shop on the South Bridge fell to this
establishment. Most of the company's
dozen shops are located on campus sites,
and academic tomes are a strong suit, as
are fine collections of contemporary
novels and sports books. This busy
branch also has a good line in top author
events.
www.blackwell.co.uk

Borders
Outskirts, Map 1
Fort Kinnaird Retail Park, Newcraighall Road,
0131 657 4041
Mon–Sat 9am–10pm, Sun 10am–8pm
It's been just six years since Borders made
its first move on the UK, after a
successful quarter of a century selling
books to Americans. Brothers Tom and
Louis Borders were the guys behind the
now megastore which promises over
130,000 different books, CDs, DVDs,
videos and a café plus a vast selection of
mags and papers. Regular events include
discussion groups, quiz nights and
children's storytimes.
www.borders.co.uk

Carson Clark Gallery
Old Town, Map 2 I5
181–183 Canongate, 0131 556 4710
Mon–Sat 10.30am–5.30pm
Maps, glorious maps. And globes. And
there are also also some cosy paintings of
animals, aerial sketches of Edinburgh
from 1868 and fun political drawings
from the days before Donald Rumsfeld
and John Prescott made the satirists' jobs
easy. The value of the goods indoors make
it perfectly understandable why there's a
sign that requests patrons not to bring in
ice-creams or wear muddy boots.
www.carson-clark-gallery.co.uk

Deadhead Comics
Old Town, Map 2 G7
27 Candlemaker Row, 0131 226 2774
Mon–Wed/Fri 10am–6pm, Thu 10am–8pm,
Sat 10am–6pm. Closed Sun
Fancy a bit of Ultimate Daredevil Elektra
or Hellblazer Haunted? Well, why
wouldn't you? The perfect stop off for the
fan of graphics of superheroes and icons
old and new. For those who think that
Spider Man is just Toby Maguire in a
tight-fitting outfit, an education awaits.
www.deadheadcomics.com

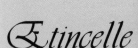

Ottakar's
City Centre, Map 2 F5
57 George Street, 0131 225 4495
Mon–Wed/Fri/Sat 9am–7pm, Thu 9am–8pm,
Sun 11.30am–5.30pm
On a former James Thin site, this store
trades on three floors with a coffee shop
on the first. An excellent children's
section and a comprehensive swathe of
Scottish books give the stock an edge. Big
author events are organised in conjunction
with venues like the Assembly Rooms
opposite – Quintin Jardine and Janet
Evanovich are two of the most recent.
Smaller affairs with writers like Paul
Johnston and John Connolly entertain
punters in the shop itself.
www.ottakars.co.uk

Waterstone's
City Centre, Map 2 E5
128 Princes Street, 226 2666
Mon–Sat 8.30am–8pm, Sun 10.30am–7pm
So important is Waterstone's to JK Rowling
that she chose the West End branch to
appear at midnight on the last HP day, as
no one was really calling it. Indeed, you
have to wonder what we ever did for
bookshops before we slipped a volume or
two into those neat black and gold bags.
Author events are big here and every genre
of books is tackled somewhere. Two
smaller branches on George Street and the
east end of Princes Street.
www.waterstones.co.uk

Word Power
Southside, Map 2 H7
43 Nicolson Street, 0131 662 9112
Mon–Sat 10am–6pm
'Books to change the world' is the Word
Power tagline. And with its unrivalled
collection of quality radical stock, we can
just about forgive it for having *Harry Potter*
on its shelves. Self-respecting fans of
Noam Chomsky, Bell Hooks, John Pilger or
Alice Walker should certainly be buying
books here. Each May, the shop organises
the Edinburgh Independent Radical Book
Fair, which has grown in quality and stature
every year since its 1997 debut.
www.word-power.co.uk

Department Stores

Harvey Nichols
City Centre, Map 2 G4
30–34 St Andrew's Square, 0131 524 8388
Mon–Wed 10am–6pm, Thu 10am–8pm, Fri/Sat
10am–7pm, Sun noon–6pm
When fashion heaven Harvey Nichols
opened with star-studded ceremony in
2002, much was expected. The flagship
outlet at the entrance to the Walk (the first
street to be built in Edinburgh since the
18th century), it was to lead the way
towards Edinburgh becoming a high class
shopping destination. And it is fabulous.
Four floors of designer decadence with rail

to rail lables from the top drawer. Duffer St
George, Prada, Amanda Wakely, Alexander
McQueen, Jimmy Choo et al are beautifully
presented. Live DJs on Saturdays and a
sunny penthouse brasserie/restaurant.
www.harveynichols.com

Jenners
City Centre, Map 2 G5
Princes Street, 0131 225 2442
Mon–Wed 9am–5.30pm, Thu 9am–7.30pm,
Fri/Sat 9am–6pm, Sun noon–5pm
As the oldest department store in the UK,
you might expect Jenners to be stuffy.
Quite the contrary. Opened in 1838, it now
has an international reputation for quality
and style. In direct competition with
Harvey Nic's round the corner, it has make-
up galore, a new jewellery section, both hip
and conservative fashion, as well as the
best toy department in town, haberdashery,
art and carpets. Cafe and ladies lunching
place.
www.jenners.com

John Lewis
City Centre, Map 2 H4
St James Centre, 0131 556 9121
Mon–Wed 9am–6pm, Thu/Fri 9am–8pm, Sat
9am–6.30pm, Sun 11am–5pm
With a company ethos of 'never knowingly
undersold', you can expect good value from
John Lewis. This branch recently
completed a £25m refurbishment and
extension, making it Scotland's largest
department store. With its bright,
contemporary layout and full range of
lifestyle products – interiors, fashion,
electrical goods, haberdashery, toys and
furnishings – it is not surprisingly a local
favourite. The penthouse café has
spectacular views over the Forth.
www.johnlewis.com

Fashion

Arkangel
West End, Map 2 C6
4 William Street, 0131 226 4466
Mon–Wed/Fri 10am–5.30pm, Thu
10am–6.30pm, Sat 11.30am–5.30pm
Supplying some labels exclusively in
Scotland, this bohemian boutique mixes
contemporary ladies' items with a small
collection of vintage classics. British
designers stocked include Anonymous,
Marilyn Moore and Harrison, plus
cashmere goodies by Scottish designer
Rosemary Eribe and a to-die-for range of
jewellery from Paris.

MY FAVOURITE SHOP
Bachelor Pad
"It's just full of funky, unusual
objects.'
Trendy Wendy, DJ

Concrete Wardrobe
Old Town, Map 2 H6
317–319 Cowgate, 0131 558 7130
Tue–Fri noon–6pm, Sat noon–5pm
Sharing a shop with interiors treasure
Concrete Butterfly, this is about as far
from high street homogenisation as you
can get. Set up by fashion designers Fiona
Mackintosh and James Donald, the store
opened in 2001 as an experiment and has
been going strong ever since. Focussing
solely on local designers, it stocks, among
others, imaginative lace by Holly Fulton,
quirky resin jewellery by Kaz Robertson
and a tweed inspired range by Roobedo.
Pricey, but gorgeous.
www.concretebutterfly.com

Corniche
Old Town, Map 2 H6
2–4 Jeffrey Street, 0131 556 3707
Mon–Sat 10am–5.30pm
Corniche is Edinburgh's original designer
mecca, stocking brands like Katherine
Hamnett, Vivienne Westwood, Jean Paul
Gaultier and Yohji Yamamoto. A petite,
upmarket boutique with 25 years in the
business, it's also very friendly. Menswear
next door sells clothes of similar calibre,
including labels by Pauline Burrows and
Thierry Mugler.

Cruise
City Centre, Map 2 E5
94 George Street, 0131 226 3524
Mon–Fri 10am–6pm, Thu 10am–7pm, Sat
9.30am–6pm, Sun noon–5pm
Celebrating its 21st birthday this year, it's
hard to believe that this trendy label
emporium once began life on Edinburgh's
Royal Mile. Popularly associated with its
Glasgow stores, Cruise is fast building up
an Edinburgh empire – its three stores
have just been joined by another on
George Street. Italian, French and
American couture fill the shelves of its
minimalist, hyper-stylish stores. 31 Castle
Street is a four-floor ladies' clothing shop,
featuring designer collections, jean labels,
footwear and accessories. 14 George
Street has four floors dedicated to men's
designer fashions, while St Mary's Street
specialises in men's jean labels.

Cult Clothing
Old Town, Map 2 H6
7–9 North Bridge, 0131 556 5003
Mon–Wed/Fri/Sat 9.30–6pm, Thu 10am–7pm,
Sun noon–5pm
This English company has stolen the
hearts of Edinburgh's trendy young things

with its clubby atmosphere and towering
rails of own-brand T-shirts and urban
labels for men and women. Colours are
funky, designs hip and it stocks the lot –
Ben Sherman shirts, Paul Frank
accessories, skate shoes and itty-bitty
print halter-necks.
www.cultclothing.com

Joey D
New Town, Map 2 G3
54 Broughton Street, 0131 557 6672
Mon–Fri 11am–6pm, Sat 11am–5pm, Sun
3–5pm
Word of mouth has made Joey D
something of an icon on Broughton Street.
The shop is a boutique crossover (that's
male and female to you and me) and
stocks a mix of own brand, recycled and
customised clothes. Styles range from
retro to clubby to outrageously
flamboyant – ideal for those who want to
be seen. Open for over four years, it's
highly original – the £20 Shoe Lounge is
unmissable.
www.d54.net

Odd One Out
Old Town, Map 2 G6
16 Victoria Street, 0131 220 6400
Mon–Sat 10am–6pm, Sun noon–5pm
Shops don't come much more individual
than this. A mass of über-trendy,
independent labels adorns its male and
female collections. Downstairs in
menswear are collections by Silas, MHI,
Aem-Kei, Academic, and a new range by
Michael Kellar. Upstairs, you'll find Lady
Soul, Sessun and Zakee Sharif for women.
Vixy Rae launched her own label in 2003.
www.oddoneout.com

Swish
Old Town, Map 2 G6
24 Victoria Street, 0131 225 4413
Mon–Wed/Fri/Sat 10.30am–6pm, Thu
11am–6.30pm, Sun noon–4.30pm
Formerly Wacky Co, this is a stylish,
trendy, with a healthy dose of fun.
Ladieswear labels include Soochi, Gsus
and Psycho Cowboy. Menswear is more
limited, but T-shirts are resoundingly
funky. Little nippers get a look in with
adorable Brand New T-shirts, and a shoe
and bag section has recently opened
upstairs. Cheap it ain't – but you pay for
this kind of serious street cred.

Walker Slater
Old Town, Map 2 G6
20 Victoria Street, 0131 220 2636
Mon–Wed/Fri/Sat 10am–6pm, Thu
10am–7pm
Opened in 1994, this traditional tailoring
shop with some style offers the full
wardrobe of knitwear, suits, MacIntosh
coats and cufflinks. Emphasis is placed
on personal detailing, which gives
options on everything from cuff details

MY FAVOURITE BUS

Number 11
'This bus just goes everywhere
you could possibly need to go.'
Fergus, age 14

Farmers' Market under the shadow of the castle, page 133

to lapel width. Walker Slater has over 5000 cloths to choose from, but can source more unusual materials if required.
www.walkerslater.com

Zara
City Centre, Map 2 E5
100–106 Princes Street, 0131 240 3230
Mon–Wed, Fri–Sat 9.30am–6pm, Thu 9.30am–8pm, Sun 11am–5pm
Zara is high street fashion with a difference. Its colourful, striking designs and good selection of basics all come with beautifully low price tags. The three-story shop stocks a limited range for men and children. A continental and decidedly more hip alternative to reliable ol' M&S.
www.zara.com

Flowers

Flowers by Maxwell
City Centre, Map 2 E5
32b Castle Street, 0131 226 2866
Mon–Fri 9am–5.30pm, Sat 9am–3pm
Thomas Maxwell has been luxuriously floral decorating for around 34 years, but has kept up with the trends. A bespoke service tailors to specific needs. With a preference for seasonal varieties (not always the case in this hothouse era), the tied bunches are heavenly.

Stems
West End, Map 2 E7
22–24 Grindlay Street, 0131 228 5575
Mon–Fri 10am–5.30pm, Sat 10am–1pm
The original flower arrangements here are bespoke and range from traditional and elegant to tropical and wacky. Established seven years ago, the company specialises in arrangements for corporate events.

Food and Drink

Argyle Place – Fruit & Veg
Southside, Map 2 G10
Mon–Sun 8.30am–8.30pm
Argyle Place, separated from central Edinburgh by the Meadows, has been one of the most popular places to buy fruit and vegetables in the city for years. There are three markets, side by side – Nadia's 18 Argyle Place, 0131 228 1946; Tse's (23 Argyle Place, 0131 228 1841 and Al Haj 25/26 Argyle Place, 0131 229 8376 – and while the majority of their food comes from Slateford's fruit market, they each have individual specialities. Tse's supplies to almost every Chinese restaurant in the Lothians. Haji's has a growing, cosmopolitan delicatessen behind the pavement vegetable displays. Don't expect the spotless, supermarket kind of fruit and vegetables – instead pick, choose and be rewarded with flavoursome produce.

Au Gourmand
New Town, Map 2 F2
1 Brandon Terrace, 0131 624 4666
Mon–Fri 8am–10pm, Sat 8.30am–10pm, Sun 10am–6pm
Finding good quality French cheeses and breads isn't difficult in Edinburgh now that Au Gourmand has set out its stall. It's stuffed with French specialities and hard-to-get cheeses such as Matocq (from the Pyrenees). Bread and patisserie are baked daily using French flour, and can be taken away or accompanied by a coffee in the café at the back of the shop. Charcuterie and terrines share the deli counter with Provençal olives and rows of moutardes, huiles, vinaigres, sirops, miels and delicious confitures line the walls.
www.augourmand.co.uk

Cadenhead's Whisky Shop
Old Town, Map 2 J5
172 Canongate, 0131 556 5864
Mon–Sat 10.30am–5.30pm
Established by William Cadenhead in 1842 and now owned by Springbank distillery, this is Scotland's oldest independent bottler. Cadenhead's cask strength whisky, gin and cognac are undiluted and unfiltered to retain their natural constituents. Whiskies are bottled from individual casks, meaning that no batch is the same and flavours vary from one bottle to another. Cadenhead's has a worldwide reputation and its homely shop is frequented by visitors and connoisseurs alike.
www.wmcadenhead.com

Crombie's of Edinburgh
New Town, Map 2 G3
97 Broughton Street, 0131 557 0111
Mon–Fri 8am–6pm, Sat 8am–5pm
While neighbourhood butchers continue to decline, Jonathan Crombie's business just keeps growing. A rare combination of tradition and innovation, the shop was founded by Jonathan's grandfather in 1956. Though you'll find award-winning pastries from the World Pie Championships, the real stars are the sausages – from Lucifer's matchsticks to basil, beef & blackberries and Pinchos

Muranos; they're available UK wide from the website. Haggis, ready meals, salads, beef, game and poultry are all prepared on the premises and sourced impeccably.
www.sausages.co.uk

The Cuttea Sark
Old Town, Map 2 G6
26 Victoria Street, 0131 226 6245
Mon–Sat 9.30am–5.30pm, Sun noon–5pm
Victoria Street is full of specialist shops (and tourists to admire them), so John Bowman's tea and coffee haven fits in well. His shelves are filled with caffeine-related accoutrements: graters, whisks, filters and drainers, cups and mugs, pots, cafétieres and percolators – even a £900 futuristic Swiss machine. Jars of loose tea and coffee in copious varieties are available from behind the counter. Look out for the fiendishly expensive Jamaican Blue Mountain coffee and Japanese and African teas.

Eddie's Seafood Market
Southside, Map 2 G10
7 Roseneath Street, 0131 229 4207
Tue–Sat 8.30am–6pm
Eddie's feels like a fish market in miniature. Supplier to many of Edinburgh's best restaurants, the place overflows with sealife: lobsters and langoustines meander around a large tank

while exotic sea-creatures, including air-freighted delicacies such as Brazilian snapper, spill from boxes on the floor. Scotland's waters provide most of the fish, however, with shell-fish high on the list. Very busy at times, Eddie's is an exotic and energetic fishmonger.

Farmers' Market – Edinburgh
West End, Map 2 E7
Castle Terrace, 0131 652 5940
First and third Sat of every month, 9am–2pm
Every fortnight, the city's farmers' market sets up its stalls under the castle. Now there's a medieval touch. One of the largest in Scotland, with around 40 traders, it pedals everything home-grown – Highland beef, wild boar, organic eggs, beer, juice and veg, fresh shellfish and the life-saver on a winter's day – hot 'hog roast' rolls. It's almost always busy, so if you want something specific it pays to get there early to avoid the queues.
www.edinburghcc.com

Henderson's
City Centre, Map 2 F4
92 Hanover Street, 0131 225 6694
Mon–Wed noon–3pm, Thu–Sat noon–9pm, Sun noon–7pm
This Edinburgh institution has a canteen-style salad bar and takeaway/deli. A vegetarian and organic food specialist, the shop stocks home-baked bread, dry goods like olives, nuts and grains, local vegetables, eggs and additive free meals like their own make tasty Moroccan stew. They also sell freshly made sandwiches.
www.hendersonsofedinburgh.co.uk

Lupe Pintos
West End, Map 2 E9
24 Leven Street, 0131 228 6241
Mon–Wed/Sat 10am–6pm, Thu/Fri 10am–7pm, Sun 12.30–5.30pm
A culinary trip to Mexico inspired Rhona Robertson and Doug Bell to open this fiery deli. Eleven years on it's still loved for its range of hard-to-get Mexican ingredients and tequilas. Potent chillies are stars of the show, strongly supported by a cast of Mexican, American and Spanish goods. Thai, Japanese and Jamaican items also sold. Look out for *Two Cooks and a Suitcase*, a travel book by the owners, which includes recipes.
www.lupepintos.com

IJ Mellis Cheesemonger
Old Town, Map 2 G6
30a Victoria Street, 0131 226 6215
Mon–Sat 9.30am–6pm, Sun noon–5pm
Buying ready-packed coloured cheddar from a supermarket seems daft when there are three Mellis shops in town offering fully matured fresh farmhouse cheeses. With years of knowledge, Iain Mellis knows exactly what makes a good

cheese, and only selects the best British and European varieties for his shops. He also has a hand in ripening them in his maturing rooms. The variety is astounding. All three shops have a Dickensian feel where aroma is high on the list of sensual delights. Other branches at 6 Bakers Place, Stockbridge (0131 225 6566) and 330 Morningside Road (0131 452 8697).
www.ijmellischeesemonger.com

Peckham's
Southside, Map 2 D10
155–159 Bruntsfield Place, 0131 229 7054
Mon–Sat 8am–midnight, Sun 9am–midnight
The company's first foray out of Glasgow, this shop is now established at the heart of a thriving local foodie quarter. There's a decent deli counter and lots of wine. Downstairs is a fully fledged bistro-restaurant, Peckham's Underground. The Stockbridge branch at 48 Raeburn Place, 0131 332 8844, continues the successful combination of deli goods, wine, and this time with a smaller, street-side cafe. The latest arrival, opened this year, is on the Southside at 49 Clerk Street.
www.peckhams.co.uk

Real Foods
New Town, Map 2 H3
37 Broughton Street, 0131 557 1911
Mon–Wed/Fri 9am–7pm, Thu 9am–8pm, Sat 9am–6.30pm, Sun 10am–6pm
An Edinburgh stalwart, RF is busier than ever. Both branches are in vibrant residential areas, near the city centre. Nuts, seeds, spices, grains and dried fruit are packed daily by nimble fingers, while flour, cereals and muesli can be bought by the kilo. There's pretty much everything you'd expect from this kind of shop – fresh organic fruit, veg and bread, sauces, spreads and soya products, along with organic wines and spirits. Other branch at 8 Brougham Street, 0131 228 1201.
www.realfoods.co.uk

Relish
Leith, Map 3 I3
6 Commercial Street, 0131 476 1920
Mon–Wed 8.30am–8pm, Thu–Sat 8.30am–9pm, Sun 10am–8pm
Relish is stylish with tall shelves and sharp lighting. Already attracting Leithers with its above-average sandwiches and coffee, it stocks serious foodie goods like truffles and oils alongside fun foods like spreadable marshmallow. Cured meats and continental cheeses are sold from the deli counter and a few tables allow sampling on the spot. You can also order fabulous takeaway food from the Michelin-starred restaurant Martin Wishart.
www.relish-food.com

Royal Mile Whiskies
Old Town, Map 2 I6
379–381 High Street, 0131 225 3383
Mon–Sat 10am–6pm, Sun 12.30–6pm
Attracting serious whisky drinkers from
around the world, this shop sells around
1000 malt whiskies and bourbons from
around Scotland, Ireland and further afield,
some of them dating back to 1897.
Collectors' items aren't cheap (peaking at
£10,000 for a 1937 Glenfiddich) but there
are plenty of single malts around the
£20–£30 mark. Staff are rigorously trained
and will direct you to the business' other
venture, the Cigar Box, for a selection of
top-notch cigars.
www.royalmilewhiskies.com

Valvona & Crolla
City Centre, Map 2 I3
19 Elm Row, 0131 556 6066
Mon–Sat 8am–6.30pm, Sun 11am–5pm
'Est 1934' is proudly displayed on the
front. Go inside and you'll find a modern
deli fit for any urban sophisticate. This
celebrated family business sells the freshest
of cheese, meat, pasta, sauces, veg from
Italy, olive oil and vinegars, wines and
bread made on the premises. People come
from all over to fill their baskets or sip a
cappuccino in the backstore café (see
Café). Regular wine and cheese tastings
and cookery demonstrations by well known
names are held in the 70-seat theatre and
food can be ordered on an impressive
website.
www.valvonacrolla.com

Villeneuve Wines
New Town, Map 2 H3
119a Broughton Street, 0131 558 8441
Mon–Thu 10am–10pm, Fri/Sat 9am–10pm,
Sun 1–8pm
There's a distinct interest at this award-
winning shop in small producers and cult
wines, such as the Opus One from Napa
Valley at £175. But both the Haddington
and Edinburgh branch have plenty more
affordable offerings from around the world,
all of which have been through the quality
test before reaching the shelves. The
website is good and you can also subscribe
to their monthly newsletter *'The Nose'*.
www.villeneuvewines.com

Interiors

Designshop
Southside, Map 2 I10
116–120 Causewayside, 0131 667 7078
Tue–Sat 11am–6pm
Since opening in February 2002, this shop
has doubled its floorspace and is full of the
very best in 20th century design –
furniture, lighting, accessories, textiles,
books and toys. The Foscarini lighting is a
talking point, with the Bubble and Coco
models taking centre stage.
www.designshop.eu.com

Inhouse
New Town, Map 2 E4
28 Howe Street, 0131 225 2888
Mon–Wed/Fri 9.30am–6pm, Thu 10am–7pm,
Sat 9.30am–5.30pm
The buyers for Inhouse could show mass-
producing interiors companies a thing or
two about good design. Step inside its
Tardis-like entrance, and enter a world
where innovation and style reign
supreme. Stocking everything from
contemporary sofas and retro lighting to
Jeff Koons espresso cups and Alessi
kitchenware, it's packed with beautiful
goods for the home. Expensive, but its
covetable wares are irresistable.
www.inhousenet.co.uk

Tangram
Old Town, Map 2 H6
33–37 Jeffrey Street, 0131 556 6551
Tue–Fri 10am–5.30pm, Sat 10am–5pm
Known for its 'less is more' window
displays, Tangram's contemporary
lighting, furnishing and textiles by
designers like Ingo Maurer and
companies like Vitra, are sparsely
displayed: the result screams quality and
exclusivity. The shop named after a
Chinese puzzle also creates interiors for
art spaces, hotels, cafés and corporate
clients.
www.tangramfurnishers.co.uk

dba lighting
Leith, Map 3 H5
222 Leith Walk, 0131 555 4499
Mon–Sat 10am–6pm
It was the work of dba which led one
over-excited style commentator to
proclaim that lighting was the new
rock'n'roll in property development. Set
up in 1986 by David Brown, the company
specialises in bespoke lighting design for
both domestic and corporate clients.
Having recently moved to state of the art
premises, the store offers everything from
a £60 table lamp to contemporary
chandeliers at £3000.
www.dba-lighting.com

Jewellery

Etincelle
West End, Map 2 B6
45 William Street, 0131 220 0320
Mon–Sat 9am–6pm, Sun 11am–3.30pm
'Sparkle' in French, Etincelle opened in
2003 and stocks the highly coveted US
products by Besso and Tarina Tarantino –
oft seen glittering on the bods of
Cameron Diaz and Jennifer Lopez.
Opened by husband and wife team
Catriona McCallum and Gavin MacLean,
it also sells vintage items, designer
accessories and bridal pieces. Look out
for the intricate Butler and Wilson floral
confections.
www.etincelle.co.uk

Cymbols at Drum Central. See music shops, page 134

Galerie Mirages
New Town, Map 2 C3
46a Raeburn Place, 0131 315 2603
Mon–Sat 10am–5.30pm, Sun 12.30–4.30pm
Shiela Dhariwal set up shop in this old bakehouse 15 years ago, selling jewellery and artifacts from Asia. Stock now includes designer jewellery from Europe, Britain, America and Africa, reflecting contemporary trends for chunky, beaded or sleek styles. The selection of silver is not matched anywhere in the city and semi-precious stones are abundant. With prices from £6.50, this shop will keep you coming back.
www.galeriemirages.com

Joseph Bonnar
City Centre, Map 2 F5
72 Thistle Street, 0131 228 2589
Mon–Sat 10.30am–5pm
Joseph Bonnar, a well kent dealer, opened this bijoux shop over 30 years ago, establishing himself as the purveyor of the biggest collection of antique jewellery in Scotland. Fine quality adornments are sourced from all over the country and cover all periods. Prices are inevitably quite high.
www.silvercard.co.uk

Palenque
Old Town, Map 2 H6
56 High Street, 0131 557 9553
Mon–Sat 10am–6pm, Sun 11am–5pm
Window displays with sweet, floaty mini-exhibitions don't get much prettier this. Inside, the range of contemporary silver jewellery is stylish, handcrafted and affordable (prices start at £3). Owned by David and Susi Heard, the shop specialises in pieces from Susi's native Mexico. Other branch at 99 Rose Street, 0131 225 7194.
www.palenque.co.uk

Rosie Brown
New Town, Map 2 D3
51 St Stephen Street, 0131 226 3774
Mon–Fri 10am–5.30pm, Sat 10am–6pm
Co-owned by Catherine Gill, a retail jeweller since the age of 17, these two shops (other branch at 137 Bruntsfield Place, 0131 226 3774), trade in delicate, feminine jewellery, beautifully displayed behind glass. Stocking chunky designs by Kenzo, contemporary styles by Scarlett Jewellery and the very quirky, very hip work of Adele Taylor, it makes for a sweet and contemporary package.

Watch
Old Town, Map 2 G7
3 Forrest Road, 0131 220 5414
Mon–Sat 10am–6pm
You've got the Luis Vuitton clutch, the Gucci sunnies and the Prada pumps. Chances are you'll want a fabulous timepiece to go with it – look no further than Watch. The design-led store has been open for five years and stocks trendy fashion brands including Starck, Diesel, Fossil, Baby-G, Swatch and Dolce & Gabbana. Prices will be matched by lower ones found elsewhere.
www.watchco.net

Malls

Ocean Terminal
Leith, Map 3 G1
Ocean Drive, 0131 555 8888
Mon–Fri 10am–8pm, Sat 10am–7pm, Sun 11am–6pm
Edinburgh's newest shopping centre is also the most pleasing to the eye. Designed by the Conran group, the interior boasts lots of swanky leather sofas, a cinema, Zinc Bar and Grill as well as (among others) Debenhams, French Connection, Gap, Bear Factory, Marks & Spencer's Simply Food. The Royal Yacht Britannia (see Attractions) is boarded from the centre and there are regular Vegas club nights. Available for hire as a venue, the centre hosted events during the 2003 MTV Europe Awards.
www.oceanterminal.com

Princes Mall
City Centre, Map 2 G5
Princes Street, 0131 557 3759
Mon–Wed/Fri/Sat 9am–6pm, Thu 9am–7pm, Sun 11am–5pm
A contemporary, underground mall at the east end of Princes Street with high street chains like Oasis, New Look and Body Shop, plus a large and noisy foodcourt. There's also a discount USC and branded urbanwear store Xile. Costa coffee on the top floor is a good bolthole when it's raining in town.
www.princesmall-edinburgh.co.uk

Blackfriars Music for folk music and instruments

Music Shops

Blackfriars Folk Music
Old Town, Map 2 H6
49 Blackfriars Street, 0131 557 3090
Mon–Sat 9.30am–5.30pm
A bit of a cornerstone in folky circles, Blackfriars sells a humungous range of traditional folk instruments including harps, bodhrans, fiddles, mandolins and bagpipes. It also stocks a varied array of CDs and books of traditional Scottish music.

Drum Central
Southside, Map 2 I9
61 South Clerk Street, 0131 667 3844
Mon–Sat 10am–6pm
Everything to do with percussion from the full drum kit to cow bells. Opened five years ago, this local company will sell you a starter kit for £260, but can also supply the best professional brands which can sting you for £1000s. Another speciality is instruments from around the world – Latin, Asian, African. This outfit services professional bands on tour and handles repairs.
www.drumcentral.co.uk

Mev Taylor's Music Shop
West End, Map 2 C7
212 Morrison Street, 0131 229 7454
Mon–Sat 9.30am–5.30pm
Enjoying the peculiar honour of being the biggest retailer of saxophones in Scotland, Mev Taylor's also sells a vast range of accessories, cases and books, as well as stocking a decent range of other brass and woodwind. It's big on guitars too, with a healthy choice of acoustics and electrics and a decent range of amps to help you get heard above the rabble.
www.mevtaylors.co.uk

Rae Macintosh Music
West End, Map 2 D6
6 Queensferry Street, 0131 225 1171
Mon–Fri 9am–5.30pm, Sat 9am–5pm, Sun 11am–5pm
Definitely the best place in town for folk sheet music. It has reams of the stuff, but is slightly disorganised, so you'll have to rake about for what you want. The staff are very helpful, so if your life is not complete without the music to 'The Skye Boat Song' or 'Ae Fond Kiss' then fill yer boots.

Scayles Music
Southside, Map 2 I8
50 St Patrick Square, 0131 667 8241
Mon–Sat 10am–6pm
Multi-purpose instrument retailers with an emphasis on acoustic and electric guitars. It also stocks a lot of traditional folky stuff though, as well as a decent range of software products, percussion and effects. Pleasantly un-muso staff are extremely civilised, and you're guaranteed that if they can't help you, they'll know a man who can.

Sound Control
Old Town, Map 2 H6
17–21 St Mary's St, 0131 557 3986
Mon–Fri 10am–6pm, Sat 9am–5.30
As the UK's biggest chain of music retailers, Sound Control offers everything a musician could possible desire or need. When a band gets signed to a major record label this is usually the first place they blow their advance. Drums, guitars, keyboards and DJ equipment by all the biggest names are available, along with accessories and other music must-haves.
www.soundcontrol.co.uk

Stringers

City Centre, Map 2 G4

13 York Place, 0131 557 5432

Mon–Sat 9.30am–5.30pm

Scotland's biggest retailer of stringed instruments is staffed by string players who offer expert advice. The shop offers a repair and restoration service and stocks a wide range of instruments, including violins, violas, cellos and bass. There are also two rooms where customers can try out instruments in private before purchase.

www.stringersmusic.co.uk

The Wind Section

City Centre, Map 2 G4

5a York Place, 0131 557 6543

Mon–Sat 9.30am–5.30pm

This specialist music shop deals with brass and woodwind sales and repairs. Instruments for sale include trumpets, trombones, tubas, saxophones, clarinets and bassoons. Also available is a repair service, covering everything from on-the-spot jobs to complete overhauls of instruments. There's a sound-proof studio where customers can try before they buy too.

www.thewindsection.com

Record Shops

Avalanche

Old Town, Map 2 G6

60 Cockburn Street, 0131 225 3939

Mon–Sat 10am–6pm

The Avalanche mini-chain isn't too hot on dance, but if it's indie you want this should probably be your first stop, whether you're looking for Blur or something that would have John Peel scratching his head. The Cockburn St HQ stocks CDs, DVDs, vinyl and tapes, while an expanded 17 West Nicolson St (0131 668 2374) is good for CDs and vinyl, with a fair bit of hip hop and electronica.

www.avalancherecords.co.uk

Backbeat Records

Southside, Map 2 off I10

31 East Crosscauseway, 0131 668 2666

Mon–Sat 10am–5.30pm

You can hardly see into this place for the Dylan posters but this tardis-like store brims with 1970s classic rock, reggae, folk and soul alongside a number of new releases. There's a good mix of vinyl, CDs and boxed sets, and this is a great place for a browse, although the staff are not the most amiable in town. If it's old and you can't find it anywhere else, you'll probably source it here.

Coda

City Centre, Map 2 G5

Princes Mall, Princes Street, 0131 557 3090

Mon–Sat 9.30am–6pm, Sun 11am–5pm

The Princes Mall branch has a good selection of discounted and chart CDs, plus assorted accessories, though it's not so

good for dance or hip hop. Perched on the corner of Bank Street, the other Coda (0131 622 7246) specialises in Scottish folk, country and classical music, with a comprehensive selection of each and knowledgable staff thrown in gratis.

www.codamusic.co.uk

Fopp

City Centre, Map 2 F5

7–15 Rose Street, 0131 220 0310

Mon–Sat 9am–9pm, Sun 11am–6pm

Specialising in insane bargains, the Fopp ethos is to buy 'em in bulk and pass the savings on to the customer. As much famed these days for its ultra-cheap books and films as it is for its CD and vinyl collections, the two shops (other branch at Cockburn Street, Old Town, 0131 220 0133) between them cover most genres of music, concentrating on indie, hip hop and dance stuff. What's more, the Rose Street branch even has a bar, so you can sip on a cold one, while there are decks on hand for you to listen before buying.

www.fopp.co.uk

HMV

City Centre, Map 2 E5

129–130 Princes Street, 0131 225 7008

Mon/Wed/Fri 9am–6pm, Tue 9.30am–6pm, Thu 9am–8pm, Sat 9am–6.30pm, Sun 11am–6pm

CDs, videos, games and connected merchandise are housed in two huge shops from this international retailer. The Princes Street branch is the largest of the two (other branch in St James Centre, City Centre, 0131 556 1236), with a basement filled with the latest releases on vinyl. Not the cheapest, and not the best for traditional music, but useful and handy nonetheless.

Hog's Head

Southside, Map 2 I9

62 South Clerk Street, 0131 667 5274

Mon–Sat 10am–6pm, Sun 1–5pm

Alarmingly dark but actually a fairly welcoming place situated in the heart of the university area. One of the biggest dealers in everything second hand, from CDs to videos, DVDs and tapes with the focus on rock but enough of everything else to warrant a root about the racks.

www.hogs-head.com

McAlister Matheson Music

West End, Map 2 E7

1 Grindlay Street, 0131 228 3827

Mon–Wed 9.30am–7pm, Thu/Fri 9.30am–7.30pm, Sat 9am–5.30pm

This is a friendly wee shop, a bit off the beaten track, and has been around for a dozen years or so. It stocks an expansive range of traditional Scottish music as well as running the gammut of styles when it comes to classical releases, almost entirely on CD.

www.mmmusic.co.uk

Record Shak
Southside, Map 2 I9
69 South Clerk Street, 0131 667 7144
Mon–Sat 10am–6pm
Groovy narrow shop with loads of
bargainous CDs and tapes, plus some
surprisingly good vinyl, especially if
you're wanting to fill in gaps in rock
classics from the 60s, 70s and 80s – Neil
Young, Santana and John Coltrane all
live here. Otherwise, the focus is largely
on indie, with a decent mix of dub, jazz,
soul and reggae. It also sells a lot of
extraneous stuff like T-shirts, hoodies,
posters and limited edition CD box sets
too.

Rhythm Rack
West End, Map 2 C7
159 Morrison Street, 0131 538 7155
Mon–Sat 10am–6pm, Sun 1–5pm
Stuck halfway between Haymarket and
the city centre, this place is worth the
walk as it has a fine selection of second-
hand CDs and vinyl. It also stocks a
reasonable range of new releases.
www.rhythmrack.com

Ripping Records
Old Town, Map 2 H6
91 South Bridge, 0131 226 7010
Mon–Wed 9.30am–6pm, Thu 9.30am–7pm,
Fri 9.30am–6pm, Sat 9.30am–6pm, Sun
noon–5.30pm
Peddling a fairly unexceptional range of
albums at not particularly bargain prices,
Ripping is a vital part of Edinburgh's
music scene because it acts as pretty
much *the* place to buy gig tickets in the
capital - check the regularly updated
website.
www.rippingrecords.com

Underground Solu'shn
Old Town, Map 2 G6
9 Cockburn Street, 0131 226 2242
Mon–Wed 10am–6pm, Thu 10am–7pm,
Fri/Sat 10am–6pm, Sun noon–5pm
Walls are adorned with signed 12"s from
the various DJs who've passed through
the doors – this is the kind of place
where punter and performer meet. Staffed
by Edinburgh DJs – who raft the quality
club nights in the city – this friendly shop
has a great range of house, techno, drum
& bass and hip hop, on good old
fashioned vinyl. Plenty of listening decks
and the staff's encyclopaedic knowledge
rarely disappoints.

Vinyl Villains
City Centre, Map 2 I3
5 Elm Row, 0131 558 1170
Mon–Fri 10.15am–6pm, Sat
10.15am–5.30pm, Sun noon–4pm
A wee treasure trove of a place. Second-
hand albums and 12"s (including lots of
that relic of a bygone era: picture discs)
go for a reasonable price, and although

its stock is far from comprehensive, there
are more than a few juicy rock, indie and
pop bargains to be snapped up. Only a
stone's throw from the centre of town,
too.

Virgin Megastore
City Centre, Map 2 E6
125 Princes Street, 0131 220 2230
Mon 9am–6.30pm, Tue 9.30am–6pm, Wed
9am–6pm, Thu 9am–8pm, Fri 9am–6pm,
Sat 9am–6.30pm, Sun 11am–6pm
While you are inside this huge store
you'll find, as the name suggests, a mega
range of all things aural and visual on
every different sort of format. As you'd
expect from a chain, Virgin stocks a wide
range of all the new releases as well as a
fairly decent back catalogue. Nice
classical and jazz sections are a bit over-
priced.
www.virgin.ac.psiweb.com

Über Disko
Old Town, Map 2 G6
36 Cockburn Street, 0131 226 2134
Mon–Thu 10am–5.45pm, Fri/Sat
9.30am–6pm
It may look fairly bare when it comes to
stock but you gotta ask for what's behind
the counter if you want the newest and
bestest from the worlds of house and
trance from the Über-Disko boys and
girls. Despite their limited musical remit,
they really know their stuff and are also a
handy source of local clubbing gossip
and advance tickets, even if there isn't a
huge amount of space to hang out.

Scottish

Geoffrey (Tailor) Kiltmakers & 21st Century Kilts
Old Town, Map 2 H6
57–59 High Street, 0131 557 0256
Mon–Wed/Fri/Sat 9am–5.30pm, Thu
9am–7pm, Sun 10am–4pm
This family business has long served
Edinburgh inhabitants and a plethora of
tourists. The shop offers daytime and
evening wear, plus increasingly popular
Jacobean and Trews outfits. A full outfit
costs from around £500, but this spot
offers a hire service, as well as a database
of tartans. The store's 21st Century Kilts
division makes traditional kilts, but using
materials such as denim, wool, leather
and even PVC. Madonna and Robbie
Williams are both fans.
*www.geoffreykilts.co.uk/www.21stcentury
kilts.co.uk*

Hawick Cashmere Company
Old Town, Map 2 F7
71–81 Grassmarket, 0131 225 8634
Mon–Sat 10am–6pm, Apr–Dec Sun
11am–4pm
Opened in 1991, this shop carries on a

softly, softly company tradition begun in 1875. In spacious surroundings, there are hundreds of styles (classic and contemporary) and colours of the rainbow to choose from. All jumpers are made in the Borders.
www.hawickcashmere.com

Hector Russell
Old Town, Map 2 H6
137–141 High Street, 0131 225 3315
Mon–Sat 9am–5.30pm, Sun noon–5pm
Hector Russell specialises in bespoke tailoring in tartan. Quality is paramount and the company can meet almost any sizing or pattern requirement. In recent years, films such as *Braveheart* have made the one-piece kilt and plaid, or Feileadh-Mhor, increasingly popular. A full outfit costs from around £550. Other branch at 95 Princes Street, City Centre (0131 225 3315).
www.hector-russell.com

Museum of Scotland Shop
Old Town, Map 2 G7
Chambers Street, 0131 247 4128
Mon/Wed/Thu–Sat 10am–5pm, Tue 10am–8pm, Sun noon–5pm
A large shop selling museum branded gifts as well as specially commissioned crafts with an emphasis on affordability. Reproductions of the Lewis chess pieces and Rob Mulholland metalwork are some current buys. The most popular souvenirs are the Dialect Sayings mugs and T-shirts, printed with dictionary definitions of Scottish words like crabbit, skiver and glaikit – look them up.
www.nms.ac.uk

Secondhand Books

Peter Bell
Old Town, Map 2 F7
68 West Port, 0131 556 2198
Mon–Sat 9.30am–5pm. Closed Sun
Stocking several thousand antiquarian/second-hand titles, this shop specialises in scholarly books on the humanities, especially English history, literature and biography and Scottish history, literature and philosophy. If your own particular bent is the Victorian period, you're in for a treat.
www.peterbell.demon.co.uk

Second Edition
New Town, Map 2 E2
9 Howard Street, 0131 556 9403
Mon–Sat 9.30am–5.30pm. Closed Sun
This family business opened its doors in 1978 and is hot on collectors' items. Its specialities are Scottish, military, travel, children's and illustrated books but you'll find everything here from *Ancient Freemasonry and the Old Dundee Lodge* to *Know your own Ship*. And its address is just a hop, skip and a jump from the

childhood home of Robert Louis Stevenson which gives it that little bit extra.
www.secondeditionbookshop.co.uk

Shoes and Bags

Helen Bateman Shoes
West End, Map 2 C6
16 William Street, 0131 220 4495
Mon–Sat 9.30am–6pm
Situated on the close-knit mini-fashion quarter of William Street, this shop sells things of individuality and beauty. Ready-to wear is upstairs. A secret bespoke room is downstairs. Colourful shoes, beaded shoes, stilettos and boots are Bateman branded and designed exclusively for this elegant but friendly shop.
www.helenbateman.com

A D Mackenzie & Co
Old Town, Map 2 G6
34 Victoria Street, 0131 220 0089
Mon–Sat 10am–5pm
If, like any non-label-obsessed traveller, you baulk at the site of LV-emblazoned luggage, then the traditionalism of A D Mackenzie is probably more your bag. Established 25 years ago after starting out as a saddle-makers, the company produces beautiful leather travel bags, briefcases and handbags, handmade on the Isle of Arran. Most products are made specifically to order. Very *All Creatures Great and Small*.
www.mackenziebags.co.uk

Office
City Centre, Map 2 F5
79a Princes Street, 0131 220 4296
Mon–Wed/Fri/Sat 9am–6pm, Thu 9am–7pm, Sun 11.30am–5.30pm
Faithful shoppers come to worship in their droves at its fashion footwear altar opened in late 2003. It's a case of survival of the fastest when it comes to bagging the latest designs in shoes, sandals, boots and trainers. Limited seating and the bustling atmosphere make peak shopping a nightmare, but with the wealth of colourful designs on offer – Adidas, Rocket Dog, Camper to name a few – at reasonable prices, the extra effort is worth it.
www.office.co.uk

MY FAVOURITE SHOP

Paddy Barrass, 15 The Grassmarket
'Wonderful clothes, shawls and linen. I bought my wedding dress, an original by Darlings, here.'
Yvette Jelfs, milliner

Shoe worshippers head for Helen Bateman, page 137

Schuh
City Centre, Map 2 E5
6–6a Frederick Street, 0131 220 0290
Mon–Wed 9am–6pm, Thu 9am–8pm, Fri/Sat
9am–6pm, Sun 11am–6pm
The first Schuh store opened in 1981 on
Edinburgh's North Bridge (it's still there).
Now it's a massive chain, with around 34
stores UK wide sporting the very latest in
footwear fashion. You'll find a mix of own
brand footwear for men and women, plus
designs by Fcuk, Diesel, Acupuncture,
Camper, Hush Puppies, Puma and Adidas.
Schuh also exclusively stocks sports Red
or Dead. It's very affordable, so an Imelda
Marcos shoe wardrobe is within easy
reach. Other branches at Frederick Street
and Ocean Terminal.
www.schuh.co.uk

Specialist

Aha Ha Ha Joke shop
Old Town, Map 2 G7
99 West Bow, 0131 220 5252
Mon–Sat 10am–6pm
Aha Ha Ha is a laugh a minute. As you
might expect, it stocks the usual favourites
– whoopee cushions, fake ciggies, chest

wigs and plastic poos. Aspiring gangster's
moll or big chief? You can purchase either
from the large selection of costumes.

The Big Park
New Town, Map 2 G3
73 Dublin Street, 0131 558 9360
Tue–Sat 10am–6pm
A little out on a limb, this boutique is
dedicated to bringing the outdoors indoors
with a range of garden accessories and
furnishings. Mammoth coloured
washbaskets, contemporary outdoor
lighting, potty-like Finn Stone chairs and
Cath Kidston bags are all crammed in.
Owned by husband and wife team Pete (a
landscape architect by trade) and René
Mullin, it's a real hidden treasure.
www.thebigpark.com

Hilary's Bazaar
Old Town, Map 2 G7
27 George IV Bridge, 0131 556 7976
Mon–Wed/Fri/Sat 10am–6pm, Thu
10am–7pm
One of Edinburgh's more off the wall
shopping experiences. Dedicated to belly
dancing, it stocks a range of Oriental
clothes sourced from Egypt, Turkey and

India and rich in vibrant reds, purples and golds. Exotic jewellery and instruments also sold. Owner Hilary Thacker is committed to popularising the dance form in Edinburgh, through videos and literature in the shop. She holds regular classes at Dance Base (see Sport).
www.hilarysbazaar.com

Party Mania
Southside, Map 2 H8
30 West Nicolson Street, 0131 667 6020
Mon–Sat 9am–6pm
Truly a one-stop party shop, Party Mania stocks everything you could possibly need for a stylish bash. Every shade and size of balloon, including metallic helium, is stocked. The list then becomes endless – tableware, party bag fillers, wedding favours, banners, fancy dress (a limited collection) and a wonderful selection of masks – pure inspiration for a masquerade party, if ever there was one.
www.partypartyparty.co.uk

Whiplash Trash
Old Town, Map 2 G6
53 Cockburn Street, 0131 226 1005
Mon–Wed/Fri/Sat 10.30am–5.30pm, Thu 10.30am–6pm
Whiplash Trash is a 'soft-core' sex shop. With its tongue firmly in cheek, it sells a range of sex paraphernalia to titillate even the most prudish shopper. From Penis Pasta and fun T-shirts to full leather gear and vibrators, its stock is varied and fun. Situated amidst the trendy, alternative shops of Cockburn Street, it is a den of iniquity that positions itself just on the right side of good taste.

Wind Things
Old Town, Map 2 G7
Grassmarket, 0131 622 7032
Mon–Sat 10am–5.30pm, Sun noon–5pm
Blustery weather makes Wind Things specially suited to the city. Unashamedly dedicated to windy indulgence, the shop sells everything from basic kites to wind buggies, land boards, frisbees, boomerangs and juggling equipment. Owners Stuart Potter and Miles Ford pride themselves as being Scotland's largest kite specialist. Kites start from as little as £15, but the more advanced technology could give your credit card a serious bashing.
www.windthings.co.uk

Sport

Blacks Outdoor Leisure
City Centre, Map 2 I3
13–14 Elm Row, 0131 556 3491
Mon–Wed/Fri/Sat 9am–5.30pm, Thu 9am–6.30pm, Sun noon–4pm
Founding father Thomas Black retired from life on the high seas to become a sailmaker on the Clyde, setting up business in 1861. His son took over,

bought ski equipment companies and expanded to become one of the largest outdoor specialists in the country. Known for the hardiness of its equipment, the stores sell brands such as Berghaus, Sprayway, Karrimor and Lowe Alpine. Other branch at 24 Frederick Street, City Centre (0131 225 8686).
www.blacks.co.uk

Boardwise
Old Town, Map 2 E7
4 Lady Lawson Street, 0131 229 5887
Mon–Sat 10am–6pm
Dedicated to snowsports, skateboarding and surfing for the hip set, this shop stocks equipment, accessories and the latest footwear – think slacker-beloved brands such as Billabong, O'Neill, Vans, Roxy and We. Staff are particularly clued up on the latest places to go, second hand goods and special offers.
www.boardwise.com

Edinburgh Bicycle Co-operative
Southside, Map 2 off E10
8 Alvanley Terrace, Whitehouse Loan, 0131 228 3565
Mon–Sun 10am–6m
Edinburgh's premier cycle shop with own brand machines. Well established and thriving, it has a buzzing workshop, large stock, lots of gear and runs classes and events. A must for all lovers of two-wheelers.
www.edinburghbicycle.com

Focus
Old Town, Map 2 F7
44 West Port, 0131 229 9009
Mon–Sat 10am–6pm, Sun 1–5pm
If you know your trucks from your decks then you're likely to find something to suit on the racks of Focus Pocus. The skatewear and urban store is more into the gear than the equipment, so it's all about looking the part. Brands stocked include Fenchurch, Planet Earth, Stussy, Blueprint and DC.
www.focuspocus.co.uk

Route One
Old Town, Map 2 G6
29 Cockburn Street, 0131 226 2131
Mon–Sat 9.30am–6pm, Sun 11am–5pm
Route One is the joker in the pack of serious sports shops. From the bright purple exterior to its stylish merchandising, it's all about fun, fun, fun. Skatewear, BMX bikes, frisbees, bright T-shirts and the latest must-have skate shoes fill the place. Expect to see skater-boi brands such as Dogtown, Fuct, Paul Frank and Quicksilver. There are small collections for ladies and children and staff are super-helpful. There's even a section dedicated to 'wallets and bling'.
www.routeone.co.uk

Tiso

Leith, Map 3 H3

41 Commercial Street, 0131 554 0804
Mon/Tue/Fri/Sat 9.30am–6pm, Wed
10am–6pm, Thu 9.30am–7.30pm, Sun
11am–5pm

'The Outdoor Specialist'. And true to its
name, the two large branches (other
branch at 125 Rose Street, City Centre
(0131 225 9486) sell everything you need
for walking, hiking, skiing and camping.
Rose Street has recently been
refurbished. Leith, meanwhile, is more
than a store – you can try almost
anything out before you buy. It has mini
climbing walls, rock pools to test water
resistance, a café, daily pilates and yoga
classes, plus regular events and organised
walks and talks.
www.tiso.co.uk

Vintage Clothing

15 The Grassmarket

Old Town, Map 2 F7

15 The Grassmarket, 0131 226 3087
Mon–Fri noon–6pm, Sat 10.30am–5.30pm

Paddy Barrass has provided the
discerning shopper with fine vintage
clothing and materials for over 30 years.
Named after its owner, the shop sells
everything from linen and lace items to
top quality dresses and ball gowns. A
sense of history pervades the store and
the level of personal attention and
customer service is excellent.

Armstrongs

Old Town, Map 2 F7

83 Grassmarket, 0131 220 5557
Mon–Thu 10am–5.30pm, Fri/Sat 10am–6pm,
Sun noon–6pm

It's not an obvious tourist destination, but
Armstrongs should be listed as the city's
greatest clothing museum. Established in
1840, its two branches act as a vast
emporium of vintage, retro and
traditional garb. The range is simply
overwhelming (sometimes with odour to
match). The Grassmarket branch, with its
voyeuristic changing facilities, is bigger,
stocking a good range of accessories,
dress shirts, bags and shoes. Southside
(66 South Clerk Street, 0131 667 3056)

MY FAVOURITE FIND

Lindsay Crawford

'I discovered this place on
Dublin Street the other day.
Crawford stocks unique
knitwear sourced from Paris,
Milan and Barcelona. And she
tells you if things simply don't
suit.'
Helen Bateman, Helen Bateman

---

is smaller, more ordered and has an
impressive selection of leather coats and
formal dresses.
www.armstrongsvintage.co.uk

Gladrags

New Town, Map 2 E2

17 Henderson Row, 0131 557 1916
Tue–Sat 10.30am–6pm

Kate Cameron baulks at the term
'second-hand clothes' and her shop
occupies the very highest end of the
vintage market. Only the best 20th
century stuff hangs here – dresses, coats,
underwear, feathers, linen – a dressing up
dream for women of style. Cameron
herself is a passionate and well-informed
buyer with as much charisma as her
beautiful goods. She also stocks an
exquisite line in glittering antique silver
and glass.

Godiva

Old Town, Map 2 F7

54 West Port, 0131 221 9212
Mon–Fri noon–6pm, Sat 11.30am–6pm

Not as vast as Armstrongs, nor as elegant
as Gladrags, this little shop has a
personality of its own. Affordable, with a
pleasing range of coats, trousers,
eveningwear and classic shirts, it has a
particularly covetable bag collection.
Owned by Fleur McIntosh, the shop has
just added a range of clothes recycled
and customised by local fashion students.
The perfect store for a one-off item.
www.godivaboutique.co.uk

Herman Brown's

Old Town, Map 2 F7

151 West Port, 0131 228 2589
Mon–Sat noon–6pm

Owned by Anna Nicholson, Herman
Brown's has been in existence for over
20 years. Retro to modern clothing,
jewellery and accessories are the
speciality, and it's easy to while away an
hour browsing the racks, glass cabinets
and displays in-store. Unlike other
second-handers, the shop is never
cluttered or over-stocked, allowing you to
select in comfort.

Rusty Zip

Old Town, Map 2 G7

14 Teviot Place, 0131 226 4634
Mon–Thu 10am–5.30pm, Fri/Sat 10am–6pm,
Sun noon–6pm

Owned by the Armstrongs chain, the
Rusty Zip is another perfectly
proportioned second-hand clothing store.
Its collection of good quality leather
coats is impressive, and so are the knick-
knacks – including wigs, feather boas
and novelty scarves – that adorn the
interior. It's a tight squeeze moving
between the rails, and you need a ladder
for a proper look, but it's well worth a
Saturday afternoon browse.

The Pentlands, page 153

escape

escape

beaches

Edinburgh is surrounded by beaches. North or south, you don't have to travel far before you hit golden sands. Cramond is the nearest, but if you've got the time it's worth going further afield for the best stretches. Water sports, boating, swimming, picnics, horse-riding, castle-building, rock-pooling – all is possible. Remember to take your sandwiches and wind-break.

Aberlady
Out of town, Map 1
East Lothian. 15 miles east of Edinburgh on A198
Once upon a time the authorities here took to clamping down on nude sunbathing. Now they've mellowed, just about. Provided you keep it all in the best possible taste, you can strip off discreetly among the dunes. This beach gets pretty busy in summer, so make sure you bag your spot early. And if it's birds you're interested in, this stretch of sand is right next to an RSPB nature reserve.

Coldingham
Out of town, Map 1
Borders. 45 miles south of Edinburgh on A1107
Worth the hike from Edinburgh, this is one of the east's cleanest beaches, receiving a tick in 2003 from the Marine Conservation Society. A pristine, cosy spot with a picturesque café, beach huts and maze of rock pools, the sheltered bay is popular with bathers and aqua divers. Surfers tend to use Pease Bay, 10 miles north along the coast.

Elie
Out of town, Map 1
Fife. 45 miles north of Edinburgh on A917
Rich, golden sands and 19th century village elegance combine to make Elie a very pretty resort indeed. Dunes and a shallow bay mean it is sheltered and safe for bathing and there is a watersports centre. Though closer to Edinburgh, it has a reputation for attracting well-heeled holiday makers from Glasgow. The Ship Inn, right on the beach, is a popular pub serving hearty meals.

Gullane
Out of town, Map 1
East Lothian. 20 miles north east of Edinburgh on A198
Gullane is everyone's favourite. Long, wide stretches of sand, rock pools and dunes bring families, dogs, horses and water sports fans back again and again all year round. Though colder and choppier than the west, it is also excellent for windsurfing and kiting (no changing facilities). There is an ice-cream van in the grassy car park in summer. Or stop off at Luca's, Musselburgh's famous parlour at 32–38 High Street.

North Berwick
Out of town, Map 1
East Lothian. Train to North Berwick or 25 miles east of Edinburgh on A198
This string of lovely beaches has views of the islands of Fidra, the Lamb and Craigleith. West Bay is slightly rocky, next to a golf course and much frequented by owners of black labradors. The town's main beach is sandier, wider and adjoins a cute park with benches and putting greens. East Bay continues past the Scottish Seabird Centre (see Days Out) with an open view to gannet-laden Bass Rock. Look out for the Luca's ice cream van here in season.

Windsurfers on Gullane beach

Portobello

Outskirts, Map 1
East Lothian. 5 miles east of Edinburgh on
A199
Edinburgh's local seaside resort has a
mile of levelled beach and stone
promenade built for Victorians, and is
now used by locals with or without dogs
and children. Joggers and skaters come
here but cycles are verboten. 19th century
swimming and turkish baths, now in fine
order since refurbishment (and with cafe)
are half-way along and open to the public
daily (Portobello Swim Centre 0131 669
6888).

Seacliff

Out of town, Map 1
East Lothian. 28 miles east of Edinburgh on
A198
A real stunner, with dramatic cliffs, sands
and the looming ruin of Tantallon Castle
next door. One of the less well-known
beaches in the area, it has received a tick
from the Marine Conservation Society.
Walkers can call by for free, but parking
the car costs around £2 at the local farm
which owns the beach. Horses are a
common sight and watersports are
permitted. To find out more about the
birds and animals that live on the east
coast, visit the Seabird Centre at North
Berwick, only three miles from here.

Silversands and Aberdour

Out of town, Map 1
Fife. Train to Aberdour or 18 miles north of
Edinburgh on A921
A town blessed with two cosy beaches.
Silversands, just north of the main street
down a signposted track, is a stretch of
sand with a bucket and spade, ice-cream
van, kids in cold water atmosphere.
Aberdour beach, at the heart of the
village) offers variety in modest
proportions, with sand, rock pools and a
small harbour. Best of all is the high cliff
path which conveniently begins at the tiny
harbourfront ice-cream shop/café
(summer only) leading to the rocky
outpost at Hawkcraig Point.

Yellowcraig

Out of town, Map 1
East Lothian. 22 miles east of Edinburgh off
A198
Yellowcraig (singular, contrary to local
colloquialism) is rumoured to be the
inspiration behind Robert Louis
Stevenson's *Treasure Island*. Flat, with
dunes and long stretches of sand, it is
sheltered and looks out to craggy Fidra
Island and its lighthouse. Impromptu
parties, conveniently facilitated by a
barbeque area, are de rigeur on this beach
and those with experience will know that
the sunrises are spectacular. Popular with
walkers who can go all the way to
Gullane beach from here.

boats

You can see the sea from all over
Edinburgh. Just stand at any
junction on George Street and it's
there, at the bottom of the hill,
shining and separating the city from
Fife. The port of Leith, now part of
the city, has working docks and
though the once thriving fishing
industry at Newhaven has gone, the
harbour there still welcomes small
craft. Most of the boats below call
the Firth of Forth home, but we've
included a couple of trips based on
the Forth and Clyde canal which is
newly restored and begins at Ratho,
near the airport. If you prefer not to
get on a boat, but want to catch
sight of the gannets, seals and
puffins that live on islands near
Edinburgh, look up the Daytrips
section, Scottish Seabird Centre,
North Berwick, page 149.

Bass Rock

Out of town, Map 1
The Harbour, North Berwick. 25 miles east of
Edinburgh off A1, 01620 892838
Sailings: Apr–Oct Mon–Sun 11am/2pm,
weather permitting (phone to confirm)
Adult £6, child £3
This one falls into the real sea-faring
catagory – a lovely hand-built wooden
boat, low in the water, which takes up to
66 people round the islands of North
Berwick. Fred Marr began these trips
many years ago – his son is now skipper.
And if you're left gasping for more, you
can book a special trip (parties only)
landing on Bass Rock where gannets rule.

Falkirk Wheel

Out of town, Map 1
Lime Road, Tamfourhill, Falkirk. 30 miles west
of Edinburgh off M9, Junction 5,
01324–619888, Booking Line 08700 500 208
Boat trips: Apr–Oct 9.30am–5pm; Nov–Mar
10am–3pm. Visitor Centre: Apr–Oct
9am–6.30pm; Nov–Mar 10am–5pm (last
entry half an hour before closing)
Boat trip: adult £8. Visitor centre: free
A Millennium project triumph – it's the
only rotating boat lift in the world,
replacing 11 locks that joined the Forth
and Clyde canals. The thing itself is
spectacular, somewhere between Escher
and NASA's imaginations, built by
Edinburgh architects. Best of all, you can
actually take a 45 minute trip on the
wheel. Gently turning 35 metres into the
air, the boat settles back to let you off at
the café in the visitor centre.
www.thefalkirkwheel.co.uk

Sula II on the Bass Rock trip

Inchcolm Island
Out of town, Map 1
The Harbour, South Queensferry. 9 miles
north west of Edinburgh off A90, 0131 331
4857
Check website for departure times
Adult £11, child £4.50, conc £9
Chugging out and back to Inchcolm, the
Maid of the Forth is a beginners' boat,
great for all ages. Taking up to 200
passengers a time, she meanders under the
Forth Railway Bridge, among yachts and
tankers, and on to the seals and abbey
ruins of the island. With an hour and a
half exploration time, it's worth
remembering to pack a picnic as the little
bar on board serves only snacks and
drinks. All details of special sailings,
including jazz cruises and private hire, on
the website.
www.maidoftheforth.co.uk

Isle of May
Out of town, Map 1
The Harbour, Anstruther, Fife. 50 miles north
of Edinburgh off M90/A921, 01333 310103
Sailings: May–mid Jul Mon–Thu/Sat/Sun; mid
Jul–Sep Mon–Sun. Check website or phone
for departure times
A special place, famous for its puffin and
seal colonies (best seen May/June), the
Isle of May is an hour and a half from
shore. Once there, the trip allows two
hours to explore an archeological dig,
lighthouses, stoney beaches and grassy
slopes. The small, double decker May
Princess carries up to 100. Bring your
own picnic – the bar serves drinks only.
As this is a tidal dependant, family-run
business, booking is advised.
www.isleofmay.com

Rosyth-Zeebrugge Ferries
Out of town, Map 1
Rosyth Harbour. 13 miles north west of
Edinburgh off A90, first exit on Fife side of
Forth Road Bridge, 0131 234 0870
Sailings: Mon–Sun 5pm (2 hour check in)
Tickets: £54–£484
There's a deal on this two-year old service
for everyone – you can spend as little as
£54 (return, upright seating off-peak) or as
much as £484 (return, luxury cabin, peak
time) depending on your fancy. The ferry
leaves Rosyth at 5pm, arrives Zeebrugge
11.30am. Book advised during school
holidays.
www.superfast.com

The Edinburgh Canal Centre
Outskirts, Map 1
The Bridge Inn, 27 Baird Road, Ratho. 14
miles west of Edinburgh off M8, Junction 2,
0131 333 1320/1251
Cruises: Mon–Sun, phone for details
Restaurant cruises: adult from £24.
Sightseeing cruises: adult £6, child £4,
family £15. Children's cruises: child from
£8
Five minutes from the airport, Ronnie
Rusack's long-established business is all
about Sunday lunches, pints, families and
messing about on the restored canal. As
well as a restaurant/bar on land, three
boats are in service – the art deco beauty
Ratho Princess and two restaurants, Pride
of the Union and Pride of Belhaven.
Themed cruises are popular – Murder
Mystery, Sightseeing, Summer Grills, Tea
Dances, Christmas Cruises or book
privately and dream up your own.
Booking essential.
www.bridgeinn.com

daytrips

If you must get away from this beautiful city, there are plenty of attractions close to home. Glasgow, a city of a very different flavour, is only an hour by car or train and explorable countryside even less. Look up the Beaches and Boats sections as well as checking out some of the inland destinations mentioned below.

Castles and Historic Houses

Abbotsford House
Out of town, Map 1
By Melrose. 38 miles south of Edinburgh off A7, 01896 752 043
Mar–Oct Mon–Sat 9.30am–5pm; Mar–May/Oct Sun 2– 5pm; Jun–Sep Sun 9.30am–5pm. Nov/Mar groups by appointment
Adult £4.50, child £2.25
Sir Walter Scott's home, thrillingly still owned and lived in by his sparky great great great-daughter, has escaped the history industry and is all the more magical for it. The spirit of the great man of letters is still very much alive in this solid, baronial residence which he had a hand in designing and rooms are much as they were when he lived here. The author was an inveterate collector of all things Scottish – this is the place to see Rob Roy's purse and a lock of Bonnie Prince Charlie's hair. Romance is definitely in the air.
www.melrose.bordernet.co.uk/abbotsford

Blackness Castle
Out of town, Map 1
Blackness. 18 miles east of Edinburgh off A904, 01506 834807
Apr–Sep Mon–Sun 9.30am–6.30pm; Oct–Mar Mon–Wed/Sat 9.30am–4.30pm, Thu 9.30am–12.30pm, Sun 2–4.30pm (last entry half an hour before closing)
Adult £2.20, child 75p, conc £1.60
A dark, boat-shaped building that once guarded entry to Blackness, seaport to nearby Linlithgow, this well-preserved castle is bulky and bare. Its lack of fancy boudoirs is what makes it fun – during 500 years service to kings and country it has been both prison and ammunition depot, making it a rare place for playful pirates. Views of the firth and Forth bridges are stunning and there's a tiny shop.
www.historic-scotland.gov.uk

Find Edinburgh's castles and historic houses in Culture, page 33

Dirleton Castle
Out of town, Map 1
Dirleton. 23 miles east of Edinburgh off A198, 01620 850330
Apr–Sep Mon–Sun 9.30am–6.30pm; Oct–Mar Mon–Sat 9.30–4.30pm, Sun 2–4.30pm (last entry half an hour before closing)
Adult £3, child £1, conc £2.30
A pretty, romantic castle, Dirleton has an architectural history stretching back over 700 years, but is best known for its gorgeous gardens, first cultivated in the 16th century. As well as an old bowling green, restored Victorian garden and 'arts and crafts' garden, this place lovingly nurtures the longest herbaceous border in the world – and that's official, according to the *Guinness Book of Records*.
www.historic-scotland.gov.uk

Falkland Palace
Out of town, Map 1
High Street, Falkland, Fife. 38 miles north of Edinburgh off A912, 01337 857397
Mar–Oct Mon–Sat 10am–6pm, Sun 1–5pm (shop open during winter)
Adult £3.50, child £2.60, family £9.50
A turreted, fairy-tale renaissance castle where Mary, Queen of Scots spent happy days. The state rooms inside are respectably fine, but it's the exterior (with parts dating from 1501) and gardens which are most prized here (plants for sale on site). The Real Tennis court, built in 1539, is unique, and hosts international championships of this early version of the game. The Palace of Magic festival in August is an annual event organised by the National Trust for Scotland. Phone for details. Falkland village itself is a gem, with quaint gift and antique shops and a choice of tearooms.
www.nts.org.uk

Floors Castle
Out of town, Map 1
Floors Castle, Roxburghe Estates Office, Kelso. 45 miles south east of Edinburgh off A68, 01573 223333
Easter–Oct Mon–Sun 10am–4.30pm
Adult £5.75, child £3.25, family £15
Designed and built in 1721 by two Georgian greats, Adam and Playfair, Floors is a splendid family home, with state rooms furnished with fine antiques and thousands of acres with signposted walks. The largest inhabited castle in Scotland, it is maintained by the Duke and Duchess of Roxburghe, who have made it their business to add a smart tearoom, gift shop and garden centre with an adventure playground. Phone or check website for details of the many musical, equestrian and theatrical events.
www.floorscastle.com

Linlithgow Palace
Out of town, Map 1
Kirkgate, Linlithgow. By train or 18 miles west
of Edinburgh on A803, 01506 842896
Apr–Sep Mon–Sun 9.30am–6.30pm;
Oct–Mar Mon–Sat 9.30am–4.30pm, Sun
2–4pm (last entry half an hour before closing)
Adult £3, child £1, conc £2.30
Even in its partly ruinous state (it was
burned out in 1746) you still get a real
feel for the comfortable life led in this
palace. Built round a central courtyard
with a fountain that flowed with wine at
the birth of Mary, Queen of Scots, there
are enough nooks and turnpike stairways
to make a great game of hide and seek.
Look out for the ladder window glazed
with coloured glass and the charmingly
named vomitorium. Linlithgow has plenty
of eating places and a lovely loch.
www.historic-scotland.gov

Melrose Abbey
Out of town, Map 1
Abbey Street, Melrose. 37 miles south east of
Edinburgh off A7, 01896 822562
Apr–Sep Mon–Sun 9.30am–6.30pm;
Oct–Mar Mon–Sat 9.30am–4.30pm, Sun
2–4.30pm (last entry half an hour before
closing)
Adult £3.50
Melrose is one of the prettiest towns in
the Borders, not least because of this
serene, ruined abbey dating from the early
15th century. Statues of saints and
gargoyles have miraculously survived
centuries of soldiers' and reformers'
attentions. Look out for the site of a
casket reputed to contain Robert the
Bruce's heart. A similar tranquility can be

found in the adjoining Priorwood Garden
(open all year) and across the road in the
studied simplicity of Harmony Garden, a
National Trust for Scotland property
(open Easter–Sep). A pleasant triumverate
of contemplative places.
www.historic-scotland.gov.uk

Stirling Castle
Out of town, Map 1
The Esplanade, Stirling. 37 miles north west
of Edinburgh off M9, Junction 10, 01786
450000
Apr–Sep Mon–Sun 9.30am–6pm; Oct–Mar
9.30am–5pm
Adult £7.50, child £2, conc £5.50
More domestic than military, this castle
on a rock rivals its Edinburgh counterpart.
Historic Scotland has been zealous in its
restoration: the 15th century Great Hall
shines in pristine golden glory and
medieval kitchens have been reinvented to
the hilt. Best of all is a wander round
cobbled courtyards and the romantic
flower garden where views are not only
dramatic but also cover some of the most
important territory in the history of
Scotland. Events through the year include
historical re-enactments. There are shops
and a café and weddings and conferences
are bookable.

Tantallon Castle
Out of town, Map 1
Near North Berwick. 28 miles east of
Edinburgh off A198, 01620 892727
Apr–Sep Mon–Wed 9.30am–4.30pm, Thu
9.30am–12.30pm, Sun 2–4.30pm
Adult £3, child £1, conc £2.30
A magnificent windswept ruin of a place,

SCOTTISH VIEWPOINT

The gates of Traquair, closed until Bonnie Prince Charlie returns, page 148

teetering on a promontory overlooking the North Sea. Earthwork defences and ramparts are a reminder of a turbulent past – it was the stronghold of the Red Douglas clan for centuries. On a clear day views of the Bass Rock are fabulous, but don't fret about the weather – this place is just as gob-smacking, perhaps more so in the mist.
www.historic-scotland.gov.uk

Traquair House
Out of town, Map 1
Innerleithen. 29 miles south of Edinburgh off A703, 01896 830323/785
Easter–Sep Mon–Sun noon–5pm; Jun–Aug 10.30am–5.30pm; Oct 11am–4pm
Adult £5.75, child £3.20, £16.75
The gates of this 17th century house are famously locked until Bonnie Prince Charlie returns. But through an alternative entrance, you'll find a thriving family estate with its own brewery (Traquair House Ale) and an established, well-attended summer fair (first weekend in August) which combines theatre, music and dance with craft stalls. Inside the house are secret stairs, spooky cellars, a painted, 18th century library and the room used by Mary, Queen of Scots. Check website for details of other events.
www.traquair.co.uk

Country

Dawyck Botanic Gardens
Out of town, Map 1
Stobo, Peebleshire. 30 miles south west of Edinburgh on B712, 01721 760254
Apr–Sep Mon–Sun 10am–6pm; Mar/Oct Mon–Sun 10am–5pm; mid–end Feb/mid–end Nov Mon–Sun 10am–4pm
Adult £3, child £1, family £7
Dawyck is a world class arboretum. You can hug conifers dating back to 1680 and gawp at some of the tallest trees in Britain. The biggest celebrity in this forest of superlatives is the magnificent Dawyck Beech, hard to miss on account of its size. Rare plants, specimen trails and the world's first ever funghi reserve make this an essential destination for nature lovers. Guided walks are lead by experts and there is a tearoom and shop selling plants.
www.rbge.org.uk

Loch Lomond
Out of town, Map 1
Loch Lomond Shores, Balloch. 70 miles west of Edinburgh on M9 to Stirling, A811 to Loch Lomond
Part of Scotland's first national park, this picturesque loch is a great getaway. But bear in mind it's not entirely unspoiled. The Loch Lomond Shores development (Mon–Sun 10am–6pm) has plonked a

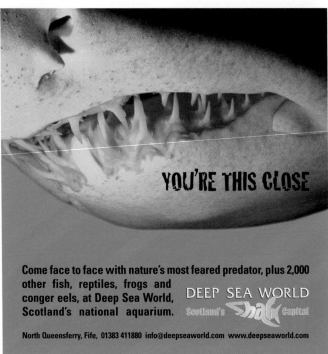

major retailing boulevard, headed by posh shop Jenners, right next to Balloch village. If you prefer the great outdoors, contact Can You Experience Loch Lomond (01389 602 576, www.canyouexperience.com) which offers weekend breaks, day hiking trips, canoeing and mountain biking by the hour from £18.
www.lochlomondshores

Portmore Game Fisheries
Out of town, Map 1
20 Avon Grove, Penicuik. 10 miles south of Edinburgh off A701, 01968 675684
Mon–Sun Apr–Oct
Fishing: from £19 per day
Three miles of bank fishing and 12 boats on a scenic little loch – booking is advised. Local brown trout are stocked alongside hard-fighting rainbow trout and freshwater barracuda. A day session (four fish limit) costs £18 and boat hire (two rods/10 fish limit) is £38. Gamefish (6a Howe Street, 0131 220 6465) is a good source of equipment and information, while inner city fishing is available on the Water of Leith (permits from 0131 455 7367, www.wateroffleith.edin.org).
www.portmore.co.uk

RSPB Vane Farm and Loch Leven National Nature Reserve
Out of town, Map 1
Kinross. 27 miles north of Edinburgh off M90, Junction 5, 01577 862 355
Visitor centre Mon–Sun 10am–5pm. Reserve dawn–dusk
Adult £3, child 50p, family £6
Hoaching with birds, this reserve has woodland trails, a hill path with fabulous vistas and a wetland trail down to all those fowl on the loch. In one of the three hides, you can spy on tufted duck, lapwings, redshanks and, in winter, up to 20,000 pink-footed geese. Even if twitching isn't your bag, the sheer numbers make this an impressive place. Café, shop and exhibition are housed in the cottage and there's a picnic area outside. Check website for details of events, including bat nights and crafts fairs.
www.rspb.org.uk

Scottish Seabird Centre
Out of town, Map 1
North Berwick. 25 miles east of Edinburgh on A198, 01620 890202
Easter–Oct Mon–Sun 10am–6pm; Nov–Easter 10am–4pm
Adult £4.95, conc £3.50, family £13.50, weekly tickets and annual membership
Great architecture, a sea view café and sealife in the raw have conspired to make this five-star attraction a hot family destination since it opened in 2001. The spectacular Big Brother for birds – three giant screens showing live webcam

coverage – homes in on the Isle of May seals, Craigleith puffins and Bass Rock gannets. It's much more exciting than it sounds, particularly if you time it right and stop by at nesting, hatching or birthing times.
www.seabird.org

Glasgow

CCA – Centre for Contemporary Art
Out of town, Map 1
350 Sauchiehall Street, Glasgow. By train or 45 miles west of Edinburgh off M8, Junction 18, 0141 352 4900
Tue–Thu 11am–11pm, Fri/Sat 11am–midnight, Sun 11am–6pm
Free (charge for special exhibitions and events)
With the internationally reknowned, Charles Rennie Mackintosh-designed Glasgow School of Art just a hop up the hill, this arts centre (formerly Third Eye Centre) has been at the heart of Glasgow cultural life for nearly 30 years. As well as hosting über-trendy art award Beck's Futures, it complements its many exhibitions with film screenings, video installations and music. Refurbished into a paragon of cool, it houses one of the city's most contemporary bars, artist-designed, naturally. The award-winning restaurant, Tempus, is a minimalist's dream with food to match.
www.cca-glasgow.com

Glasgow Museum of Transport
Out of town, Map 1
Kelvin Hall, 1 Bunhouse Road. By train or 46 miles west of Edinburgh off M8, Junction 18, 0141 287 2720
Mon–Thu/Sat 10am–5pm, Fri/Sun 11am–5pm
Free
Little boys' paradise, the popular Museum of Transport sets the scene with a reconstruction of a 1938 Glasgow street with lovingly preserved steam locomotives, horse-drawn trams, vintage buses, motorbikes and cars. The Clyde's proud shipbuilding history and a shoogle round the origins of the city's Clockwork Orange underground are other highlights. There are snacks on site, but it's not far to 87 Byres Road and the nostalgic booths of the family-run University Café (opened in 1918).
www.glasgowmuseums.com

Glasgow Science Centre
Out of town, Map 1
50 Pacific Quay, Govan. By train or 49 miles west of Edinburgh off M8, Junction 20, 0141 420 5000
Science Mall Mon–Sun 10am–6pm
Adult £6.95, child £4.95, family £18.95
To really appreciate Scotland's reputation for producing great inventors and

engineers, a visit to Glasgow's Science Centre is a must. Its shaky 400ft tower notwithstanding, the Science Centre has been a welcome addition to the city presenting brave new worlds of science and technology in an entertaining, accessible way, particularly through the panoramic screenings of the gargantuan 80x60ft IMAX cinema (admission extra).
www.gsc.org.uk

Heritage and Museums

Bo'ness and Kinneil Railway
Out of town
Bo'ness Station, Union Street. 22 miles west of Edinburgh on A706, 01506 822298
Apr–Oct Sat/Sun; July/Aug Mon–Sun. Trains at 11am, 12.15pm, 1.45pm, 3pm, 4.15pm
Check website for ticket prices
These old giants take passengers on a sedate seven mile round trip to Birkhill. If you fancy something themed, you can go for a day out with Thomas, join the Diesel Gala or take the Easter Egg or Santa Train (which you can't get on for love nor money unless you book in advance). The Scottish Railway Exhibition is part of the trip and if that isn't enough, you can opt to visit the fire clay mine at Birkhill which goes deep under the Avon Gorge. Trips further afield, using old railway stock, are also organised by the Scottish Railway Preservation Society, keepers of this site.
www.srps.org.uk

Museum of Flight
Out of town, Map 1
East Fortune Airfield, East Fortune. 23 miles east of Edinburgh off A1, 01620 880308
Easter–Jun Mon–Sun 10.30am–5pm; Jul/Aug Mon–Sun 10.30am–6pm; Nov–Easter Mon–Sun 10.30am–4pm
Adult £3, child free
A hands-on and climb-in museum on the site of a 1915 fighter base. Inside the hangars, you'll find the Puss Moth, Dragon, the oldest existing Harrier Jump Jet, a Spitfire and a Messerschmitt Me 163 Komet: over 50 planes make this the biggest aviation collection in the UK and a must for planespotters. There is a café and this is also the site of the huge, open air East Fortune Sunday Market. Flying and other (vintage cars, fire engines) events take off year round.
www.nms.ac.uk/flight

New Lanark World Heritage Site
Out of town, Map 1
New Lanark Mills, South Lanarkshire. 35 miles south west of Edinburgh on A70, 01555 661 345
Mon–Sun 11am–5pm
Adult £5.95, child £3.95, family £16.95
This beautifully restored 18th century model village near the Falls of Clyde is a cracker. The embodiment of his vision of industrial life, it is a thought-provoking reminder of mill manager Robert Owen's progressive ideas. The audio-visual presentation *Annie McLeod's Story*, recounts mill life through the spirit of a young girl, but the real star of this experience are those heavenly tenements built into a gorge where the roar of the falls never stops.
www.newlanark.org

Preston Mill and Phantassie Doocot
Out of town, Map 1
East Linton. 24 miles east of Edinburgh off A1, 01620 860426
Apr–Sep Thu–Mon noon–5pm
Adult £3.50, child £2.60, family £9.50
This is a blissful, bucolic spot with the mill wheel still turning, white ducks on the pond and the jaunty, 17th century building close to but perfectly hidden from the road. Now owned by the National Trust for Scotland, it is still in creaky, working condition. Watching the Heath Robinson machinery is fun and you can't help wondering how they got those mill stones upstairs. There's a small shop and tea can be taken in the pretty village next door.
www.nts.org.uk

Scotland's Secret Bunker
Out of town, Map 1
Crown Buildings, Troywood, near St Andrews, Fife. 50 miles north of Edinburgh off A915, 01333 310301
Apr–Oct Mon–Sun 10am–6pm (last entry 5pm)
Adult £6.95, conc £3.95
This strange relic of the Cold War is hidden 100 feet under an innocuous looking farmhouse near St Andrews. Built as a hideout for the Scottish government and BBC in the event of a nuclear attack, the facilities would have been cutting edge in the 1950s, but now look more like the set of an early Bond film. Although some ropey-looking old shop models dressed as military workers are a bit amateurish, this building – only removed from the Official Secrets Act quite recently – provides a genuinely fascinating insight into feelings about nuclear war half a century ago.
www.secretbunker.co.uk

MY FAVOURITE PLACE

Arthur's Seat (Holyrood Park)
'You can see all of Edinburgh, but you feel like you're in the middle of nowhere.'
Tim Makin, DJ, Smokey & the Bandit

parks

City Parks

Blackford Hill and Hermitage of Braid
Southside, Map 2 off F10
Access from Observatory Road, Cluny Gardens or Hermitage of Braid, 0131 447 7145
Contact Ranger Service for guided walks
Rising from the genteel streets of Morningside, this is the real thing – a country park in the city with windswept hillside paths walking up to some cracking views. Kids and grannies love Blackford Pond's sheltered benches, ducks and swans. In the valley to the east, historic Hermitage House is now a base for the Countryside Ranger Service.
www.cecrangerservice

Bruntsfield Links
Southside, Map 2 E9
Melville Drive to south, Bruntsfield Place, Terrace and Crescent to north
In the 18th century golf was invented in Scotland, and the deer and boar were shunted out to make way for several hallowed clubs. Today, a short nine hole course and putting green (see Sport) remains within the boundaries of a 30 acre city park. Both park and course are chocka all year round and there's a dog-free play area for small children.

Calton Hill
City Centre, Map 2 I4
Main entrance just past 29 Waterloo Place
One of Edinburgh's famous city centre hills, this is in a class of its own. Rising from the east end of Princes Street, its cluster of monuments and 200 year old observatories perched on top create an atmosphere which is eccentric, not to say downright odd. The twelve columns of Edinburgh's Disgrace (1822), so called because of controversy over its completion, is a favourite for photoshoots. Views are spectacular and the hill's rough terrain is used regularly for pageants and performances. See Beltane in Festivals.

Holyrood Park
Old Town, Map 2 J7
Entrances at Holyrood Road, London Road, Dalkeith Road and Duddingston Road West
Road through park closed Sun
This is Edinburgh's *Central Park* – the place where everyone goes. 650 hectares of raw landscape, including the famous 250m climb of Arthur's Seat, are stretched out behind the Royal Mile. Hunting ground to kings and burial site for plague victims, it was a favourite haunt of Mary, Queen of Scots, Sir Walter Scott and Bonnie Prince Charlie. Now it's a place to walk, jog, climb, exercise the dog, roll Easter eggs, picnic, feed the swans (on one of three lochs) and celebrate (Arthur's Seat is scaled by revellers on May Day and Hogmanay). The Scottish Parliament, Palace of Holyroodhouse and Edinburgh

The palm house at the Royal Botanic Garden, page 154

University are all lucky neighbours of this spectacular resource. Parking near palace and at all lochsides.

Inverleith Park
New Town, Map 2 B1
Access from Inverleith Place, Fettes Avenue and Arboretum Road

A bustling Victorian city park encircled by tall trees and sliced down the middle by a wide pedestrian boulevard. There's lots going on here – allotments, petanque club, weekend model boat meets on the pond, bowling, cycling, jogging, football craziness and a pretty good children's playground. When you're out of puff, there are even a few secluded spots for taking a break. An ice cream van is stationed at the east gates in summer opposite the neighbouring Royal Botanic Garden.

Leith Links
Leith, Map 3 J5
Access from John's Place, Links Gardens and Seafield Place

It used to stretch all the way to Portobello, has seen duels and executions, and was also James VI's favourite golf course. Excitements on this scale (though it has more recently been home to the chainsaw acrobats of Archaos during the Fringe) are all in the past, and it now has fun play equipment, allotments, cricket and football pitches, putting and bowling and hosts the Leith Festival. See Festivals.

The Meadows
Southside, Map 2 G9
Bounded by Melville Drive

Jawbone Walk must be one of Edinburgh's most heavily beaten tracks, leading tenement-living Marchmont dwellers through the Meadows to work in town and university every day. On the site of the drained Borough Loch, this 18th century park with its 1200 mature trees (the pink cherries are heavy-laden in spring) is now much used for football, cricket, tennis (see Sport), bowling, frisbee, jogging, kids (small playpark) and just hanging out. The Meadows Festival (see Festivals) is held in first week of June.

Country Parks

Cammo House
Outskirts, Map 1
Cammo Estate, bordered by Cammo Road, off Queensferry Road, 0131 447 7145

Unpublicised but not unloved, this country park in town was Scotland's first landscaped garden, created by Sir John Clerk in the 18th century. Already run down, it transferred from private to council ownership in the 1970s and has since let its hair down to become lovely, wildish parkland. As well as the ruins of the house itself, there are woodland walks and 100 hectares of open space. A place to discover.
www.cecrangerservice.co.uk

Corstorphine Hill
Outskirts, Map 1
Access and car park from Clermiston Road North, 0131 447 7145
Contact Ranger Service for badger walks

Top of the hill country, mostly wooded, this 75 hectare park is home to Edinburgh's best known badger community. Surrounded by city, this is a wild place you can really get lost in. Upgrading is in progress.
www.cecrangerservice.co.uk

Play at Victoria Park, page 154

Craigmillar Castle Park
Outskirts, Map 1
Craigmillar
Craigmillar Castle Park pretty much has it all – remarkable views, wildlife and winding paths for walking the environs of Craigmillar Castle (see Castles and Historic Houses). 60 hectares of wilderness provide ample space for those escaping city hustle. And keep your eyes peeled – there are buzzards and roe deer in those hills.

Cramond Foreshore Walk
Outskirts, Map 1
Cramond Village to Granton Point
No sandy beaches, but breezy seaside paths lead away from one of Edinburgh's oldest villages to the meadow and woodlands of Gypsy Brae, a good place for playing and picnics. At low tide it's especially fun to hike out to Cramond Island. The River Almond Walk starts among the yachts in the small harbour and there is a pub with plenty of parking.

Dalkeith Country Park
Outskirts, Map 1
Dalkeith. 7 miles south east of Edinburgh off A68, 0131 654 1666
Aug–Oct Mon–Sun 10am–5.30pm
Adult/child £2, family £7
Climb high into the tree canopy and slide down the huge slides – even adults are tempted. The best adventure park in or around town, this forest fun is run by the Buccleuch estate. Equipment is regularly updated and added to. Nearby, caves on the South Esk river and a stunning 600-year-old oak wood provide unique trails for bikes and walkers. Horses, ducks, picnic facilities, café and shop are all on site. Don't miss the derelict 1840s conservatory and its dark, underground cellar. Spooky.
www.dalkeithcountrypark.co.uk

River Almond Walkway
Outskirts, Map 1
From Cramond Village to Cammo Park
A walk on the wild side of the city with clifftop woodlands, ponds, meadowland, wildflowers and riverbank life. Less of a park than a journey, this trail makes a good family ramble with rough paths, stairs and a touch of the countryside.

MY FAVOURITE PARK

Princes Street Gardens
'It's really hot there in summer and you can get a sandwich from Marks & Spencers and sit on the grass hill. Then you can roll down it.'
Faith, age 10

city5s
GO FLY A KITE

■ **Arthur's Seat, Holyrood Park**
The city's highest climb (280 metres of extinct volcano). Panoramas!

■ **Calton Hill**
Fly in full view of Edinburgh's main thoroughfare, Princes Street. Gaze out to sea too.

■ **Meadows**
More trees here, but it's the kind of place where anything goes. Frisbees might be safer.

■ **Blackford Hill**
This wild place, in gentile Morningside, is perfectly open for kite experts.

■ **Portobello Beach**
Get the sea breezes into your lungs and your kite (see Beaches).

Vogrie Country Park
Out of town, Map 1
By Gorebridge. 5 miles south of Edinburgh off the A68/A7, 01875 821 990
Mon–Sun 7.30am until one hour before sunset
Parking £1
Take the kids for a crash around this former estate – 105 hectares of wooded Victorian parkland with ponds, rivers and meadows. Great adventure playground replete with the essential death slide, crazy golf and a tea room in which to catch your breath.

Water of Leith
Citywide
From Leith docks to Balerno, 0131 455 7367
Visitor centre open Apr–Sep Mon–Sun 10am–4pm; Oct–Mar Mon–Sun 10am–4pm
Adult £2, child £1.20, family £7
The upgrading of the Water of Leith Walkway is finally complete. And what a spectacular success it is: 35 kilometres of riverbank pathways suitable for cyclists and walkers begin in the Pentlands, meander through Balerno village, take in the city centre and end at Leith docks. Kingfishers have been sighted and brown trout are now common – fishing permits (see Sport) are available from the visitor centre, a newly-designed building with the river's history unplugged. A treasure.
www.waterofleith.edin.org

Gardens

Dunbar's Close Garden
Old Town, Map 2 I5
Royal Mile, next to Canongate Kirk
A tiny, secret retreat – somewhere for the folk next door at the new Scottish Parliament to get away from it all. Formally laid out with box parterre and clipped yew, it reflects a 17th century style when long gardens like this would have been common in this area. Possibly a bit isolated for some, it's a contemplative place for a takeaway lunch from one of the nearby cafés.

Malleny Garden
Outskirts, Map 1
Balerno. 8 miles south west of Edinburgh off A70, 0131 449 2283
Mon–Sun 10am–6pm, or dusk if earlier
Honesty box £2
A National Trust for Scotland walled garden spilling over with roses and old-fashioned herbaceous borders. Four 400-year-old yew trees provide architectural drama and surrounding woodlands offer peaceful walks. Did you know that there was such a thing as the National Bonsai Collection for Scotland? Well, it's here too.
www.nts.org.uk

Princes Street Gardens
City Centre, Map 2 E6
South side of Princes Street, intersected by the Mound
A cherished asset, this garden runs full length along Edinburgh's main shopping street. Bridging the Old and New Towns it is spectacular – a deep valley with rosebeds, lawns and over 2000 trees. One of Britain's first public parks, it was built in the hollow of a drained loch. Separated down the middle by the National Galleries' complex, the east side boasts the Scott Monument (see Architecture), while the west has the oldest floral clock in the world, 101 years old in 2003, the Ross Theatre (see Music), and a small, busy playpark. In December and early January, the east side hosts the city's Capital Christmas (see Festivals).

Royal Botanic Garden
New Town, Map 2 D1
Access from Inverleith Row and Arboretum Place, 0131 552 7171
Mon–Sun open at 9.30am all year. Closes 4pm Nov–Jan, 5pm Feb/Oct, 6pm Mar/Sep, 7pm Apr–Aug
Free
Busier than ever, the Botanics always seems peaceful. Unarguably the most beautiful formal park in Edinburgh, it is also a serious garden, renowned for its botanical collections and as a research centre, second only to Kew. The tallest Palm House in Britain has recently been restored and the world famous rock garden (a favourite of hide-and-seekers) stars 5,000 plants. Inverleith House (see Art Galleries) is an exhibition venue of reknown and the Terrace Café offers lunch and snacks. Note there are no bikes, picnics, sports or dogs allowed – just feast on all that horticultural eye candy.
www.rbge.org.uk

Play Parks

King George V Park
New Town, Map 2 F2
Bounded by Eyre Place and Scotland Street
A great big chute takes you from Scotland Street down into this little hollow, a favourite playpark for kids all over the city. Swings and roundabouts with a difference, mostly for the under tens, are safe and away from roads. Grassy, with paved paths for cyclists of all ages.

Saughton Park and Fort Saughton
Outskirts, Map 2 off A9
Bounded by Balgreen Road, Stevenson Drive and Water of Leith
A multi-purpose park with open spaces, playing fields and sports centre. It is perhaps best know outside the neighbourhood though for its spectacular showpiece rose garden (13,000 plants), and for its offshoot Fort Saughton, a spacious, creative playpark, with lots of active fun for the under tens.

Victoria Park
Leith, Map 3 D3
Bounded by Newhaven Road and Craighall Road
A neighbourhood park near the Water of Leith, Victoria is visited by non-locals for its up-to-the-minute playpark. Mobbed by kids after the three local schools are out, it has a selection of brightly coloured, new-fangled slides, wobbly things, climbing and hanging bits. Compact, but well-designed for a crowd, this fenced-off area has seating for adults and keeps the little monkeys busy for hours.

Woodcraft

Four Winds Inspiration Centre
New Town, Map 2 C2
The Pavilion, Inverleith Park, Arboretum Place, 0131 332 2229
Phone for opening times
As well as carving up the city's diseased, dead elm wood into useful commodities like mushroom sculptures, this is the place to collect new-age skills. Spinning, weaving, beading, furniture-making and all sorts of wholesome crafts are offered in day or block classes. Site is next to Inverleith Park. Check website for the year-round programme.
www.four-winds.org.uk

The Caledonian Hilton, page 157

staying over

staying over

hotels & b&bs

Edinburgh can have over a million guests staying over. Angelina Jolie likes the Balmoral. Tony Blair chose the Howard last time. The newly glammified country house, Prestonfield, has entertained Elton John. Bohemians and shy celebs might prefer a boutique hote. And then there are the legions of b&bs, many of them excellent, lots of them city central. We've put together a few recommended ones here. VisitScotland will fill in the gaps: Brochure hotline: 08705 511 511 Tourist Information: 0131 332 2433

Expensive

The Balmoral
City Centre, Map 2 G5
1 Princes Street, 0131 556 2414
Double room: from £160
With the best address in town, this is the five-star choice of the Manolo heeled – Kylie and Angelina Jolie slept here during their 2003 MTV awards visit. Presiding over the east end of Princes Street, next to Waverley Station, this Victorian pile (see Architecture) is topped with Edinburgh's answer to Big Ben, traditionally set a few minutes fast to keep train travellers on time. Number One, a popular, wallet-fleecing, fine dining room is one of the very few Michelin-starred restaurants in town. Afternoon tea is served daily 3–5pm in the splended Palm Court.
www.roccofortehotels.com

The Bonham
West End, Map 2 C5
35 Drumsheugh Gardens, 0131 226 6050
Double room: from £195
Traditional with high ceilings, wood panelling accented with colour, deco furniture and Scottish art combine to create one of Edinburgh's most popular and artfully designed boutique hotels. A discrete place with award-winning style, quiet but city central, it is a bolthole to actors, high-fliers and those who just love the perfect place. The restaurant, much used by non-residents, serves contemporary, organic food in simpatico surroundings.
www.thebonham.com

The Caledonian Hilton
City Centre, Map 2 D6
4 Princes Street, 0131 222 8888
Double room: from £215
The 'Caley', as it's known locally, is an Edinburgh institution – a grand dame celebrating 101 years in service. Eight storeys of red sandstone, it dominates the west end. Inside, period features – a sweeping, central staircase, 50s wildlife murals, 20s kitsch in the Pompadour restaurant – make it other than ordinary. Hilton, the new owner, is sticking with traditional lines on the whole, but has refurbished 50 of the 250 bedrooms in contemporary comfort. Afternoon tea served daily. Leisure club with swimming pool.
www.hilton.com/caledonian

Channings
New Town, Map 2 B4
15 South Learmonth Gardens, 0131 332 3232
Double room: from £185
Once home to polar explorer Sir Ernest Shackleton, Channings is now a boutique hotel, owned by the company that has made such a success in town with the Bonham and the Howard. In a quiet Victorian terrace, near the city centre, it has panoramic views from its top floors. Recently refurbished, a contemporary, creamy feel is creeping in, though antiques and tartan remain in parts. Four-posters and baths built for two are bliss. Channings and its lighter-style sister Ochre Vita are restaurants run to high standards, by ex-(fitz)Henry chef, Hubert Lamort. A classy, comfortable hideaway.
www.channings.co.uk

The Glasshouse
City Centre, Map 2 H4
2 Greenside Place, 0131 525 8200
Double room: from £175
Controversial and sexy, this five-star hotel combines the facade of an old church with a contemporary glass structure to dramatic effect. Two minutes from Princes Street, it occupies the fifth and sixth floors of the Omni Leisure Complex, which opened in 2003. Guests of this stylish hotel, which cost £7m, can enjoy a two-acre rooftop garden, as well as membership of the Holmes Place gym next door. There is no restaurant.
www.theetoncollection.com

The Howard
New Town, Map 2 F3
34 Great King Street, 0131 557 3500
Double room: from £275
The ultimate boutique hotel. Like its sisters the Bonham and Channings, it makes the most of its historic interiors. Converted from several Georgian townhouses, just 15 rooms, some of them luxury suites, accommodate well-kent faces like Sean Connery and Tony Blair, in the best possible taste. Room service is available at all times. Richly furnished with antiques, paintings and chandeliers, this is an establishment at the top of its range.
www.thehoward.com

Parliament House Hotel
City Centre, Map 2 H4
15 Calton Hill, 0131 478 4000
Double room: from £160
Named a few years back when the new
Scottish Parliament had planned to sit in
the next door Royal High School, this
restored townhouse hotel, part Georgian,
part Jacobean, is traditionally furnished in
colourful style. Seconds away from the
Princes Street throngs, it offers a
comfortable, quiet retreat. Best rooms are
those with views over the city. A bright
basement bistro provides breakfast.
www.scotland-hotels.co.uk

Prestonfield
Southside, Map 2 off K10
Priestfield Road, 0131 225 7800
Double room: from £225
If you're feeling indulgent, where better to
stay than in the heavenly historic setting of
Prestonfield? Recently bought by James
Thomson, proprietor of the Witchery
restaurant, it has been given a fabulous
£2m face lift, touching up its luxurious
original 17th century interiors and new
wing. Guests have included Benjamin
Franklin and more recently Elton John.
www.prestonfield.com

The Scotsman
Old Town, Map 2 H6
20 North Bridge, 0131 556 5565
Double room: from £145
Not long ago this building was full of
journalists beating deadlines: it is now
one of Edinburgh's top hotels. Retaining
some fabulous original features – the
name of the venerable *Scotsman* itself,
the marble staircase and wood-panelled
editor's office (book it for the night) –
the new incumbents have created a smart
hotel with tailored lines and serious
comfort. Some rooms have views and
there is a glamorous spa with a steel
pool.
www.thescotsmanhotel.co.uk

Sheraton Grand
West End, Map 2 D7
1 Festival Square, 0131 229 9131
Double room: from £180
A modern, upmarket business hotel, this
one of a chain caters to the surrounding
financial district. Overlooking Festival
Square, it is next door to a cultural
cluster that includes the Traverse, Usher
Hall, Royal Lyceum and Filmhouse.
ONE spa, at the top, attracts lots of non-
residents and is possibly Edinburgh's

Colonial welcome at the Original Raj, page 161

most glamorous pampering place, complete with open rooftop hot pool. Days and half-days (from £40) are positively snapped up.
www.sheraton.com/grandedinburgh

The Witchery by the Castle
Old Town, Map 2 F6
352 Castlehill, 0131 225 5613
Suite: from £225
There are just seven exclusive suites in this 16th century merchant's house, once a meeting place of satanists. Richly romantic in reds, black and gold, they cater for those who wish to indulge in style. No room service, but there are galley kitchens in some rooms. Downstairs one of Edinburgh's most popular up-market, magical restaurants serves its own brand of classic Scottish cuisine.
www.thewitchery.com

Moderate

Apex International Hotel
Old Town, Map 2 F7
31–35 Grassmarket, 0131 300 3456
Double room: from £120
One of four Apex hotels in the city, this former university building has a welcoming glass frontage and airy design. Rooms with castle views are slightly pricier than standard but with two double beds, potentially economic. Surrounded by the historic Grassmarket, close to clubland and over the hill from Princes Street, this is a pretty handy spot to land. The hotel restaurant Agua, serves international grub at easy prices (£9.95 for three courses).
www.apexhotels.co.uk

Bank Hotel
Old Town, Map 2 H6
1 South Bridge, 0131 556 9940
Double room: from £110
If you're looking for somewhere a little different, this central inn could be just the thing. As the name suggests, it was once a counting house – it now has nine comfy, quirky rooms, each themed round a famous Scot. It's a playful idea executed with some taste. Charles Rennie Mackintosh, David Livingstone and John Logie Baird are among the chosen few. Breakfast is served in the bank manager's office.
www.festival-inns.co.uk

Christopher North House Hotel
New Town, Map 2 D4
6 Gloucester Place, 0131 225 2720
Double room: from £120
A cosy little place near Stockbridge, an area with a friendly, village atmosphere and a colourful collection of specialist food shops, cafés, boutiques and good pubs. Understated on the outside, North's is decorated full-on inside with plush drapes, striped wallpaper and gilded mirrors. The name, incidentally, is taken from the pseudonym of a celebrated Edinburgh writer who lived here.
www.christophernorth.co.uk

The George Hotel
City Centre, Map 2 F5
19–21 George Street, 0131 225 1251
Double room: from £105
Hub of the social side of the annual Television Festival in August, this lavishly decorated Georgian hotel services Edinburgh's classiest shopping street. A modern extension stretches out back, so ask if you want one of its older rooms – many of them have dreamy views of the Firth of Forth or the castle. The cosy tartan bar and two restaurants, Le Chambertin and Carvery, are run on traditional lines. An old favourite, now run by Intercontinental.
www.edinburgh.intercontinental.com

Greens Hotel
West End, Map 2 A6
24 Eglinton Crescent, 0131 337 1565/6311
Double room: from £140
Another in the legion of attractive Georgian townhouses in quiet, convenient locations not far from the city centre. Many rooms have views of the not too distant coast and hills. Decor here is elegantly traditional. Evening meals, conference and meeting facilities all available on a small scale.
www.crerarhotels.com

Malmaison
Leith, Map 3 I3
1 Tower Place, 0131 468 5000
Double room: from £125
One of Edinburgh's first contemporary hotels, Malmaison still sets standards for reliable chic. Formerly a seamen's mission, the red sandstone building has a plum position at the heart of Leith's restaurant district, overlooking the docks. Rooms have bold, colourful style, many with sea views. Much frequented by non-residents, the Brasserie is sophisticated and serves accomplished meals, while the adjoining café-bar spills into the courtyard on warm days.
www.malmaison.com

Newington Cottage
Southside, Map 2 J10
15 Blacket Place, 0131 668 1935
Double room: from £80
A Regency cottage with tranquil gardens, in a leafy conservation area within walking distance of the city centre. Rooms are very spacious and lavishly furnished. A really splendid hideaway.
www.newcot.demon.co.uk

The Point Hotel
West End, Map 2 E7
34 Bread Street, 0131 221 5555
Double room: from £105
A hip, hot hotel. Designed and owned by architect Andrew Doolan, the Point has been fashioned from a Co-op department store to incorporate 140 beautiful bedrooms in shock block colours. On ground level, the spacious restaurant and bar are frequented by a youthful, local office crowd. The look is New York and the food is good Scottish contemporary at fantastic prices (around £15 for three courses). Monboddo, next door, is a cocktail kind of bar. Now one of a crowd of boutique hotels, the Point is still first choice for arty types.
www.point-hotel.co.uk

rick's
City Centre, Map 2 E5
55A Frederick Street, 0131 622 7800
Double room: from £117.50
Cashmere blankets and rich, minimalist style make this boutique hotel good value city centre luxury. Built into a Georgian block, the interior is seriously 'designed' with wood and tan downstairs and soft lilac looks in the 10 bedrooms. The groovy basement restaurant/bar is packed at weekends, a fact that does not disturb those relaxing above – rooms are well away from the action. Popular with visiting celebrities, this is the perfect base for a *Sex in the City* shop in George Street's fashion strip – the Manolo Blahniks are at the far end in Harvey Nic's.
www.ricksedinburgh.co.uk

Inexpensive

Ailsa Craig Hotel
New Town, Map 2 J4
42 Royal Terrace, 0131 556 1022
Double room: from £50
This independent guest house is on a quiet terrace close to the Playhouse Theatre. A 1820s family town house, it has traditionally styled interiors which complement its neo-classical architecture.
www.townhousehotels.co.uk

Bar Java
Leith, Map 3 I3
48/52 Constitution Street, 0131 553 2020
Double room: from £60
The people at Bar Java aren't just in the business of providing pints: this cosy bar situated in the lively area of Leith also offers reasonably priced accommodation only a mile from the city centre. The small, informal hotel bit has nine tastefully decorated rooms. Facilities are pretty basic and include a shared bathroom but there are extensive refurbishments in the offing.
www.hotelbarjava.com

The Green House
Southside, Map 2 C10
14 Hartington Gardens, 0131 622 7634
Double room: from £30
In leafy Bruntsfield, an area with boutiques and good restaurants, this vegetarian guest house is a 20 minute walk from Princes Street. Based in a family home, rooms are bright and airy with original features and pleasant furnishings. The breakfast menu is a whopper for lovers of the full B&B experience. A vegetarian society award winner. Two yoga centres close by (see Sport).
www.greenhouse-edinburgh.com

Grosvenor Gardens Hotel
West End, Map 2 B7
1 Grosvenor Gardens, 0131 313 3415
Double room: from £55
A Victorian town house in a quiet street, just across the road from Haymarket Station and minutes from the city centre. Some good restaurants, cafés and two of Scotland's national galleries are right on your doorstep. No smoking throughout, the house is richly furnished along traditional lines.
www.stayinedinburgh.com

Ibis
Old Town, Map 2 H6
6 Hunter Square, 0131 240 7000
Double room: from £50
Next to the historic Tron Kirk and just off the Royal Mile, this basic hotel is an ideal base for exploring the city's numerous attractions. Bright, modern and still new, it has good facilities and some tasty views across the city.
www.accor-hotels.com

International Guest House
Southside, Map 2 I10
37 Mayfield Gardens, 0131 667 2511/9833
Double room: from £35
Close to the trees and green of the Meadows, this lovely Victorian town house has traditional features top to bottom with en-suite facilities adding up to date comfort. Ample private parking for guests. Evening meals on request.
www.accommodation-edinburgh.com

MW Guesthouse
Southside, Map 2 K10
94 Dalkeith Road, 0131 662 9265
Double room: from £50
Crisp linen and a contemporary colour scheme mark this guesthouse out from the rest. 14 ensuite rooms, all named after famous Scotch whiskies, are all so tastefully decorated they are show house perfect. Some rooms have views of Salisbury Crags and Arthur's Seat, as well as details like traditional shutters and marble fireplaces.
www.mwguesthouse.co.uk

Original Raj
West End, Map 2 off A7
6 West Coates, 0131 346 1333
Double room: from £40
With a white elephant in its front garden and chunky furniture from Jaipur inside, the Original Raj is like no other Edinburgh hotel. Owned by locally renowned chef Tommy Miah, who also runs the popular Raj restaurant in Leith, it has a pretty spicy dining room too. The 17 richly coloured rooms are great value and keep you only minutes away from the city centre.
www.rajempire.com

Premier Lodge Hotel
West End, Map 2 E8
Lauriston Place, 0870 990 6610
Double room: £54
A spanking new gaff right next door to Edinburgh College of Art, this hotel is part of a chain, but offers good quality city centre accommodation for tight budgets. Unlike the other premier branch at 94–96 Grassmarket nearby, this one also has an integral snazzy bar, Bar Est.
www.premierlodge.co.uk

Six Mary's Place
New Town, Map 2 C3
Raeburn Place, Stockbridge, 0131 332 8965
Double room: from £60
Recently refurbished Georgian town house, with modern decor in keeping with the style of the property. Period features and access to a beautiful garden. Very friendly service and free internet access for guests. Smoke-free environment and vegetarian breakfast available.
www.sixmarysplace.co.uk

Stuart House
New Town, Map 2 G2
12 East Claremont Street, 0131 557 9030
Double room: from £70
A friendly, family guest house in a Georgian terrace house with all the trimmings – high ceilings, shutters and cornices. No smoking with free street parking, it is only 10 minutes' walk from the city centre.
www.stuartguesthouse.com

Travel Lodge
Old Town, Map 2 H6
33 St Mary's Street, 0870 191 1637
Double room: from £52.95
This modern hotel is off the Royal Mile and close to many attractions. All rooms have double beds but there are also family and disabled rooms available. The café and bar are open until 11pm for guests.
www.travelodge.co.uk

Once you're settled in, turn to Bars & Pubs page 81, Cafes and Takeaways page 92 and Restaurants page 100

self**catering**

Freewheelers head for the city's many hostels which are cosy, amazingly priced and not just for students - most now have rooms as well as dorms. We've included camping and apartments in this list for a full range of options.

Apartments

Canon Court Luxury Serviced Apartments
New Town, Map 2 F2
20 Canonmills, 0131 474 7000
Apartments: from £67 per night
These five year old apartments on the edge of the New Town provide good, central accomodation: 42 one and two bed flats with parking and twice-weekly servicing. Special deals at certain times of year. Facilities round here are hotting up with the impressive, newly opened Union Yoga and Au Gourmand deli satisfying very different corporal needs.
www.canoncourt.co.uk

No 5 Self-Catering Apartments
Outskirts, Map 1
5 Abercorn Terrace, Portobello, 0131 669 1044
Double room: from £80 per week. Flat: from £150 per week
If you do like to be beside the seaside, check out these self-catering flats in Portobello, just a couple of miles from central Edinburgh. Two flats (each one sleeping three) and three studio rooms fill up a large Victorian building set back from the main road. No smoking and a garden for residents' use.
www.numberfive.com

Royal Garden Apartments
City Centre, Map G4
2 York Buildings, Queen Street, 0131 625 1234
Apartments: from £90 per night
City centre one and two bedroom apartments and penthouses in a recently refurbished Georgian building facing the sandstone bulk of the National Portrait Gallery. Café, beauty therapy and a private garden are available for guests' use.
www.royal-garden.co.uk

Royal Mile Residence
Old Town, Map 2 H6
219 Royal Mile, 0131 226 5155
Double room: from £175 per night
Sporting vast views of the city, these brand new, super- designed, two-bedroomed apartments are

breathtakingly expensive. For the king's ransom, all mod cons are at your disposal, including the use of the Escape Health Club at the nearby, equally luxurious, Scotsman Hotel.
www.royalmileresidence.com

Camping

Marine Drive Camp Site and Caravan Park
Outskirts, Map 1
35–37 Marine Drive, Davidsons Mains, 0131 312 6874
Tent pitches: from £4 per night, plus supplement per person. Caravan pitches: from £9 per night, plus supplement per person
In sight of the sea and among wide open spaces, this is a bustling, popular site, so much so that during summer the camping area allows only backpackers – no cars. A well-equipped place, booking is essential.

Mortonhall Caravan Park
Outskirts, Map 1
38 Mortonhall Gate, Frogston Road East. 4.5 miles south of Edinburgh on A701, 0131 664 1533
Tent pitches: from £9.75 per night
Caravans, cars and backpackers are all welcome to this leafy park on the fringes of the city. Plenty of woodland walks, golfing next door and nearby off-site restaurants. There is an excellent city bus service and booking is recommended for August.
www.meadowhead.co.uk

Hostels

Brodie's 2
Old Town, Map 2 H6
93 High Street, 0131 556 2223
Dorm bed: from £10.50. Rooms: from £35
Opened in 2003, this new concept hostel mixes dorms with smart, double ensuite bedrooms. More weekend away than backpacker, it has all the communal charm of a traditional hostel with a little contemporary style. The original Brodie's, at 12 High Street (0131 556 6770), is more olde worlde with exposed beams

and fireplaces. Access to kitchen, lounge and internet is free for all in both hostels.
www.brodieshostels.co.uk

Caledonian Backpackers
West End, Map 2 D6
3 Queensferry Street, 0131 226 2939
Dorm bed: from £10. Rooms: from £32
Two hostels at either end of Princes Street, just about as central as you can get. Queensferry Street has 280 beds and the good old Mathers Bar below. East Princes Street Backpackers (5 West Register Street, 0131 556 6894) has 106 beds and is in the same block as the Café Royal pub. Both have full facilities. So, great locations, great bars.
www.caledonianbackpackers.com

Edinburgh Backpackers Hostel
Old Town, Map 2 H6
65 Cockburn Street, 0131 220 1717
Dorm bed: from £13. Rooms: from £39.50
How do these hostels do it? Fabulous locations, historic buildings: this company has a branch just off the Royal Mile, on Edinburgh's best known alternative shopping street and another to the west of the city centre (6 Douglas Crescent, 0131 225 6209) in beautiful Dean Village. Cockburn Street has 100 beds and 17 twin rooms. Belford was formerly a church and has 120 beds, some in rooms with gothic vibes. Both have all facilities. Book ahead in summer.
www.hoppo.com

Edinburgh Bruntsfield Youth Hostel
Southside, Map 2 E10
7 Bruntsfield Crescent, 0870 004 1114
Dorm bed: from £11
The long-established Scottish Youth Hostel Association has a couple of large hostels in areas not far from the city centre. Bruntsfield has 126 beds and is close to the frisbee-filled Meadows. 18 Eglinton Crescent (0870 004 1114) has 150 beds. Both have all facilities and booking during Jul/Aug is recommended.
www.syha.org.uk

Historic doorway into Macbackpackers High Street Hostel

Edinburgh Central Youth Hostel
Southside, Map 2 H6
Robertson's Close, Infirmary Street, 0870 004 1115
Jul/Aug only
Single room: from £20
As well as two dorm hostels, SYHA also manages several buildings offering summer-only rooms. University halls of residence the rest of the year, they are all comfortable, well-equipped and close to the city centre. Central Hostel (Robertson's Close, Infirmary Street, 0870 004 1115) has 100 single rooms within large flats. International (Kincaids Court, Guthrie Street, 0870 004 1117) also has 100 rooms and Pleasance (New Arthur Place, 0870 004 1118) contains new flats in a very central location.
www.syha.org.uk

Edinburgh University Pollock Halls
Southside, Map 2 J9
18 Holyrood Park Road, 0131 667 1971
Easter/summer only
Single room: from £27
Brand new digs with all mod cons in this university village right on the edge of Holyrood Park. The Commonwealth Pool next door will keep you fit and studentland shopping is just around the corner. More apartment than hostel accommodation.
www.edinburghfirst.com

High Street Hostel
Old Town, Map 2 H6
8 Blackfriars Street, 0131 557 3984
Dorm bed: from £12
This is a rambling old building, reputed to have Mary, Queen of Scots' connections. Just off the Royal Mile, it's in the hub, but on a quiet street. Macbackpackers, a great outfit which also offers custom built tours of Scotland, have another two hostels nearby. Royal Mile Backpackers (105 High Street, 0131 557 6120) is cosy with only 38 beds, while Castle Rock (15 Johnston Terrace, 0131 225 9666) is a biggie with 290 beds and views of the castle. All facilities are offered in the main hostels with the smaller one sharing.
www.macbackpackers.com

St Christopher's Inn
Old Town, Map 2 G6
9–13 Market Street, 0131 226 1446
Dorm bed: from £15
Right next to Waverley Station, this hostel is well equipped on street level with two bars and a café. Run by the international Famous company, it has dorm beds and private rooms.
www.st-christophers.co.uk

travel

By plane or rail, Edinburgh is an easy place to get to. And once you're here, it's a compact city to navigate. This listing will help you get around, but take our advice, walking is just the best.

Air

Edinburgh Airport
Outskirts, Map 1
7 miles west of Edinburgh, off A8, 0131 333 1000
You can reach Edinburgh's dinky, but ever-growing airport by bus, car or taxi. Bus: Lothian Buses operates Airlink services from outside the city centre's Waverley train station (30 minute journey). Adult £3.30 single, child £2/£3, open single £5. An option saver incorporates travel on Airlink with regular fleet buses. Parking: for the one hour option, expect to pay from 90p for up to 30 minutes. In BAA's main car park the charges are currently around £6.70 per day, irrespective of time period. Secure Airparks have a huge car park a few miles west of the airport, with a connecting shuttle mini bus. Taxi: expect to pay around £20 each way to and from town. Tourist Information: in the international arrivals hall. Left Luggage and Lost Property: between check-in and international arrivals hall on the ground floor. Shops: up the escalators you'll find a small, gifty branch of Jenners department store, a chemist and a newsagent. Food: the food court is expensive and fairly bland. Costa Coffee on the ground floor is your best bet if you're stuck waiting.
www.BAA.com

Bike

Spokes
Citywide
0131 313 2114
There are 140 km cycle routes in the city with more planned. Part of this network is covered by cycle lanes on main roads which have no division between cyclist and cars. Safer alternatives are cycle paths like the Innocent Railway Path and Water of Leith Walkway. For comprehensive information on city cycling and the Lothians, contact Spokes, the Lothian Cycle Campaign, which produces the Edinburgh Cycle Map and Midlothian Cycle Map – pick this up from bike shops, bookshops or Spokes itself. If you need to build your confidence or are new to cycling, Spokes operates a 'buddy' system.
www.spokes.org.uk

Sustrans
Citywide
The charity Sustrans is designing and developing the National Cycle Network. So far this includes 10,000 miles of cycle path, including both off-road and traffic-calmed road routes. Routes 1 and 75 go through Edinburgh, with Route 1 running to Aberdeen and 75 linking the capital with Glasgow. Sustrans also publishes maps of the Cycle Network and offers advice on Safe Routes to School projects.
www.sustrans.co.uk

Bus

Edinburgh Bus Station
City Centre, Map 2 G4
St Andrew Square, Busline enquiries 08705 50 50 50
This is the place to come to if you're travelling out of town. The new bus station, incongruously sited next door to fashion mecca, Harvey Nics, opened two years ago and is much sleeker than the open air one it replaced – more a city terminal now and infinitly more comfortable. A newsagent and left luggage lockers are the terminal's only facilities, but the station is surrounded by shops and places to eat. Citylink, National Express and Stagecoach run services to all parts of the country from here. Check website/phone for timetable details.
www.citylink.co.uk

Lothian Bus Company
Leith
Annandale Street, 0131 555 6363
With its distinctive maroon and white livery, this is Edinburgh's main company. It still has plenty of double deckers plying the city routes, supported now by a new fleet of single decker, low-floor, easy access buses. Lothian claims to have all prime journeys covered, running buses on them at least every 15 minutes. Rival company First Buses (01324 611 111) runs a limited service in town, concentrating on routes throughout the Lothians, Borders and Central Region. Fares for adults and children work on a stage principal starting at 60p for 1–2 stages. Pay the driver (no change given) and ask if you're not sure how much. There is also a useful £1.80 day ticket. Concession holders pay a flat fare and travel free in some cases. A number of saver tickets – weekly, monthly, yearly – are available for frequent travellers and are available from the Lothian Buses Travelshops at 27 Hanover Street and 31 Waverley Bridge. And how do you catch the bus? It's always wise to hail your bus with an outstretched arm: there's nothing worse than watching it sail merrily by. Greenways – dedicated bus lanes on main routes – are unique to the city and mostly coloured grass green, not a pretty sight.

They are useful though, allowing buses, taxis and cyclists to move unobstructed on the inside track.
www.lothianbuses.co.uk

Traveline
Citywide
Traveline, 0870 608 2608
Mon–Sun 8am–8pm
If you're planning a journey and are going to be using public transport, Traveline provides impartial advice. The information you recieve is based on details published in current timetables. It can also provide advice regarding travel in Scotland, England and Wales.
wwwtraveline.org.uk

Car

Edinburgh City Car Club
Citywide
31 Argyle Place, 0845 458 1784
Membership from £11 per month
If you don't own a car, but would like easy access to one, best to join the City Car Club, run by a private company with the support of the City of Edinburgh Council. Membership starts at £11 per month, with charges for time and mileage on top. You can book a car from dedicated bays around town, a few weeks in advance or as little as half an hour before you need it. See For Hire.
www.smartmoves.co.uk

Parking
Citywide
Despite what it feels when you're crawling along Queen Street at peak times, the city doesn't really suffer from gridlock. If you keep to the limits, getting from A to B isn't too much of a chore. Watch your speed though – manned speed checks could be right round the next corner. The real headache is parking. Within the two parking restriction zones in the city centre – Central and Peripheral – prices vary, but expect to pay no less than 30p for every 15 mins. In the Central zone, restrictions generally apply Mon–Sat 8.30am–6.30pm, while restrictions vary in the Peripheral zone. The alternative is to use one of the multi-storey or one-level car parks around the city. They have a combined total of 5,975 spaces, so with fingers crossed, you might just find one. For more information you can get a copy of the Edinburgh City Car Club and Parking Guide, tel 0131 469 5400.
www.edinburgh.gov.uk/parking

Parking Tickets
Citywide
City of Edinburgh Council, 0131 469 5400
You have been warned. The City of Edinburgh Council is not lenient when its parking restrictions are flouted. Parking

attendants patrol the streets, while police traffic wardens enforce regulations on the city's Greenways. There is a raft of misdemeanours that could result in a parking ticket. These include parking on double yellows at any time (single yellow lines have restricted parking – check nearby notices); parking outside the bay markings – and that means any part of your vehicle outside the bay; parking on a bay designated for disabled badge holders without a current badge; parking a car/van in a designated solo motorcycle bay; parking in a resident permit holders' bay without a valid permit. If you do receive a ticket and feel it was unfairly issued, you can challenge it. You have to do this in writing to the Notice Processing Centre, City of Edinburgh Council, PO Box 17065, Edinburgh, EH11 3YU. You cannot make a challenge by phone.
www.edinburgh.gov.uk/parking

Taxi

Taxi
Citywide
Traditional black cabs are still the taxi of choice in Edinburgh. There are plenty of ranks in the city centre or you can flag them down from the pavement. Alternatively, they can be ordered by phone for which you will pay a supplement. Taxis in this city are not cheap and you will rarely pay under a fiver. There are a number of reliable companies. City Cabs 0131 228 1211 has

many cars but is often busy. Capital Castle 0131 228 2555 is a good bet. Limousines and mini-bus hire are also available. Phone Platinum Limo Company 0131 336 3993 if you want a stretch. Festival Cars supply vehicles for larger parties 0131 552 1777.

Train

Haymarket Station
West End, Map 2 B7
Haymarket Terrace, 0845 748 4950
Satellite to Waverley in the city centre, this small Victorian station services the west end of town and is included on most routes running west and north.

Waverley Station
City Centre, Map 2 G5
Waverley Bridge, 0845 748 4950
Just off Princes Street, Waverley serves the East Coast main line to London as well as connecting to the West Coast main line via Glasgow. Scotrail services depart Waverley for destinations throughout Scotland, while local services go to East and West Lothian. Various renovations have been undertaken over the years, including the most recent addition of a Marks & Spencer Simply Food shop where travellers can now grab snacks, sandwiches and groceries. Those who see modern-day convenience as a threat to traditional station aesthetics need not worry though: the past survives in the main building with its ceiling of cherubs and the glass-covered structure of the station itself.

Edinburgh's brand new bus station

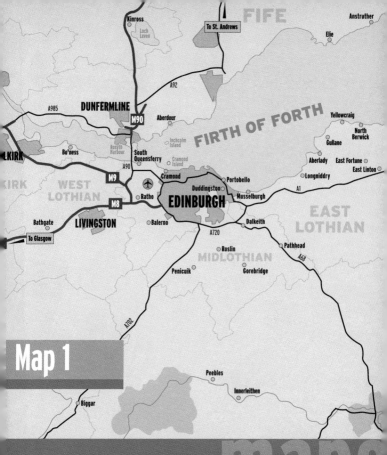

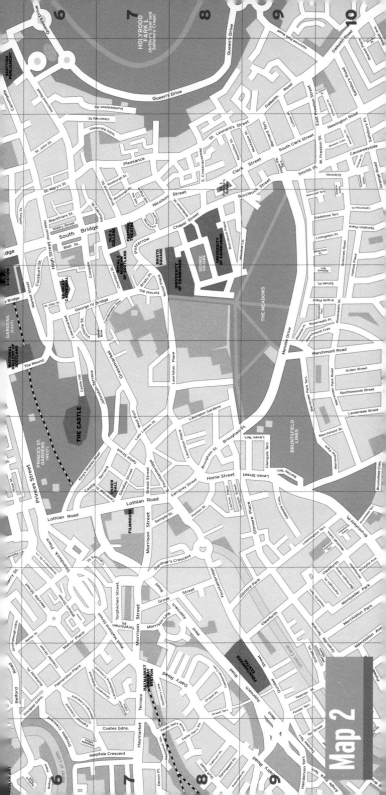

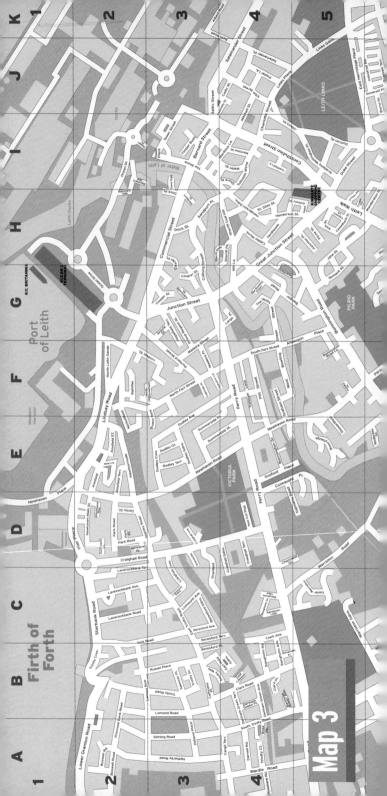

EDINBURGH EDINBURGH

AN INSIDER'S GUIDE TO EDINBURGH WWW.MYVISITSCOTLAND.COM

Live it. Visit Scotland.
visitscotland.com 0845 22 55 121

index

index

index

Edinburgh
City Guide

This indispensable pocket guide to Edinburgh is new from *The List*, Scotland's leading arts and entertainment magazine. [...] date and easy to use, this information buster will get you t[...] and beaches, galleries and museums, hotels and hostels, s[...] pubs, clubs, festivals and more. Whether you're local or jus[...] visiting, don't be without it.

- ● culture
- ● out & about
- ● eating & drinking
- ● shopping
- ● escape
- ● staying over

£4.95

Edinburgh City Guide is a first edition and a new title in *The List* pocket guide series. All guides are £4.95.